COUNTDOWN TO STATEHOOD

Palestinian State Formation in the West Bank and Gaza

Hillel Frisch

State University of New York Press

Published by
State University of New York Press, Albany

Printed in the United States of America

For information, address the State University of New York Press,
State University Plaza, Albany, NY 12246

Production by Diane Ganeles
Marketing by Nancy Farrell

Library of Congress Cataloging-in-Publication Data

Frisch, Hillel.
Countdown to statehood : Palestinian state formation in the West Bank and Gaza / Hillel Frisch.
p. cm. — (SUNY series in Israeli studies)
Includes bibliographical references and index.
ISBN 0-7914-3711-6 (hc : alk. paper). — ISBN 0-7914-3712-4 (pbk. : alk. paper)
1. Palestinian Arabs—Politics and government. 2. Nationalism—Palestine. 3. Munaẓẓamat al-Taḥrīr al-Filasṭīnīyah. I. Title. II. Series.
DS119.7.F75 1998
956.94'0049274—dc21 97-35899
CIP

10 9 8 7 6 5 4 3 2 1

Bruce Stanley
1998 London
$22

COUNTDOWN TO STATEHOOD

A volume in the SUNY Series in Israeli Studies
Russell Stone, editor

To my children
Avigail, Neomi, Yael, David, and Itamar

CONTENTS

ACKNOWLEDGMENTS

When so much of the academic's work involves criticism (as well intentioned and constructive as it may be), it is almost a relief to end one's labors with acknowledgments to others who facilitated its execution. A sense of trepidation, however, continues to linger when one realizes that inevitably I will overlook persons worthy of thanks. I begin then with an apology.

My heartfelt thanks go to the Truman Institute, its academic director, Moshe Maoz, its executive director, Edy Kaufman, and the academic committee for providing me with seed money and facilities throughout the duration of research and writing of this book. I also would like to thank members of the staff of the Truman Institute and its library—Cecil Panzer, Avraham Greenhaus, Ammon Ben-Arieh, and Ricardo Schwed—who met my many requests for research material even at the most inconvenient moments, and Haya Beckerman for editing advice. A generous grant from the Israel Academy of Arts and Sciences enabled me to complete the book.

I would like to thank Frank Dobbins, Sheldon Geller, William S. Miles, Yitzchak Naqqash, and Ira Sharkansky for commenting on portions of the manuscript and David Ricci for coming to my aid in editing and improving the book. I have gained much from their comments and criticisms. Special thanks also go to Cory Welt for his patient editing work, to Jacob Landau for his proverbial good advice, and to my wife Edna and my children, Avigail, Neomi, Yael, David, and Itamar. Aziz Haidar, ʿAbd al-Jawad Salih, Marwan al-Barghuthi, and Nabih Bashir contributed important insights whose debt I am more than happy to acknowledge. Needles to say, I take full responsibility for any defects in the book.

PREFACE

This essay on Palestinian state formation attempts to fill a significant gap in the burgeoning literature on Palestinian nationalism. While aspects of Palestinian nationalism such as national liberation, revolution, and institution building have been extensively researched, and while studies of the intifada emphasize the importance of institution building in sustaining the uprising, no one has yet explored the impact of such matters on Palestinian state building. In fact, the only European-language studies that specifically deal with the issue of statehood have been policy blueprints for attaining independence, not historically sensitive investigations that take into account the relationship between prestate institution building and eventual state formation.[1] Dealing mainly with the transfer of power and the functional and geographical boundaries of the state, those studies neglect the state-in-the-making process and its implications for state consolidation.

I, on the other hand, shall endeavor to sketch the historical development of institutions within the Palestinian national movement in its diaspora and within the Palestinian community in the occupied territories, to highlight the relationship between the two, and to link all of this to *the process* of creating and sustaining a Palestinian state. This approach emerges from the literature on state formation, and indeed my book is written with an eye toward enriching the theory of state formation, particularly as it relates to the non-European world.

To these ends, my study addresses the following questions: What relationship is there between the politicization of Palestinian society and state formation? What is the relationship between the mode of struggle and state building? How did the structural properties of Palestinian nationalism, its division between diaspora and local Palestinians, impact upon state formation? How was this reflected in PLO policies of institution building in the West Bank and Gaza? Are the "national" institutions created under Israeli rule developing into efficient state bureaucracies? Have conflict-resolution mechanisms developed that can sustain pluralism?

In what follows, Palestinian state formation will be analyzed in reference to the Zionist experience. As we shall see, the two cases contain striking structural parallels in addition to sharing geographical contiguity and historical continuity. For example, chapter 1 argues that in the modern system of nation-states, only a people making territorial claims from within a contested territory are likely to attain independence. The same chapter then shows how both national movements, arising in a diaspora setting, were faced with an imperative to territorialize.

Of course, while the Zionist and Palestinian experiences are similar, they were also significantly different. For example, the Zionists and the Palestinians confronted very different regimes, resulting in contrasting forms of territorialization. In the Zionist experience, Great Britain acted as an umpire regime and facilitated Zionist institution building. Zionist territorialization, in turn, initiated a process of state formation during the course of which a territorial leadership eclipsed the diaspora leadership. The Palestinians, by contrast, faced an adversarial nation-state bent on keeping rebellious national leaders abroad. In response, the PLO first attempted to build up a para-state in Lebanon, relying on international diplomacy to achieve territorialization there. This period is covered in chapter 2.

The PLO, however, could not escape the imperative of creating a presence in the occupied territories, generating three basic tensions between local territorialists and the diaspora, as chapter 3, on the emergence of the Shabiba youth movement and a PLO middle command, discusses. The local territorialists preferred to build public service institutions in order to ease the burden of occupation, and to create territory-wide institutions and representative frameworks that would facilitate political devolution. The PLO, by contrast, preferred diffuse institution building to centralized state building; the rise of a subordinate middle command rather than a territorial leadership; violent mobilization to institution building; and international diplomacy rather than political devolution as a means of achieving statehood.

Mirroring Israeli policy toward the occupied territories, the PLO adopted a strategy of fragmenting and diffusing territorial institutions to arrest the emergence of quasi-state institutions. There were significant costs, however, to this sort of territorialization program. Diffusion impairs the functions of institutions, weakens the possibility of creating an efficient center in the post-independence era, and encourages the growth of an opposition. The preference for violence over more functional institution building has the same effects.

Chapter 4 explores these themes by examining specific attempts at institution building in the territories, attempts such as the aborted effort to establish a Palestinian university. Although the PLO did little to thwart this venture, it became aware of the dangers of institution building independent of, or in competition, with it. This was further reflected in the relationship between the PLO and the Council of Higher Education. The politics of al-Najah National University reveal these tensions at the grassroots level, as well as the importance of diffusion as a mechanism of control.

Chapter 5 looks at state building during the intifada and focuses on the tension between political devolution and diplomacy, as well as that between the mobilization of violence and institution building. Palestinian society became increasingly politicized and rich in organizations, yet it was plagued by an absence of overarching and representative institutions. The focus on violence served to increase internal conflict. The intifada mobilized the masses but structurally it represented a retreat in the process of state formation, as an analysis of the Unified National Command communiqués demonstrates.

In chapter 6, I will analyze the impact of the Madrid peace process, from 1991 to 1993, on the relationship between the "inside" (local) and "outside" (abroad) and its influence on the state-in-the-making. A bid for power by the territorialists was closely linked to efforts to reform the PLO and combat Arafat's personal rule. The division between diaspora and territorialists only exacerbated the problem of non-institutionalization within the PLO in the diaspora.

The countdown to statehood set off in Washington by signing a Declaration of Principles in 1993 forms the basis for chapter 7. What did the Palestinians do to set up the state they were to effectively govern within five months after the signing? Palestinian efforts are compared to the moves taken by Zionist leaders between the UN decision to partition Palestine and the British evacuation. Sharp differences emerge between the two cases. In the Palestinian case, we will see that state building regressed as Arafat's neopatrimonial rule intensified and the takeover of power became more imminent. This state of affairs became the legacy of the new entity, a phenomenon all too similar to other decolonization experiences.

A comparison with other forms of state formation in my concluding chapter focuses on two principal themes: (1) the correlation between violence and institution building, and (2) the impact of neopatrimonialism in national movements in comparison to the effects of more institutionalized forms of decision making and organization. A paradox emerges: while neopatrimonial national movements that use force rather than cultivate voluntary associations and institution building can hasten resolution of external conflict, they harm the prospects of internal consolidation in the postsettlement era. Violence does increase costs for the occupier, and neopatrimonial rule allows for more rapid and decisive compromises with the enemy. The gains, however, are short-term, as independence is achieved more quickly, but stability and democratization of the emerging entity are delayed.

1

Territorialization and State Formation

The Palestinian Experience in Comparative Perspective

THE IMPERATIVE TO TERRITORIALIZE

National movements engage in two tasks: nation building, which is the creation of an identity around a common set of symbols, and state building, which is the formation of institutions to govern the polity.[1] The first may originate in a people's homeland, but it can just as easily develop in diaspora, where members of an ethnic group are often unwanted or despised. By contrast, political independence—the fundamental goal of state-builders—can only be achieved in a homeland. National movements formed in diaspora must territorialize or risk withering away.

Were one to compare the number of nation-builders and "inventors" of nations who never left their native lands to those with experience abroad, the share of the latter would be substantially higher. Frequently, in fact, it is alien intellectuals living in an imperial center or among nations more developed than their own who forge new national identities. This is hardly surprising, for those living in foreign lands are presented with intellectual opportunities to mimic the more advanced society that serves them as a cultural milieu. National ideologies and identities can thus emerge that are molded in the image of metropolitan cultures even though they are in opposition to both these cultures and the empires that foster them.[2] These identities may then be adopted by the inhabitants of their homeland. This pattern of alienation and construction of national identity widened as the division of the world into territorial states enlarged the boundaries of diaspora beyond European settings to include neighboring postcolonial states. During the era of imperialism, extreme alienation might have been likely only in a European setting, but as new states nationalized, the scope for alienation of outsiders from neighboring areas correspondingly increased.

In contrast, the principles governing state behavior and resolution of international political conflicts can explain why state building is limited to the geographic area the nation claims as its own. According to the principles of the state system, most political solutions in international affairs are territorial.[3] In those few disputed territories where no past claim to sovereignty has been conclusively accepted by the international community—as in the Palestinian case—the right to independence must ultimately be advanced by the indigenous population, not by its representatives in diaspora. It is the territorial constituency that must voice its claim to sovereignty.

At the same time, the state system contributes to the atrophy of national movements that remain in a diaspora.[4] Over time, a jealous sovereignty renders what might have been the most welcome political guest unwanted. States are especially uncomfortable playing host to national movements. Their coercive potential, insistence on secrecy, and methods of building up support within the host state, are all troublesome matters that can only be offset by a perception that their presence brings clear benefits to the host state.[5] Meanwhile, the state whose territory the national movement contests will usually act to reduce these benefits considerably. Retribution can take many forms, from minor subversion to full-scale punitive raids against the host state. Frequently, even minor subversion is costly enough to make the host reconsider its role as a sanctuary state.

For these reasons, diaspora movements must *territorialize*, either directly through transferring of leadership and resources from "outside" to "inside," or indirectly, by mobilizing the indigenous population to press a claim for independence on behalf of the national movement.[6] A voice only in diaspora remains a voice in the wilderness. National movements that remain there are fated to political failure.

This was the challenge confronted by two major diaspora national movements of the twentieth century—the Palestinian movement of the last three decades and Zionism, its earlier and closest parallel. Both movements initiated modern nation building in a diaspora and then territorialized. While Theodore Herzl, the founder of Zionism, was writing *The Jewish State* at the end of the nineteenth century and founding the World Zionist Organization in Basle, Switzerland, most of the Jews living in Palestine were patiently awaiting the coming of the Messiah.[7] Similarly, when Yasser Arafat, in the early 1960s, set up the National Palestinian Liberation Movement—Fath—to liberate Palestine from the Zionists in the name of Palestinian nationalism, most politically aware Palestinians in former Palestine were avowed pan-Arabists and passively waiting for Arab armies to liberate them. Neither the Jews of Palestine in the old Yishuv, nor Arab state Palestinians living in Gaza and the West Bank, or Arabs residing in Israel in the late 1950s, played major roles in the birth or rebirth of these nationalist movements. Indeed the rise and spread of Palestinian nationalism chronicles a complicated dialectic between the diaspora and the homeland, ranging from Lebanon to the Gulf states, from Europe to North Africa, and from the West Bank to Gaza.

In both movements, furthermore, the locus of institution building moved from abroad to the territories. By 1936, the Israeli state-in-the-making was firmly in the hands of Jewish Zionists in Palestine. As for the Palestinians, by 1988 the conflict was being played out by Palestinians in the occupied territories, mostly in the name of Palestinian particularism. And while territorialization in these two movements took a different course—for the Zionists, bringing Jewish immigrants to the Holy Land to press their claim; for the PLO, mobilizing Palestinians already in the territories to support the PLO—they shared in the long run a common journey. Only for the Palestinians the journey was much harsher, with correspondingly fewer rewards.

Context and Timing in Palestinian Territorialization

A certain detour that the Zionists never had to make reveals the relative harshness of the Palestinian journey. Before the PLO territorialized, it went through a dramatic process of *diasporization*—one relocation after another—between the nation-building era of the 1960s and the final territorialization of the movement that began in 1988 and was completed when the outside leadership arrived in the homeland and the Palestinian Authority was established there in the summer of 1994. The PLO center emerged in Gaza and Jerusalem, shifted in time to East Bank Jordan, was forced to relocate to Beirut, where it lost its physical contiguity with its "inside" population center, and was forced again to relocate, this final time to Tunis, two thousand miles away from the homeland. Why this historical detour? What were its implications for state building? Posing these questions allows us to analyze why PLO territorialization proved so much more difficult, yielded fewer diplomatic results, and led to a much more problematic political entity than had the Zionist case before it.

Probably the most important difference between the two movements lies in the nature of the regimes they encountered. The study of decolonization has shown a robust link between colonial regime type and duration, on the one hand, and intensity of conflict between national movements and states, on the other. Since World War II, national movements have fared best against *imperial* regimes that view their colonies as no more than strategic resources to secure wide-ranging geographic control.[8] Alternatively, conflict persisted on in *settled colonies*, whose European inhabitants ardently combated the liberal pressure in the home country to withdraw.[9] One very long such conflict took place in Algeria, which had many by European residents and was considered, at least for some time, to be an extension of France itself.[10] Even more protracted were the struggles against *settler regimes*, where administrative rule, formerly wielded by the imperial power, was transferred to the settlers themselves (as in Eritrea, Zimbabwe, and Namibia).[11]

Of the four types of regimes that national movements may face in the period of decolonization, however, it is the struggle against the *nation-state* that has proved most durable. Against this formidable foe, the national movement contests the state center rather than its periphery and arouses the mobilization of another "nation" against its own. In such a case, the state's organizational and logistical advantages are considerably augmented. And while European imperialists could always, however painfully, withdraw to their metropole, this option is unacceptable to the communal nation-state, which views its territory as an inviolable whole. This zero-sum perception is vividly portrayed in the Israeli-Palestinian case, where polling data, on the eve of the Madrid Conference in late 1991 that opened negotiations between Israel and its adversaries, indicated that at least two-thirds of the Israeli Jewish population felt that Palestinian statehood threatened Israeli security regardless of whatever the land mass it would cover.[12] These fears were amplified by the fact that the conflict against the PLO was closely linked to the inter state conflict between Israel and its Arab state neighbors, and by the PLO's covenantal commitment to the destruction of Israel rather than solely to its territorial diminution.[13] While the Zionists territorialized under the most benign regime possible—a British mandatory power formally committed to the creation of a Jewish national home—the Palestinians who created the PLO in 1964 battled against, in some respects, a much less flexible foe.

Timing was also important. The Palestinians sought to territorialize in an era when 157 members of the state system had divided the globe among themselves and had, as a result, excluded hundreds of national movements seeking entry. Their exclusion was justified on the grounds that the principle of territorial inviolability overrode the principle of self-determination. Here was a complete reversal of norms from the previous era, when self-determination had been the reigning principle justifying the transformation of colonies under imperial rule into sovereign states.[14] Moreover, the tendency of the state system to uphold the territorial sovereignty of existing multi-ethnic states against claims of self-determination was an outstanding feature of the post-World War II era, at least until the collapse, internally, of the USSR and Yugoslavia. Bangladesh was the only successful secession state created in that period. But even then, its success was due almost exclusively to its unique physical separation from the western part of Pakistan by India, which encouraged secession from Pakistan and the establishment of Bangladesh as an independent state.[15]

In a technical sense, the Israeli-Palestinian confrontation is not quite a conflict of secession, as Israel never achieved undisputed sovereignty over Judea, Samaria, and Gaza. That most governments, as well as foreign media, refer to these areas as occupied territories is a clear demonstration that the Israeli claim to the territories was not only disputed but, in fact, rejected. This would suggest that the international resistance to secession should not apply to this case. Nevertheless, while Palestinian claims to the territories have won much more support than most secession movements, and while the international community may have recognized, in principle, Palestinian rights to the territories, many state governments have been reticent about supporting Palestinian statehood. The world community, it seems, has appeared willing to sacrifice particular justice rather than open the Pandora's box by threatening the integrity of the existing state system.

The Dilemma of Palestinian Territorialization

Nation-states, like strong colonial powers, often force national movements into exile or, in the case of diaspora-born national movements, block the initial territorialization of leadership, manpower, and resources. This is what happened to the Palestinians: when Arafat attempted to set up base in the West Bank in 1967, Israel forced him out. A division thus developed between the "inside," the segment of the national movement fighting within the contested territory, and the "outside" leadership. As in similar cases, the Palestinians faced an increasingly acute state-building dilemma as this division solidified. The national movement had to territorialize in order to legitimize its claim to independence. This required, particularly in protracted conflicts, a territorially based organizational infrastructure. But such an infrastructure is a potential breeding ground for local challenges to the diaspora leadership.

The history of Zionism shows how territorialization can foster a strong inside leadership. Up until the end of the First World War, the Zionist movement's leadership and organizational infrastructure was based in London rather than Jerusalem, and it was led by diaspora leaders such as Chaim Weizmann and Louis Brandeis.[16] By 1935, however, it was clear that, after intensive diaspora support for colonization and local institution building, principally through the Histadrut (the central Federation of Labor) and the creation of the territorially-based Jewish Agency in 1929, the leaders who rose through these organizations prevailed over the diaspora leadership that funded them. David Ben-Gurion's assumption of the chairmanship of both the World Zionist Organization and the Jewish Agency in 1935 signified the transformation of Zionism from a diaspora-center/territory-periphery movement into a territorially centered movement. This was emphasized in 1949 when Ben-Gurion became the first prime minister of Israel, while Weizmann had to make do with the honorary but powerless title of president, an office that has yet to fill a vital role in the Israeli political structure.

Aware that they might lose control, the PLO preferred to follow the example of another diaspora-based national movement—Algeria's National Liberation Front (FLN). In the Algerian case, the diaspora leadership prevailed over its inside competitors in the consolidation of the state. In 1956, "inside" leaders convened a rump congress of the FLN near the Valley of the Soummam to contest the power of the "outsiders," some of whom had fled to neighboring states while others were sitting in French prisons. The congress attempted to "virtually eliminate the latter from the effective command of the FLN by requiring that the five-man executive be stationed on Algerian soil."[17] This was even before four of the nine historic "outside" founders had been kidnapped by France in mid-air two years later. But it was the outside—at first, exiled politicians under Ahmad Ben Bella and later the outside military wing—that prevailed.[18] Eventually, Houari Boumedienne, the chief of staff of the Army of National Liberation (the ALN) that was formed outside of Algeria along the borders of Tunisia and Morocco, seized power in a coup, placed Ben Bella under house arrest, and went on to rule until his death in 1978.[19] By contrast, the surviving guerrillas, who fought within Algeria and suffered most in the war of liberation, gained little: by 1967, there were no guerrillas left in positions of power. It was only natural that the PLO would adopt the FLN as a symbol, if not an exact model, in its fight to maintain hegemony,[20] while Palestinian territorialists looked more to Zionism as a successful model of (internal) territorialism.[21]

The Algerian outsiders triumphed against the French and their own insiders first by waiting out on the sidelines, and then by engaging in concerted negotiations with the French under intense international pressure. Perhaps this is why the PLO hesitated to try territorializing a second time and attempted, in its stead, to build a quasi-state in the diaspora. This was the historical detour mentioned earlier. It ended in 1982 when Israel forced the PLO to leave Beirut and left the organization with no other choice but to come to grips with the dilemma of territorialization and to figure out organizational strategies of mobilization that would reduce the chances that an alternative leadership would emerge in Gaza or the West Bank.

The PLO employed four techniques to create a territorial voice while avoiding the emergence of an alternative leadership. First, it encouraged antiregime mobilization and violence over the creation of institutions that could provide public services to the local population. Second, it sought to subordinate local leaders to those abroad, using neopatrimonial methods widely employed by Arab regimes toward their citizens, rather than sharing power with them. Third, it permitted institutional fragmentation instead of facilitating the creation of translocal and centralized institutions. Finally, it maintained a monopoly over international diplomacy rather than promoting political devolution from Israel from within. Generally, the territorialists, for reasons that will be amplified in the course of this book, preferred the alternative in each of these paired dichotomies. But unlike the Zionists, the PLO never transferred the bulk of its resources to the occupied territories.[22]

THE IMPACT OF ZIONIST TERRITORIALIZATION ON STATE BUILDING

As we have seen, territorialization is an imperative both for achieving independence and for maintaining hegemony within the national movement. But *how* diaspora national movements territorialize has a major effect on the *form* the future state will take. Operating under a mandate government that sanctioned the creation of a Jewish national home, Zionist territorialization was characterized by the territorialists' alliance with a diaspora and then by their ascendancy over diaspora leadership. Priority was accorded to colonization over diplomacy or war as institution building—the spawning of settlement and public welfare institutions preceded the mobilization of violence. Zionist territorialization by characterized by the creation of strong central institutions, rules, and procedures for conflict resolution over personalized and diffuse power structures.[23]

In the Zionist case, perhaps the most important element in initiating a state-building process before independence was the creation of a territorial leadership. The emergence of such a leadership may be traced back to the establishment of two territorial parties, HaPoel HaTzair and Poalei Zion, among the earliest to emerge in the Yishuv and in the Zionist movement.[24] HaPoel HaTzair was involved in the first experiments of "national" settlement, where the World Zionist Organization (WZO) provided the funds and the political party provided the manpower, the ideology, and the leadership.[25] In time, new settlements became affiliated to these parties, whose leaders included state-building visionary leaders such as Berl Katznelson, Ben-Gurion, and Yitzchak Ben-Zvi. These were the same leaders who formed Achdut HaAvodah in 1919 and the Histadrut one year later. In the 1920s, both parties monopolized labor by drawing workers into the Histadrut with the help of WZO funds. Once the two territorial parties merged in 1930, they were then ready to tackle control of the WZO and the Jewish Agency.[26] Their dominance in both ensured political control over diaspora-based financial resources and hegemony within the Yishuv as a whole. Thus the pronouncement that appeared in the official journal of Poalei Zion in 1910—"that the destiny of Zionism will ultimately be decided neither by the World Zionist Organization nor by the worldwide political and diplomatic efforts of Zionism; the outcome will be decided in the land of the Turk"—was vindicated not in 1948 but already in 1936.[27]

The ascendancy of a territorial leadership went hand in hand with territorial institutionalization or state building, which reflects a significant stage beyond mere institution building. Institutionalization or state building involves the creation of organizations that make or conform to rules that render decision making predictable, recurrent, and legitimate. Their functions are to prioritize, resolve conflicts, and allocate resources. This is typically the business of political parties, parliaments, and other representative institutions.[28]

Institution building, by contrast, is concerned with roles; the formation of organizations that are wholly functional and material; they provide power to wage the struggle against the enemy, coercion against potential internal rule breakers, or public services. Institutionalization, therefore, is a complex process that involves competing political factions, groups and ideologies. Its *political* scope is thus wider than that of institution building.[29]

The character of Zionist settlement was, in its first stage, politically diffuse and organizationally underdeveloped. The new Yishuv of the first *aliyah* (wave of immigration), a period of ethnic plantation settlement, was characterized by diffuse pre-political local government chafing under an increasingly onerous settlement administration set up by Baron Rothschild.[30] Its replacement in 1903 by the Jewish Colonial Association (JCA), an equally non-Zionist and elitist institution, hardly helped matters. What united the twenty-five new settler communities was their growing bond of dependence on an "outside" force dedicated to market profitability. The JCA eventually abandoned Palestine for what seemed then to be greener pastures in Argentina and Russia.[31]

The second aliyah's search for a solution to its market predicament set the stage for a more equitable pattern between inside and outside, but also paved the way to growing politicization and the creation of politically affiliated settlement movements in the Yishuv.[32] Institutionalization reached its peak when the territorial leadership eclipsed the diaspora leadership in the 1930s, as David Ben-Gurion and his colleagues wrested control of the Zionist movement and its resources from the diaspora leadership, while continuing to obey democratic rules of allocation that were prevalent in the WZO. The Yishuv leadership henceforth controlled resources originating in diaspora. The outside leadership, by facilitating territorial institution building, had basically engineered their own marginalization.[33]

Finally, as Shmuel Sandler has noted, the earlier the territorialization of the party and the greater the number of its cadres in Palestine as a percentage of the total party membership, the greater the party or bloc's power and, consequently, the greater its role in the formation and consolidation of the state.[34] The strength of the Labor parties, as measured in terms of election performances, was always disproportionately greater in Palestine than it was in diaspora. Thus, for example, in the elections to the Zionist Congress in 1931, Labor won 69 percent of the votes cast in Palestine but only 29 percent of the votes cast in Palestine and in the diaspora combined. By contrast, the General Zionists, the party led by Chaim Weizmann, secured only 7.8 percent of the vote in Palestine but 36 percent of the total votes. The votes cast for the revisionists was more evenly divided, accounting for 16.8 percent of the Palestinian vote and 21 percent of the total vote. It is clear that the parties that made up the Labor movement were the only predominantly territorial parties.

Their growing power signified in time the hegemony of the territorialists over diaspora.

In the post-independence era, the territorially-center/diaspora-periphery relationship basically extended to most of organized world Jewry, a process initiated in 1929 with the establishment of the Jewish Agency, which included non-Zionists from the diaspora.[35] Such a political center was later uniquely suited to meet the exigencies of mass immigration in the early years of statehood. The structure was diffuse and voluntary enough to assure pluralism, yet sufficiently institutionalized to make effective and pressing decisions, and to execute policy in a state inundated by immigrants and surrounded by enemies.

Territorialization and Palestinian State Building

Since Palestinian territorialization was very different from Zionist territorialization, it is hardly surprising that the institution-building process before and during the creation of the Palestinian Authority took a very different form from that of its predecessor. The difference was caused primarily by a more intense conflict. The more powerful the enemy, the more able it is to thwart a national movement's objectives. The more violent the conflict between the two becomes, by and large, the smaller the opportunity to engage in effective state making. This reality may be seen not only in the apposition of the Zionist and Palestinian movements but also in a comparison between India and Algeria. In the former, England was willing to accede a measure of self-government and foster relatively free municipal elections contested by the Indian National Congress. In consequence, a reasonably effective and democratic government emerged.[36] In Algeria, by contrast, the inside was effectively decimated by the French. Thus when the struggle over internal hegemony within the new Algerian state began, the "inside" was already very weak.

Crisis, often the by-product of a violent struggle for independence, accentuates the trend to autocracy. Both the PLO center and the Palestinians in the territories lived in a state of perpetual crisis, the former suffering the hardships of surviving in sanctuary states, and the latter living under a powerful military occupation. Such a condition increased the need for quick decisions, encouraged personal rule at the center, fostered mobilization over institution building (not to speak of state building), and led to organizational fragmentation in the contested territory. As fragmentation increases, the search for a political center to hold the movement together gravitates around a leader. This often gives birth to neopatrimonialism, which is so prevalent in the Third World.[37]

In the Palestinian case, neopatrimonialism rather than classic patrimonialism took hold. In the newer version, there is a constant tension between "what ought to be," as defined by modern ideologies, principally liberal democracy and public administration procedure, and "what is," that is, the power configuration existing within the organization, which almost always skewed sharply to the benefit of the chairman, founder, or ruler. In classic patrimonialism, the leader might be challenged, not because the power configuration is illegitimate, but rather because he does not use his power for legitimate ends. In neopatrimonial structures, however, the challenge actually relates to the process of acquiring power, not just the exercise of it. Never totally legitimate, the leader is frequently challenged in the name of ideologies that he presumably accepts.

To counter such illegitimacy, the neopatrimonial leader makes use of modern forms of organization as a power base to counter pressures for reform. But while the bases of support are well organized, decision-making organs are usually in disarray. In fact, the leader prevents the emergence of procedures that would govern decision making. Because the leader must worry about the loyalty of the people within the organization supporting him, a politics of diffusion, or of encouraging a multiplicity of factions, offers the leader room for maneuver between shifting patterns of coalition building. If he feels threatened, he can reduce the payoff to his own organization by distributing more to the opposition or to independents, a reservoir of individuals who can usually be bought for a price. But since the opposition is organized and also poses a threat, the leader must maintain hegemony, and not just dominance, for his organization. Neopatrimonialism is therefore a three-tier system. The ruler personalizes critical decision making; he is supported by a hegemonic organization; and, at the same time, he ensures that the political arena will remain plural and diffuse.

It is ironic that national movements that espouse modernity so often give birth to "traditional" regimes. Like many other national movements, the Palestinian yearning to modernity is reflected in the name of the national movement itself, the PLO, the correct translation of which is the Organization of Palestinian Liberation (to be distinguished from liberation by [other] Arabs). This is demonstrated even more strikingly by the way Palestinians refer to the PLO simply as the "al-munazama," the Organization. The factional clan-based fighting that had consumed the Palestinian movement from within during the Mandate had brought forth a longing for modern organization, participatory decision making, and efficient execution in both the military and political wings of the organization.

Instead of the characteristics Max Weber imputed to organizations, however, the PLO was characterized by a dominant party—Fath—that enjoyed a plurality in a multifaction environment and a leader who maintained control over an autonomous position in respect both to his faction and the overall organization. Pluralism was a balancing device that, while letting the opposition know that the dominant organization was on Arafat's side, also let Fath know that rival claimants for his patronage existed. Fath's institutionalization has always been weak, probably purposefully so. In the course of nearly thirty years of its existence, the faction convened only five general conferences (not necessarily at critical junctures), the smaller revolutionary councils rarely met, and no one is quite sure of the procedures used for selecting representatives. Arafat's system of balancing personal as well as corporate rivals, and of refraining from punishing deviants, is patterned along lines suggested by John Waterbury in a study of King Hassan of Morocco.[38] A live enemy was better than a dead one, as were weakened corporate groups more useful within the system than outside it. Arafat, Palestinian critics often assert, behaves very much like Ahmad Shuqairy, his predecessor, as a one-man show (*bi-tafarud*), but while Shuqairy was ousted, Arafat always had a quasi-organizational power base.[39] For Sabri Jiryis, "the [Palestinian] movement, more so than any time in the past seems as if it is like any other Arab regime, or like third world regimes in general which tread a path no one is sure where it will end,"[40] an organization where a "nonadministrative" (*la-idariyya*) and "nonorganizational" (*la-tanzimiyya*) mentality reigns."[41] Thus, for example, could veteran PLO activist and member of the PLO Executive Committee Abdullah Hurani declare in the summer of 1993 that neither he nor other members ever knew the exact state of the PLO's financial situation."[42]

Outside actors also had a role to play in the establishment of neopatrimonialism in Palestinian society. Conservative Arab rulers sought to draw Arafat into their fold and away from the radical leftist organizations that also operated within the PLO. They were equally suspicious of many elements within Fath itself. Needless to say, they found in Arafat a cooperative interlocutor. Since they were heavily involved in funding the organization, they could channel their money mainly to him. As a result, Arafat has always enjoyed a near monopoly of control over the PLO's financial resources (and also over those of the Palestinian Authority). Meanwhile, support from more radical Arab states assured a multiplicity of factions in the PLO, through which Arafat's neopatrimonialism could come into play. After all, multiple and competing groups form the basis of patrimonialism at the base. Thus, radical and conservative Arab states, who so often challenged each other on many other levels, unwittingly joined forces in strengthening neopatrimonialism within the PLO. The conservative states promoted it at the top through personal linkages with Arafat, while the radical states promoted diffusion at the base.

These institutional features obviously have retarded Palestinian state formation. Arafat's leadership in the PLO was institutionalized before the politicization of mass society in the occupied territories. As a leader, he was also affected most by the territorializing dilemma and, therefore, had a strong vested interest in adopting a strategy of diffuse and suboptimal institution building, of diplomacy over devolution, and of subordination rather than power sharing with territorial organizers and leaders. Ironically, however, while the neopatrimonial leader can typically make quick decisions, unencumbered by compliance to formal rules, and thereby hasten the establishment of political authority, he may do so at the expense of cheapening the quality of the final product. Territorialization, therefore, must be analyzed by the impact it has on both achieving statehood as well as the eventual form of the state.

The Legacy of Fragmentation

It would be wrong to think that the PLO actively fragmented society and local leadership in the territories so much as it maintained existing fragmentation. Joel Migdal, in his synchronic comparison of the Zionist Yishuv with Palestinian society, has pointed out how an immigrant society is more likely than a dispersed, predominantly rural society to produce a strong state with a high level of institutionalization.[43] Immigrant societies, because they can, so to speak, begin from scratch, are presented with unique opportunities to bring into being new social forms of organizational life and test their efficiency in meeting broad societal objectives. Rural societies are less flexible and cannot strike out in new directions without considerable violence directed against notables, headmen, familial groups, and other segments of society that would feel threatened by new social forms. The Zionist movement was especially innovative in creating such institutions. These institutions in turn were linked to strong state building because of the unique nature of the conflict between a minority of colonizers and an indigenous majority where land was relatively scarce. Shafir has shown that in settlement areas where the ratio between colonizers and natives was high, subsequent state capacities during consolidation were low.[44] The Palestinians, on the other hand, particularly in the West Bank, were predominantly rural, linked almost exclusively to local towns, and were characterized by high levels of emigration that fostered a high level of dependence on aid from emigrants and a sense of local parochialism ties between expatriates and villagers create.

The PLO's fears of a strong alternative local leadership also dovetailed with the interests and policies of two other external actors—Israel and Jordan. Emile Sahliyeh makes this point well:

> The conflicting interests of these three have only served to deepen disunity and fragmentation among the ranks of the local elite. Indeed, the net effect of their polices has been to weaken the position of the traditional politicians without allowing for the emergence of a new, viable leadership. In their attempt to affect West Bank internal political dynamics, Jordan, the PLO, and Israel have not confined their competition to the manipulation of economic resources and inducements. They have frequently used coercive techniques to penetrate and weaken the sphere of influence of the rival actors.[45]

Thus, for a variety of reasons—ecological, institutional, and political—the difficulties of state making for any potential Palestinian leadership were greater than the challenge to the Zionist movement had been. No wonder the PLO tried to avoid overcoming these difficulties by engaging instead in diaspora state-building, as the following chapter analyzes.

2

The PLO, Territorialization, and Palestinian State Formation

The Zionist movement successfully forged a state before its formal independence was declared. Such state building, firmly in the hands of territorially based leaders, had a positive effect on subsequent state consolidation. By contrast, Palestinian state building efforts swung in the opposite direction. It began primarily in historic Palestine in Gaza under the Egyptians, then moved to the diaspora, and only in the 1980s focused once more on the territories. The territorialization of the diaspora leadership occurred even later. This chapter examines the emergence and entrenchment of the division between the diaspora and the territorialists before the diaspora leadership realized that state building in diaspora was unfeasible and that the movement had to territorialize in order to achieve statehood. Subsequent chapters will then focus on how such diasporization impacted upon territorial institution building.

The PLO as a Diaspora Event

Egyptian historian Wahid ʿAbd al-Majid has divided the Israeli-Palestinian conflict into three periods:

1. The initial years, in which Palestinians put their faith in the Arab states to redress their historical grievances and bring them back to Palestine
2. The years 1967–1982, when Palestinians in the diaspora sought to resolve their own plight by mobilizing militarily through guerrilla action
3. The period from the fall of Beirut through the intifada, in which the local Palestinians began to take their fate into their own hands.[1]

While the third claim (which we will examine in chapter 5) has yet to be substantiated, the first two are useful frameworks for understanding the following two assertions: that the Palestinian national movement emerged as a result of efforts of others, and that, after the Palestinians organized themselves and sought independence from their former sponsors, its activities took place mostly outside of Palestine.

It was not Palestinians themselves but Arab diplomats who introduced the idea of mobilizing Palestinians around the principle of self-determination. The debate over endorsing the idea of a "Palestinian entity" was fueled by the rivalry between President ʿAbd al-Karim Qasim of Iraq and Egyptian president Jamal Abdul Nasser, each of whom at the time was vying to be the dominant leader in the Arab world. Attempting to undercut Nasser, whose conception of Arab unity was a unified pan-Arab state, Qasim called for the immediate establishment of an independent Palestinian republic in those parts of Palestine held by Arab sovereign states. He vindictively described these territories—Gaza ruled by Egypt since 1948 and the West Bank annexed by Jordan in 1950—as part of the territory that was "usurped by three thieves: one hostile to Arab nationalism, Zionism, and the other two from within the Arab camp: Egypt and Jordan."[2] Qasim's advocacy of immediate Palestinian statehood within precisely defined territory fit well with his vision of a confederation of states, as opposed to Nasser's vision of pan-Arab unity.

To counteract this Iraqi attack on Egyptian hegemony, Nasser came up with his own scheme for establishing elected, representative Palestinian institutions in Gaza, Jordan, and Lebanon collectively called the Palestinian Arab National Union (PNU) whose representatives were to later elect an Executive Committee and represent the Palestinian case in Arab and international forums.[3] In creating this vehicle to represent the Palestinians, Nasser acknowledged the mobilization of a people and development of their identity as means to achieve self-determination in the future, but he disregarded the concepts of statehood and territoriality. The PNU never amounted to much; it ceased to operate soon after founding elections were held in Syria, in June 1960, and in Gaza, seven months later.[4]

Pressured, however, to match Iraq's continued support for the immediate establishment of a Palestinian republic, Nasser on March 5, 1962 passed a law bestowing on Gaza a "constitutional order" (*al-nizam al-dusturi lil-Qitaʿ*) that declared Gaza to be "an integral part of Filastin land," and defined the Palestinians there as constituents of a "National Union" (not to be confused with the PNU, which had ceased to exist), which included "all Palestinians, wherever they [may] live."[5] This National Union soon became the Legislative Council, presided over by Dr. Haydar ʿAbd al-Shafi, who was to later head the Palestinian delegation in the Madrid and Washington peace process. Nasser thus acceded to give the Palestinians a territory but not one that formed the kernel of a state.

In 1964, Nasser formally abolished the National Union so that it would not compete with the PLO, established the same year.[6] In sharp contrast to either Jordan or Syria, Egypt passed a law in 1965 on the Palestinian Popular Organization (PPO), which was designed to both create territorially based representative forums within the PLO and to facilitate the creation of popular organizations. Though the PLO was given a relatively free hand to mobilize a base of popular support, the results were disappointing. Only 17,000 Palestinians, in a population of 400,000, registered between June 1965 and March 1966 for the elections to the PPO institutions and the PPO National Bureau that were scheduled to be held in April.[7] Egypt's noninterference in Palestinian affairs, however, came to an abrupt end when the Egyptian head of police was summarily dismissed. The secretary-general of the PPO, Abd al-Shafi, and the members of the PPO Bureau who comprised its central organ, resigned after al-Shafi had protested the participation of police in PPO meetings. They replaced them with more docile members.[8]

The PLO itself was the handmaiden of the Arab states and not a grassroots initiative. On January 1, 1964, Arab presidents and monarchs at the first Arab summit conference decided to set up an organization that would mobilize the Palestinians for the coming struggle with Israel. That decision became a reality four months later with the establishment of the PLO. Palestinians themselves had failed to take the initiative not for lack of zeal so much as for the Arab regimes' unwillingness to tolerate almost any autonomous political initiative—least of all by Palestinians.

The PLO was founded in East Jerusalem, the former government center of the British mandate and center of Arab Palestinian politics. But while most of its representatives were Palestinian residents of the West Bank, many were there in the service of the Hashemite king. Shemesh estimates that over 100 members of the first Palestinian National Council (PNC) held in Jerusalem in 1964, held positions in the Jordanian establishment.[9] Even Ahmad Shuqairy, the founding father of the PLO and first chairman of its Executive Committee, had in the past represented both Saudi Arabia and Syria as a professional diplomat. Many more attendants were less motivated by Palestinian state formation than by the prospects of liberating Palestine and merging it into a united Arab state.

Autonomous Palestinian institution building, by contrast, began in the diaspora. Fath, the first authentic Palestinian organization, emerged in Lebanon in 1959, and its success in dominating the PLO ten years later further diasporized the movement. A profile of Fath's leadership reflect its diaspora political roots. Of the four major figures in Fath, Yasser Arafat became active in politics solely in diaspora; Salah Khalaf had engaged in Palestinian politics in Cairo in the early 1950s and then only briefly in Gaza before departing for Kuwait in 1960; Faruq al-Kaddumi had left Jordan for Saudi Arabia by 1952; and Khalil al-Wazir was politically active in the Gulf as early as 1957, although he might have emigrated there even earlier.[10] Even in an enlarged look at the Fath leadership, we see that only four (Khalaf, Muhammad Yusuf al-Najjar, Salim Zaᶜnun, and Muhammad Abu Mayzar) of twenty-three Fath members designated in one study as its most prominent leaders, were actively engaged in politics in Gaza or the West Bank during the 1950s. None of them were engaged in political activities in the name of Palestinian particularism.[11] Seventeen of the twenty-three leaders had emigrated from Gaza and the West Bank as young adults in the 1950s to work as, mostly, teachers, engineers, or bureaucrats in Saudi Arabia, the Gulf states, Algeria, or West Germany.[12] Furthermore, only four Fath representatives attended the first PNC meeting[13] and, as far as can be ascertained, Fath played only a minor role in Palestinian institution building in Gaza during the last three years of Egyptian rule. Finally, Fath, unlike two prominent guerrilla factions within the PLO, the Popular Front for the Liberation of Palestine (PFLP) and the pro Syrian al-Sa^{c}iqa, did not inherit political and organizational structures from the Jordanian or Egyptian eras.[14]

A comparison between the composition of the executive committees of the PLO in the years 1964–67 and for the three years after Arafat became chairman at the 6th PNC in Cairo in January 1969 also clearly reflect PLO diasporization. Seven of the fourteen members of the first Executive Committee in 1964 were either residents of the West Bank or Gaza at the time or local political activists in the past. Five of these seven were active politicians in parts of former Mandate Palestine even before the emergence of the PLO: Haydar ^{c}Abd al-Shafi, the former president of the Legislative Council set up in accordance with the 1962 Palestinian constitution; Hamid Abu Sitta, who formed an organization representing refugee interests; Walid Qamhawi, a former Arab Nationalist Movement politician; Bahjat Abu-Gharibiyya, a member of the Jordanian Ba^{c}th party from Jerusalem; and Qasim al-Rimawi, another former Ba^{c}th member. In the second executive committee, six of thirteen were residents of the West Bank and Gaza, as were five of ten in the third.[15] Once the guerrilla factions took over the PLO in 1968, and Fath established its hegemony in 1969, the composition of the Executive Committee changed radically. In the fifth, sixth, and seventh committees, four diaspora leaders from Fath headed the list. Below them, the names changed. The powerful stayed put, while the less influential rotated. Only two members of the fifth, sixth, and seventh PNCs, Kamal Nasir, a former Ba^{c}thist, and Abu Sitta had played important political roles in organizations or parties active in the West Bank and Gaza before 1967.[16] The actual concentration of power within the organization was overwhelmingly in the hands of diaspora leadership.

During this period, the PLO also underwent considerable functional and structural change. Functionally, the PLO, founded as a civilian-military institution, was transformed almost exclusively into a guerrilla movement that focused on liberation at the expense of political representation. The PLO's structure transformed accordingly as a political framework based on the principle of geographical representation of the Palestinian people gave way to an umbrella of guerrilla organizations. The membership of the PNC declined from 396 in the founding meeting of the PLO in 1964 to 100 in the fourth PNC meeting in 1968, in which the factions in the PLO garnered 40 seats.[17]

The triumph of diaspora-based activists over territorialists like ʿAbd al-Shafi signaled the victory of those for whom violent mobilization was more important than institution building.

The Failure of Territorialization

PLO leader Yasser Arafat had the advantage of hindsight that Zionist leader Chaim Weizmann and early Palestinian Arab leader Hajj Amin al-Husayni had lacked. Weizmann's predilection for diaspora diplomacy over territorial institution building facilitated his own replacement as the leader of the World Zionist Organization. The lesson from Hajj Amin's life story was even more severe. His absence from Palestine at the critical moments of potential Palestinian state formation condemned him to an increasingly peripheral political existence.[18] The experiences of both underscored the importance of being physically present in the area, as well as of territorializing one's supporting organization.

Arafat attempted to achieve both objectives in the fall of 1967 when he adopted a strategy of guerrilla warfare, traversed the Jordan River, and set up base in the West Bank. Fath's guerrilla strategy possessed advantages over a strategy of political mobilization. In guerrilla warfare, Fath faced little internal competition. Had Arafat chosen a strategy of political mobilization, he would have had to compete with existing, though weakened, political parties in the territories.[19] Moreover, the Arab world looked to guerrilla action for salvation after the defeat of the Arab states in the Six Day War. Finally, guerrilla warfare fostered the military expertise not only needed to fight the enemy but also useful for prevailing over indigenous rivals.

This national liberation model, however, did not serve well Arafat and Fath, who had overlooked the power and determination of the nation-state. It has been estimated that Israeli forces captured 1,000 guerrillas and killed 200 more between the time Arafat moved to the West Bank and his escape back to Jordan four months later.[20] The damage inflicted against Israel hardly justified such losses. Artillery duels between Palestinian guerrillas and the Jordanian army against Israel, and raids into Israel accounted for the overwhelming number of incidents. In 1968, for example, only 33 of a total of 1,320 recorded military incidents that took place in the West Bank could be linked to internally generated guerrilla activities. The same was true of casualties. Guerrillas operating within the West Bank and Gaza killed six Israeli soldiers in 1968, while 108 died in interstate border conflagrations on the Jordanian and Suez fronts alone. And while communiqués released by the various PLO factions claimed responsibility for the deaths of 2,618 Israelis in 1968,[21] only 177 Israelis were killed in hostile activities of all sorts.[22] Such a palpable lack of success eventually generated a credibility crisis within the Palestinian resistance movement. Though revolutionary, anti-state sentiment spread throughout the Arab world after the 1967 war, the fact remains that even at the height of the Palestinian armed struggle's popularity, military conflict essentially remained an interstate phenomenon.

The PLO's failure to transplant its military operations into the territories was the first step in institutionalizing the separation between "inside" and "outside" in the emerging Palestinian political community. The loss of the Jordanian base in the summer of 1971, when Jordan evicted, killed, or imprisoned the last remaining Palestinian guerrillas (after an operation that had begun the previous September), and the PLO relocation to Lebanon completed the process. The diaspora was effectively separated from its territorial constituency and remained that way for the next twelve years.[23]

Arafat's ouster from the West Bank and his subsequent removal from Jordan revealed dramatically how much more arduous a task territorialization was destined to be than in the Zionist case of earlier years. For the Zionists, the British had been empire and umpire, facilitating the cultivation of the Jewish national home, on the one hand, and attempting to mitigate the communal conflict between the Jews and Arabs, on the other. The Zionists built up their center under British protection but mobilized independently in the face of the communal enemy. The Palestinian factions, by contrast, came face to face against a nation-state that was in the midst of mobilizing against adversarial territorial states. The models of national liberations, spun out of the experiences of declining empires and demographically outnumbered colonialists, were of little use. Worse, the PLO could not even prevail over Jordan, the weakest of the confrontation states, divided into two peoples and ruled by a monarchy. If the Palestinian resistance was no match against the combined force of community and state even when, as in the Jordanian case, the dominant community was demographically a minority, all the more futile was the continuation of armed struggle against Israel.

A Strategy of Armed Struggle and Diplomacy

No longer useful against the enemy, the ideology of armed struggle still had a role to play in coping with the dilemma of territorialization. In Lebanon in 1971 the leadership of the PLO had to figure out how to politically mobilize in the territory without cultivating an alternative leadership.

The problem was that both territorial Palestinians and Jordan had taken advantage of the PLO's weakness in diaspora to rally the inhabitants of the territories around their platforms and challenge the PLO, which still claimed to represent the Palestinians.[24] In March 1972, King Hussein announced his federal plan for a united Kingdom of Jordan. Fortunately for the PLO, Jordanian credibility and legitimacy in the territories after the events of Black

September suffered an equal, or even more precipitous, drop than that of the PLO. At the same time, territorialists advocating a Palestinian entity, a solution little different than the state of Palestine the PLO was to later seek in the Madrid peace conference, never succeeded in institutionalizing a political center. The advocates of the Palestinian entity hoped to persuade Israel to devolve power and facilitate the evolution of democratic Palestinian statehood from occupation as had the powers of the Allies in Japan and West Germany after World War II.[25] Needless to say, they were unsuccessful.

However weak the factions were at this point, they responded with alacrity to these challenges. First, they threatened "to establish revolutionary courts" and try the advocates of the Palestinian entity—a euphemism for swift punishment.[26]

Second, in a bid to enhance the representative nature of the PLO, Fath steadily enlarged the membership of the PNC from 1973 on to include more independents; by 1977, the PNC comprised over 400 members, approximately the same number of members as it had had in the mid-sixties.[27] Now, nonaffiliated members vastly outnumbered those representing the factions. At least formally, the PLO had reverted from an umbrella framework of guerrilla factions to a more centralized civilian-political center. Nevertheless, Fath continued to dominate the organization with the help of an increasing number of pro-Fath independents.

But even more dramatic was an increasing focus on diplomatic initiatives. Once again, the PLO found something that was denied to the inhabitants of the territories by both Jordan and Israel. Diplomacy thus became a substitute for the temporary loss of guerrilla action.

While the PLO was scoring victories in the regional and international arenas in 1973–74, its involvement in terrorist activity decreased considerably. It was only after the failure of the Geneva talks, harmful PLO involvement in Lebanon's internecine war, and a subsequent conflict with Syria in which the Syrians sided with the Lebanese Phalange that the PLO made strenuous efforts to organize terrorist activity in the territories.[28] Israeli data for the years 1975–76 shows a sharp rise in attempts to form local terrorist groups.[29]

The temporary decline in one functional monopoly created the need to emphasize an alternative. Nevertheless, armed struggle continued to be the PLO's major slogan, however much it was inappropriate to the situation. This ideology persisted less for strategic objectives in the struggle against Israel than with the wish to maintain hegemony over the movement.

State Building in Lebanon

In late 1975 and the first half of 1976, a wave of pro-PLO Palestinian nationalism swept the West Bank. As noted, guerrilla activity increased precipitously.

Yet unlike previous waves of guerrilla activity involving mostly cadres that originated and were trained outside the territories, this time most of the activities were generated from within the West Bank.[30] A nationalist youth that perceived the PLO as the legitimate representative of the Palestinian people had come of age. The appearance of local activists made the phenomenon of resistance more sustainable, especially since many were linked to the Palestinian National Front (PNF), the first territory-wide coalition of forces to organize within the territories for the purpose of resisting Israeli rule through political collective action (see next chapter).

Mass political protest revolving around the value-added tax that Israel sought to impose in the occupied territories added to the wave of protest. The synthesis between political nationalism and economic grievances leveled against the authorities expanded the coalition of opposition to Israeli occupation to include not only intellectuals and professionals who failed to compete in an Israeli-imposed common market, but shopkeepers as well. Both the synthesis of economic concerns and ideological positions and the effects of the emerging coalition made themselves felt in the municipal elections held in 1976, when nationalist mayors who identified with the PLO were swept into office.[31] Three years later, this same elite formed the nucleus of a territory-wide organ, the National Guidance Committee (NGC), which fought the Camp David process.[32]

These mayors, unlike their predecessors, were avid institution builders eager to embark on projects on a collective basis. Two sets of mayors, those of the twin towns of Ramallah and al-Bireh and of the adjacent cities Tulkarem and Qalquilya, agreed to establish coordinating committees, a first for the territories since occupation.[33] In Nablus, the municipality expanded its role in society. The newly elected mayor Bassam al-Shaq^ca announced the establishment of a municipal theater as well as a center that would coordinate activities between municipal organs and voluntary organizations "in the absence of the central state."[34] At least four cities publicized their desire to encourage the activities of voluntary work committees, established by the Jordanian Communist Party under the aegis of the Palestinian National Front.[35] Finally, three East Jerusalem dailies, two of which were ardently pro-PLO, followed these developments with great enthusiasm.

Yet instead of focusing on the territories and pouring resources into cadres eager to fight, students and shopkeepers willing to protest, and an elected local nationalist elite, the PLO responded with their own attempt at state building in war-ravaged, ethnically torn, and politically penetrated Lebanon. For the PLO, the maintenance of functional monopolies was more important than territorialization. Sabri Jiryis, the veteran editor of the prestigious journal *Shu^ɔun Filastiniyya*, condemned the PLO's preoccupation with the diaspora, accusing the factions comprising the PLO of "distancing themselves day by day from the essential problems."[36] Jamil Hilal, a spokesman in the PLO administration with pronounced leftist leanings concurred, but more bluntly. The PLO, as far as he was concerned, attempted to deliberately marginalize the importance of the territories when the diaspora center was so weak.[37] Presumably, the opposite should have been the case, as the time seemed propitious to transfer resources from the PLO to the territories.

Accordingly, funds flowed overwhelmingly to Lebanon. To be sure, the PLO was responding in part to a situation it had only indirectly created. The widening civil war and the withdrawal of an effective state left a vacuum in the provision of social services that the PLO felt only it could fill in order to take care of the needs of the Palestinian population.[38] The "alternative homeland" (*al-watan al-badil*) in Lebanon came to comprise 140 Palestinian Red Crescent Society clinics augmented by 47 more run by Samed, the PLO's economic arm, ten hospitals, and a vast bureaucratic network of over 8,000 employees. The PLO para-state presumably enjoyed a budget in the hundreds of millions of dollars (including constituent organizations), three-quarters of which went to support the PLO's social and administrative programs. Such a build-up amounted to state building rather than just the replacement of the Lebanese presence.[39] Moreover, this did not include the 5,000 workers directly employed by Samed or a communications network that included a Voice of Palestine radio network, several newspapers, the WAFA press agency, and a research institute.[40]

The transformation of guerrilla units into conventional army formations indicated that the PLO intended to stay in Lebanon for quite some time. By 1981, Khalidi writes that, "PLO Chairman Yasser Arafat was now a head of a state in all but name, more powerful than many Arab rulers. His was no longer a humble revolutionary movement, but rather a vigorous para-state, with a growing bureaucracy administering the Palestinians everywhere and with a budget bigger than that of many small sovereign states."[41] Khalidi was exaggerating somewhat, but PLO expenditures did stand at $233 million in the late 1970s, most of which was spent in Lebanon.[42]

It is estimated that the PLO spent at least a third of its budget to support a standing army alone.[43] This effort to establish a conventional army was another indication that Lebanon was becoming a permanent base of Palestinian nationalism. In fact, the nature of the PLO's military activities was at cross purposes to its political objectives. At the 13th PNC, held in 1977, the PLO had for the first time officially decided to create a Palestinian state. While borders were not designated, PLO leaders intimated that the state was to be created side by side with Israel rather than replace it. Nevertheless, cross-border raids or artillery into Israel's heartland along the Lebanese border suggested that the PLO remained committed to Israel's destruction. United States officials justified their persistence in not recognizing the PLO partially on these grounds.

A more basic problem for the PLO lay in its failure to grasp the near impossibility of creating a para-state in foreign territory. In Jordan, the organization had been foiled by a sovereign territorial state. In Lebanon, communal countermobilization would have compromised PLO efforts even had the Israelis not invaded Lebanon. Prior to 1982, before the PLO's effective military expulsion, communal countermobilization by newly politicized communities in Lebanon, mainly the Shiʾites, was already constraining Palestinian political action.

In historical terms, the Lebanese experiment was a costly diversion that did not take into account the conjectural context of state systems and rival micronationalism that might have accommodated incipient nation building in diaspora, but made it a disastrous arena for state building. Yet state-building efforts in the territories would only threaten the diaspora-centered leadership. A territorial elite, organized in an effective policy making territory-wide organ, could prove a threat to the PLO's centrality outside. The very success of this elite led the PLO to divert, rather than concentrate, allocations to the territories.

It was only in the wake of the 1982 Operation Galilee war, with the demise of Palestinian quasi-state-building in Lebanon, that, paradoxically, the PLO was forced by the Israelis to focus predominantly on the territories. In the war of the camps in 1985, the PLO started to acknowledge the fact that countermobilization had as deleterious an effect on para-state formation as did the state system. As the latter had rendered Jordan inhospitable, so did the first make Lebanon unbearable. Even so, the PLO maintained both a large bureaucracy and army in the diaspora. As late as 1987 the PLO, according to Jiryis, was focusing too much on the diaspora and even contemplated a return to Lebanon.[44]

State building, thus, then can become victim to the politics of national movements, if the struggle against the enemy is secondary to the struggle between contenders for the political kingdom.

Palestinian Ideology and State Formation

Zionist ideology has been acclaimed for its pragmatic thinking about building the state in incremental, evolutionary fashion; Arab nationalism, by contrast, has been criticized for being too ethereal and abstract, and thus, for failing to address the problems of transforming grand designs into concrete realities.[45] Assuming, as this perspective does, that ideas shape reality as much as they reflect it, did Palestinian thought and ideology focus or induce interest in preparing the institutional mechanisms for eventual statehood?[46]

The relationship between ideology and state formation can be analyzed along three lines

1. The intensity of the Palestinian ethos of territoriality
2. The relationship between evocative ideological symbols and institution building

3. The movement's collective cognitive focus on the state formation process in the pre-independence period.

Ethos and Territoriality

Though Zionism and Palestinian nationalism idealized the land, they related to it in fundamentally different ways. In Zionism, redemption was the central motif, and the territorial redeemers are the true bearers of nationalism.[47] For Palestinian ideology, at least until the intifada, the suffering of exile was a major theme, as was the belief that those who could deliver Palestinians from their affliction hailed principally from diaspora. It was the dispossessed refugees, in diaspora, rather than the oppressed Palestinians within Palestine, who most avidly evoked the Palestinian tragedy.[48] In Zionism, settlers in the Yishuv served as models of pioneering heroism and exemplars of a new national ethos of bold accomplishment in contrast to a withering diaspora. In Palestinian nationalism, it was the freedom fighters from the Lebanese camps rather than those demonstrating in Nablus, Ramallah, and other urban centers of the West Bank who were called upon to right an historical wrong and erase shame with the glory of struggle. The territorialists were *samid*, steadfast—a poor rival to either the Zionist *halutz* (pioneer) or the Palestinian guerrilla.

Only during the intifada was ideology fully territorialized, as the local stone-thrower emerged more glorious than the guerrilla, and the local, rather than the Lebanese, refugee camp became a bastion of Palestinian heroism. The ideology of the Fath-affiliated Shabiba movement in the territories had initiated the process of ideological territorialization when its youth committees, established in the refugee camps in the West Bank and Gaza in the early 1980s, were no longer perceived as reflections of transient camp life but as bastions of Palestinian heroism.[49] Palestinian "activism" took root in the land itself. By the outbreak of the intifada, the Lebanese refugee camp was no longer a story of heroism but a symbol of the withering of Palestinian diaspora. But unlike the Zionist case, where this theme was the ideological take-off point, in Palestinian nationalism, the concept gained currency only toward the end of the struggle for self-determination, when the possibility of achieving some kind of territorial entity in Palestine seemed real. Territoriality loomed large in Palestinian ideology, but it was a territorial focus that minimized the contribution of the territorial bearers in comparison to those in diaspora.

Ideology and Institution Building

Five years elapsed before Fath, the indigenous voice of Palestinian particularism, attained a dominant position in the PLO. Yet an ideology of *wataniyya* (nationhood) did not necessarily imply a focus on territoriality and statehood, or even a sensitivity to state formation. For, while it was true that Palestinian particularism promoted nation building, an ideology of cathartic and violent praxis was antithetical to institutionalization. Fath's appeal as a radical movement that defied existing states, and its belief in transformation through violent liberation were hardly the ideological blocks that facilitated serious thought on statehood.[50] In fact, the early writings of the organization involved repeated calls to avoid the subject lest theoretical concerns divide a vanguard that should be united by praxis itself.

This hostility to prosaic politics ran even deeper. Unlike the radical factions that encouraged political mobilization of the "proletariat," for Fath almost any form of politics was suspect. Politics bore with it the possibility of compromise on principles and objectives and opened the arena to cooptation by surrounding powers. According to Fath ideologists, the old Arab Palestinian movement succumbed to both these purported evils and paid for it in humiliating defeat. Only the strategic use and organization of collective violence could make the movement immune from these pathologies. Until 1967, Fath perceived itself as the detonator that would set off the conflagration between the Arab states and Israel. After 1967, the burden increased. Now it was to be a war of liberation in which the Palestinian guerrilla groups played the leading role.[51] The focus on the armed struggle served as a substitute for much needed discussion on institution building and the construction of territorial Palestinian society.

Liberation rather than redemption was what the diaspora center offered up until the early 1970s. Only after the territorialists responded with schemes for building national universities, nationalizing a system of higher education, and creating voluntary youth movements (see following chapters) did Palestinian ideology begin to seriously focus on the institutions of redemption.

The Focus on State Formation

Both the Palestinian and Zionist movements confronted ideological currents that diverted attention away from thinking about the process of state formation. Zionism ran the danger of being outflanked by philanthropism on the right and radical socialism on the left. The predicament facing Palestinian nationalism was no less acute, as the bear hug of Arab nationalism only gave way in later years to Islamic fundamentalism. Nevertheless, there was a key difference between the role of the state in Zionist and Palestinian ideologies. In Zionism, a strong state-centered current, which both furthered the idea as an objective and promoted coherent models of state formation, was remarkably developed. The PLO, on the other hand, never abandoned pan-Arabism, an ideology that is particularly weak on the structural and evolutionary aspects of state formation. The strong strains of pan-Arabism in the final communiqués of the sixth and seventh sessions of the PNC (convened to confront the growing crisis in Jordan) reflect how malleable ideology can be when it suits political purposes. To be sure, there was ample discussion of the state in the PLO but little on state formation as a process.[52]

To sum up, the ideological symbols with which Palestinian nationalism was infused were not inherently conducive to the articulation of state-formation processes. Founding ideas related to Frantz Fanon on the one hand and pan-Arabism on the other did not promote a state-building ideology. Diaspora concepts of uprootment and return (on an individual not a collective level) lowered the exchange value of the territorial Palestinians, as did the ideological role of armed struggle. Ideology was not solely an independent variable: the PLO prolonged the ideology of armed struggle with artificial respiration just as it perpetuated armed struggle in practice to achieve the same goal—the perpetuation of diaspora hegemony in order that it might be the prime bidder for the political kingdom. *!?

Political Fragmentation in the Territories

Fortunately for the PLO, political and ecological forces considerably helped to reduce the possibility that an alternative leadership would emerge in the occupied territories. The most devastating was the legacy of 1948. The literature emphasizes the fragmentation that took place as Palestinians fled to the various Arab states. Often overlooked is the fragmentation of those Palestinians who remained or fled to areas formerly within the Mandate. Ironically, these territorial Palestinians, divided between three hostile sovereign states, Israel, Jordan, and Egypt, were more isolated from each other than were refugees who fled to the other Arab states such as Lebanon, Syria, and the Gulf states. Two of them, Israel and Jordan, also had a clear state interest in maintaining and intensifying the fragmentation of territorial Palestinians: the Israelis regarding both their own Palestinian citizens from 1948, and the Palestinians in the territories from 1967 on; and the Jordanians, during their rule from 1948 to 1967. Because of the intrinsic importance of the West Bank, the latter's legacy is particularly important.

The Legacy of the Jordanian Regime

In an article on Palestinian state formation, Hisham Ahmad points out that the penetration of the Zionist movement into the area and the subsequent establishment of the state of Israel delayed Arab Palestinian state formation by at least forty-five years compared to other Arab states in the area. No doubt Ahmad is correct, but his analysis is incomplete as Jordan, too, played a significant role in the delay of Palestinian state formation, particularly after 1948. Their influence ran along two lines at least: (1) the relationship between state consolidation in East-Bank Jordan and the peripheralization of the area west of the Jordan River, and (2) state penetration and political, economic, and social diffusion of the West Bank that resulted in the population's thorough demobilization.

A look at demographic data reveals a striking pattern of state consolidation. While Jordan's capital Amman grew from 108,304 in 1952 to 277,344 in 1963 (an increase of 156 percent) Jerusalem's population grew from 50,000 to only 70,000.[53] Even then, Jerusalem was the only urban center in the West Bank, with the possible exception of Ramallah, to have a population-growth rate that nearly matched the national average.[54] In fact, the population increase of Amman alone was greater than the entire population increase of the West Bank during this period.

The regime encouraged massive population exit from the West Bank by heavily favoring industrial and infrastructural investment in the East Bank. In the early 1950s, one of four national projects was located in the West Bank, accounting for only 5 percent of investment.[55] The regime also encouraged the United Nations Relief Work Agency (UNRWA) and a variety of private voluntary organizations to promote vocational education that made many refugees eligible for emigration. Finally, East Bankers were favored with import permits in a service economy where inflow of funds have always exceeded domestic product.[56] The diminutive West Bank became unique in that it ruralized when surrounding societies urbanized, and hardly increased its population while the number of inhabitants in surrounding areas grew three- and fourfold.

Jordan went to great lengths to stunt the growth of Jerusalem. The kingdom scored two important political points by adopting such a strategy: the state (1) consolidated itself in the former Circassian village of Amman, rather than in the Palestinian side of the river; and (2) curtailed urbanization where Palestinian opposition to the regime was strongest.[57] Certainly, the immediate development of East Jerusalem after the 1948 war was beyond the scope of Jordan's meager resources. Even the state of Israel, despite its deep-seated commitment to the development of West Jerusalem, was unable during these years to promote a city growth rate comparable to other parts of the country.[58] Nevertheless, there are important indications, especially in the early years of Jordanian rule, that suggest a deliberate policy on the part of the Jordanian regime to downgrade Jerusalem and enhance Amman. For ten years, its city councillor requested that Jerusalem be declared a twin capital, but it was only in 1959, long after Amman's preeminence had been assured, that Jerusalem was declared the second capital of Jordan.[59] In a similar vein, a campaign to induce the government to retain some important ministries in Jerusalem failed as early as 1951, when the government began to transfer the Ministry of Education to Amman, at a time when the educational system in the West Bank was far larger and more developed than on the East Bank. Jordan also insisted that the UNRWA central office be situated in Amman despite the fact that the overwhelming percentage of its refugee clients were located in the West Bank.[60] If the relocation of the government ministries could be justified on grounds that the West Bank was more vulnerable strategically and that therefore ministerial headquarters should not be situated there, this consideration could hardly justify the relocation of UNRWA headquarters. Perhaps the most telling expression of the regime's attempts to downgrade Jerusalem was its refusal to grant permission to establish a university in the city.[61] Jordan feared that such an institution, particularly in Jerusalem, would foster a Palestinian identity around which Palestinian citizens of Jordan could crystallize.

Not only did Jordan reduce the West Bank's importance and attractiveness, it made sure it was powerless. Jordan had declared all opposition political parties illegal in 1957 and since most of that opposition was centered in the West Bank, the ban's net effect was greater there than in Jordan proper. For ten years, parties were forced to operate underground, severely undermining their effectiveness. Jordan repressed PLO institution building in the years 1964–67 with the same zeal it did the political parties, thereby preventing Palestinian institutions from taking root. When demonstrators ran into the streets in 1969, they shouted: "ʿAbdul Nasser, ʿAbdul Nasser," rather than the name of a leader from any of the emerging PLO factions.[62] So peripheralized had local society become that even when fighting on their own, they awaited a savior from distant Egypt.

Jordan actively fragmented the West Bank as well. Administratively, the Hashemite kingdom divided this small area into ever smaller administrative subdivisions. Up until 1957, the West Bank was composed of two regions (*liwa*) only, Jerusalem and Nablus. In 1957, a third was added as Hebron, formerly included within Jerusalem's domain, became a region in its own right.[63] Political considerations had something to do with this, as Jerusalem staunchly supported the Mufti, who was rabidly anti-Hashemite and an advocate of Palestinian state building, while Hebron was dominated by Shaykh Muhammad ʿAli al-Jaʿbari, the Hebron city mayor and a pro-Hashemite.

Moreover, a third administrative rung, the subdistrict (*nahiyya*), was created: two in the region and district (*qada*) of Nablus, one in the district of Jenin, and one in the district of Tulkarem.[64] The administration was further localized with the upgrading of Jenin to liwa status in a 1964 redivision. In 1965, Jenin was once again designated a district, yet the addition of a fourth administrative rung and an increase in the number of subdistricts from four to six canceled out the centralizing effect wrought by its abolition as a region.

The preservation of localism was even more evident in the government's attempts to organize labor. Only unions limited to individual towns were legal, and even then were restricted by specific trade.[65] The government obviously feared amalgamation of a potentially troublesome array of institutions. By 1967, approximately 5,000 workers belonged to unions, about 10 percent of the workforce in Jordanian industry at the time. Thirty-two out of forty-one unions were located in the West Bank, but as industrial establishments were much smaller, so were the unions. The average membership of unions in the Jerusalem-Ramallah area, where 60 percent of the unions were concentrated, was just 230. In the Nablus region, in which another 20 percent were located, union membership was far smaller, averaging 90 members per union.[66]

Finally, the Jordanian regime made sure that the provision of social services would be provided by voluntary organizations, and thus decentralized. The main providers of social welfare in the area—three federations of charitable societies in Nablus, Jerusalem, and Hebron—were all linked to the general federation in Amman but not to each other. Not one social service or public institution was centered in the West Bank. With the segmentation of the body politic and its subordination to an outside center, it is little wonder that no strong leadership with a common vision emerged to challenge Israeli rule.

The Israeli Administration

In 1967, the Israelis were to discover that the Jordanians had bequeathed a legacy that made the task of administering the West Bank relatively easy in the first seven years of Israeli occupation. So beholden were they to the Jordanians that the Israeli authorities continued the policy of the territory's former administrators.

Administratively, Israel intensified the policy of fragmentation by creating six districts in the West Bank and abolishing all hierarchies between them. In addition, Israel singled out the district of Nablus, the traditional center of Arab Palestinian nationalism, for special treatment: it was deprived of most of its territory, with land and population attached to the neighboring districts of Jenin to the north, Tulqarem to the east, and Ramallah to the south; the sparsely populated Jordan valley became a district in its own right. The timing of this decision belied its intent, for the redivision came in the wake of the Nablus general strike in 1969, the most serious attempt at mass civil disobedience in the West Bank between 1967 and the outbreak of the intifada.[67] The growth of the city of Jenin, as well as the administrative center of Salfit, a major village northwest of Nablus, formerly of that district but now placed under jurisdiction of more distant Ramallah, have been decisively attributed to Israel's interest in reducing Nablus' influence on the surrounding area.[68]

Israel assumed that localism spelled weakness and would be a disadvantage when it came to mobilizing mass resistance, unlike in the 1936 revolt when the localism of Palestinian life had served the community in good stead. Then, the British only had, at the height of the rebellion, a standing army of 20,000; Israel had at least five times that amount after 1967. In addition, with the construction of roads to most of the villages, the Israeli army had much improved access to the trouble centers of the Arab rebellion. Thus, after Fath's initial failure to territorialize, it seemed that Israeli rule would proceed uneventfully. Little did Israel realize that the PLO, through decade-long political mobilization, would be able to turn the weakness of localism into advantage during the intifada.

The Demography of Localism

Urbanization and metropolitanization characterized the states surrounding the West Bank. By contrast, the West Bank itself was one of the few relatively developed, heavily populated areas in the region in which a rural majority was maintained. This was so despite the existence of a thriving and continuous urban life. Few areas so relatively prosperous and populated and so richly urban are at the same time so local. With more than 450 official places of residence (the number of localities in Israel with four times the population), the dispersion of the population is four times greater in the West Bank than in urbanized and metropolitanized Israel. The bus lines, more so than any other single indicator, emphasize the localism and dispersion of the West Bank ecology, both in physical and administrative terms. Through the establishment of the Palestinian Authority, no Arab bus line ran through the length or breadth of the West Bank, a minuscule territory 100 miles long and 40 miles wide. In 1987, 387 buses, owned by 100 companies plied the roads. Seventy-one percent of these companies owned only one bus, and 61 percent of the buses serviced rural areas only. It took five buses to traverse the territory's length, and no one bus line covered even half of the distance in either direction.[69] Only Jerusalem served as a hub of transportation linking the city with other regional centers, and Tulkarem is the only other regional city (a definition that also includes Nablus, Jenin, Ramallah, and Hebron) that was directly linked with more than one other regional center by bus.

As table 2.1 indicates, the geographic distribution by district remained relatively stable over twenty years of Israeli rule, not allowing for the emergence of a demographic center that facilitates state formation. In general, there was little urbanization, for though urban areas grew faster than rural areas (93.1 percent compared to 76.8), the relative size of both hardly changed. Urban areas accounted for 38.8 percent in 1967 compared to 40.9 percent twenty years later, a level of urbanization substantially lower than the surrounding states.[70] Thus, the West Bank remained a predominantly rural, nonmetropolitan society. Even the urban centers, with the exception of Nablus, Hebron, and Jerusalem, were small.

The vitality of rural life and small urban centers under Israeli rule is also attested to by the data. The smaller urban localities in Jenin, Tulkarem, and Qalquilya exhibited robust growth rates, all exceeding average urban growth,[71] while under Jordanian rule, many villages, principally along the borders with Israel, suffered absolute population losses. Only 30 of 389 villages in the West Bank during this period experienced population loss, chiefly in the southern Hebron region.[72] Older villages spawned offshoots.

Table 2.1. West Bank Population by Subdistrict in 1967 and 1987, as Percentage of Total West Bank

	CBS 1967	WBDP 1987
Jenin	15.8	15.2
Nablus	17.1	17.8
Tulkarem	16.8	15.6
Ramallah	18.8	17.7
Bethlehem and Jericho	11.6	12.7
Hebron	20.0	21.0
Total	100.0	100.0

Source: Meron Benvinisti and Shlomo Khayat, *The West Bank Data Atlas* (Jerusalem: the West Bank Data Project, 1988), 29.

Emigration and Localism

Under Jordanian rule, emigration patterns also fostered political parochialism as remittances helped maintain artificially the viability of diffuse regional towns rather than foster metropolitan growth around Jerusalem, which might have been more conducive to the emergence of a national elite.[73] The regional towns were the centers of traditional urban notable power.

From 1967, geographic dispersion increased, spreading outward from the main highland region, principally to the west toward Israel, where most of the increase of employment opportunities could be found. Villages along the border and further inward enjoyed mild prosperity under Israeli rule as the West Bank workforce sought its fortune in the Israeli labor market. Little disruption occurred however, between residence and work site since most villagers commuted to work and worked side by side with fellow workers in places of employment in Israel. This was especially true of construction sites, in which nearly half of the Arab labor force from the territories were employed. While ties with the local village or refugee camp were maintained, the bonds between local notables and the proletarianized workforce were not.[74] Both trends boded ill for Israeli authorities. The urban notable had increasingly less control economically over his clients, and at the same time population dispersion substantially increased. Thus, the ability of Israel to maintain indirect intermediary rule weakened as did the means to monitor and control the political alternatives that emerged (two ingredients of control no occupying authority can do without).

But at the same time it made it difficult for a territorial leadership to emerge and engage in the establishment of translocal institutions. Even the incipient metropolitanization in the Jerusalem area due to the economic and political benefits of living in or near Jerusalem was offset by considerable institutional dispersion in the West Bank itself. Such dispersion benefited neither Israel nor the local elite, but rather the PLO, which penetrated it, as we shall see, through the help of front organizations.

The United Nations Refugee Relief Works Association (UNRWA) and the Private Voluntary Organizations (PVOS)

Foreign voluntary organizations and the UNRWA further fragmented and localized authority within the occupied territories. With the exception of states suffering massive natural calamities, prolonged civil war, or both, it is rare for relief agencies to possess budgets amounting to over one-third of the total governing authorities' expenditures. Nevertheless, this was the case with the UNRWA and the civil administration. In 1992, UNRWA's total budget stood at $128.6 million while the 1993 budget of the Israeli civil administration stood at $282.5 million, and it was the second largest employer after the government.[75]

Private voluntary organizations (PVOs) have also been especially active in the occupied territories. This is a legacy of the Jordanian era. Jordan was one of the only states in the Middle East that did not try monopolizing the provision of social services through state agencies but preferred to allow both foreign and indigenous private voluntary organizations to provide many of these services. These PVOs advocated a small-scale project-by-project approach that focused on direct contact with the clients and beneficiaries.[76] Even though many of the funds were channeled into areas where they enjoyed some autonomy, such as higher education and social and sports organizations, it was difficult, if not impossible, for a local elite to form around projects funded by these organizations.[77]

The Politics of Diffusion, PLO Penetration, and Mobilization

Just as Israel benefited from Jordanian policies of depoliticization and peripheralization in the West Bank, so in turn did the PLO benefit from the policies of its predecessors and rivals. Yet it benefited from the *cumulative* effects of such policies only when it began to penetrate the occupied territories in the mid- and late-1970s.

The PLO's legitimacy, formally won at the 1974 Rabat Conference, facilitated its hegemony and penetration even more. Unlike Jordan, which enjoyed only conditional legitimacy when it ruled the West Bank, and Israel, considered by territorial and diaspora Palestinians alike an illegitimate foreign occupier, the PLO became the sole representative of the Palestinian people.

The legacy of occupation worked to the PLO's advantage in at least three ways. First, as weak and as diffuse as the PLO may have been, the political elite in the occupied territories was even more diffuse, unorganized, and fragmented. Had the Jordanians not dealt so harshly with political parties and made politics such a personal, local, and factional game, opposition to the PLO might have been more intense. Israel intensified this effect through deportation—the physical exile of the political elite, many of whom were pan-Arab establishment figures. Second, because of Jordanian, Egyptian, and Israeli repression in the territories, the PLO by necessity became the first political center of the Palestinian community. Once in the seat of power, it became far more difficult to mount a challenge to its supremacy. Both of these impinged negatively on the possibility of territorial state formation by local Palestinians themselves.

Third, the legacy of demographic and political diffusion facilitated mobilization initiated and supported by the PLO. Israel incorrectly thought that such diffusion would help pacify the population. That might have been the case had there not been a competing outside agent emotionally and ethnically close to the indigenous population that could, through small-scale allocations and organization, win the hearts and minds of the inhabitants of many West Bank localities. Even before the intifada, Israel's control of the hinterland and the refugee camps became tenuous. The diffusion of the population rendered the provision of public services costly to the state but relatively cheap for the PLO.

The legacy of Jordanian and Israeli policies thus weighed heavily against any attempts by the locals to work together to develop centralized institutions. At the same time, demographic dispersion facilitated PLO penetration and mobilization of the population. The next chapter focuses on how the PLO secured resistance on the inside without generating territorial competition that would challenge the hegemony of the outside.

3

Territorializing the PLO

The PLO and Mass Mobilization

The institutionalization of the PLO as a diaspora center had significant effects on potential state building in the West Bank. In the following four chapters I analyze the ramifications of the wedding between the diaspora center and Palestinian politics in the territories as it was reflected in leadership, institution building, and resource-utilization patterns. Though these three dimensions are treated separately, a basic theme runs through all of them, namely, that in sharp contrast to the Zionist experience in the later stages of territorialization, political mobilization has increased fragmentation without engendering territorial center-building. The more mobilized, organized, and ideologized the inhabitants of the West Bank and Gaza became, the more the diaspora center favored political mobilization to institution building and social control. The PLO subordinated the politicized segments of the West Bank rather than cultivating the local leadership, fragmented institutions instead of amalgamating them, and finally, preferred diplomacy to political devolution, a facet that will be explored in greatest depth in chapters 5 and 6 on the intifada and the negotiations process. Such patterns reflect a personalistic state-building process that, I will argue in the final chapters, is ill equipped to foster state consolidation should a Palestinian state come into being.

Regimes have different goals for their populations and employ divergent means to achieve them.[1] As an occupying state, Israel often used naked coercion to demobilize Palestinian society and prevent state building. Jordan at times suppressed the population but generally only after cooptation failed to achieve the same results.[2] The PLO shared with these two regimes the goal of avoiding locally initiated Palestinian state building yet differed from both in its imperative to territorialize—to mobilize the inhabitants of the territories in order to prove to the world that they supported its claim as sole representative of the Palestinian people.

The inhabitants of the territories, by contrast, had other priorities, which stemmed from a different calculus. They not only harbored long-term goals for independence but had to conceive strategies to survive occupation. This meant establishing institutions that a laissez-faire occupation did not foster. Where mobilization exposed the local population to Israel's punitive measures, institution building facilitated the creation of local power bases to challenge the PLO monopoly, encouraged the possibility of devolution at far less human and material cost to the local inhabitants than armed struggle, and cushioned the harshness of occupation. Thus, a sharp asymmetry of interests characterized PLO-territory relations—the outside's gain was the inside's loss and vice versa.[3]

How the PLO prevailed upon the inhabitants to take the more expensive mobilization route is basically a story of building an alliance with a small, but growing, disenfranchised segment of political society—the students that flocked to the colleges set up by the middle-class elite they were to replace. For them, mobilization was rewarding. The change in the priorities of the politicized segments in the West Bank, from institution building to mobilization, is reflected in the ability of Fath to skip over the urban elite and ally itself with the newly educated. The creation of the Shabiba movement and the fostering of the middle command that led it reflected this alliance. Institution building was subordinated to mobilization by a middle command that, in its turn, was subordinated to the PLO factions.

Long before the emergence of Shabiba, however, there were challengers who gave priority to institution building and who had to be removed, coopted, or eclipsed.

Removing Territorial Challengers—The Palestinian Entity Idea

Violence or steadfastness—these were the choices the PLO offered the inhabitants of the territories in the first years of Israeli rule. Either join the guerrillas or remain passive. There was, however, a third way—state building based on the Zionist precedent. This was the frame of mind adopted by the advocates of political devolution, notables, intellectuals, and professionals who believed it possible that Israel would gradually devolve rule to local Palestinians and therefore sought ways to engage in state building that would facilitate the process and consolidate the state. The advocates of this approach were divided into two loosely knit groups: supporters of the Palestinian entity who advocated territorial state building and political devolution from the occupation power, and who were of high social status, and the younger institution-builders who not only sought an answer to the occupation, but also saw the need for social transformation that would undo the deliberate attempts of Jordanian-backed notables to reassert their authority as social, economic, and political intermediaries.[4] The two groups crystallized around the East Jerusalem newspapers *Al-Quds* and *Al-Fajr*, respectively.[5] *Al-Quds*, the sole survivor of the Jordanian purge of the Palestinian press, adopted a line supportive of state building, though this was hardly the central theme of the newspaper.[6] The same was true of the first ten issues of the *Al-Fajr* daily, which appeared in the first three months of 1972 (after which the PLO took over the newspaper).

Two conceptual threads unified this otherwise fragmented elite. First, both groups believed that territorial Palestinians had to become masters of their own fate. Second, they both championed the emergence of a liberal democratic entity. For the first group in particular, the devolution of power from occupation to democracy in postwar Germany and Japan provided a model they hoped would be emulated in the occupied territories.[7] But outside interference, as well as inter- and intragroup rivalries, scuttled any hope of their realizing the idea of devolution into statehood beyond its appearance on the printed page.

Nablus mayor Hamdi Kan^{c}an and the veteran mayor of Hebron (and Ja^{c}bari clan leader) Shaykh Muhammad ^{c}Ali al-Ja^{c}bari were two of the first group's most prominent members. Kan^{c}an's first foray into territorial politics began with a long article in *Al-Quds* on January 1, 1969, that called for local municipal elections to help foster a local leadership. That leadership, he proposed, would then take part in the future peace process over the territories. The proposal came in the wake of a visit of George Scranton, the governor of Pennsylvania, toward Israel. Scranton, who was known for his critical attitude toward Israel and therefore popular among Arab politicians, was the personal envoy of U.S. President Richard Nixon. To the dismay of Kan^{c}an, Scranton met solely with personalities known for their strong links to the Jordanian king and who supported the unity of the two banks, the basic position, in principle, of the United States. In his article, Kan^{c}an claimed that these people hardly represented the population of the West Bank and that elections should take place to resolve the issues of representation. This position was shared by the newspaper editors as well.

Especially as it was voiced by the mayor of the largest and most prosperous town in the West Bank, the article generated much interest. Nevertheless, the affair proved to be little more than a tempest in a teapot. After a quick visit to Beirut, in which he met PLO faction leaders, Kan^{c}an retracted his proposal and denied having any association with the idea of an independent Palestinian entity, a concept that he had never explicitly spelled out, but that had been read between the lines by the pro-Jordanian and the PLO.[8] An especially vicious attack in *al-Difa^{c}*, the official Jordanian newspaper, followed suit.[9] On March 12, 1969, Kan^{c}an, succumbing to pressure from both sides, resigned from office.[10] PLO factions had made common cause with Jordan in order to obstruct state-building efforts among local Palestinians. It was to become an all-too-familiar phenomenon in the years to come.

Abstaining from regional politics for over two years, Kan^{c}an resurfaced in August 1971, with another article published in *Al-Quds* containing similar ideas to those he had voiced previously.[11] The timing must have been a crucial element of his plan. Only days before, the remainder of the

Palestinian resistance had been forced out of Jordan. Jordan, itself, was preoccupied, suffering under the brunt of an Arab state boycott for this action. The time seemed propitious to create a local leadership in the territories that could negotiate political devolution. The difference this time was that Israel responded in the affirmative to such prompting and issued a statute on November 26, 1971, announcing the holding of local elections in the West Bank the following March.[12] But once again, internal Palestinian opposition foiled the Kan^{c}an plan. When Kan^{c}an drew up an electoral list to contest the elections, he was bombarded by threats of violence that culminated in the burning of a pharmacy of one of the candidates on the list.[13] On March 20, 1972, a mere eight days before the elections, Kan^{c}an withdrew from the race, despite considerable arm-twisting by the Israeli authorities to stand firm.[14] This decision marked the end of his involvement in politics.

Al-Ja^{c}bari's involvement was slightly less sporadic and regional than Kan^{c}an's. His major efforts consisted of convening large assemblies in the Hebron area that culminated in the establishment of a Public Interests Committee (lajnat al-masalih al-^{c}amma), a proposal to set up a radio station, and a request to establish a political party.[15] The last two requests were turned down by the authorities. Despite his daring, he frequently denied positions once they became known to the general public.[16] In later years, he justified his erratic political behavior on the basis of Israeli lack of support.

A striking feature of those in support of a Palestinian entity was their inability to operate in unison.[17] When Al-Ja^{c}bari assembled the Hebron notables, Kan^{c}an was absent from the political arena. Similarly, when Kan^{c}an published his articles calling for elections, al-Ja^{c}bari opposed them.[18] But this opposition in no way inhibited al-Ja^{c}bari from initiating similar efforts after he won the 1972 elections unopposed.[19] Even those who coined the idea of the Palestinian entity, Dr. Hamdi al-Taji al-Faruqi, a physician from Nablus and a former member of the pan-Arab Jordanian Ba^{c}th party, ʿAziz Shahada, a Christian lawyer from Ramallah, and journalist and writer Muhammad Abu Shilbaya, the most prolific of the three, rarely wrote at the same time.

The behavior of the young intellectuals who published and wrote in *Al-Fajr* was no different. While *Al-Fajr* is often described as a PLO invention, it began as a local locus of potential opposition, and was only later coopted by the PLO. Joe Nasr, its publisher, envisioned the creation of a political party, but adamantly opposed al-Ja^{c}bari.[20] In fact, the published diatribes of the newspaper against the Hebron mayor might have been behind Nasr's mysterious murder in 1974, presumably at the hands of Jamil Hamad, *Al-Fajr*'s editor and chief publicist.[21] According to the Nasr family, al-Ja^{c}bari, in collusion with Jordan, paid Hamad to murder Nasr. Jordan, the royal family in particular, was the other major target of Hamad and Nasr's barbs.[22]

Other intellectuals, most notably Salim Tamari and the Marxist ʿAdil Samara, took a more long-range view, suggesting in the pages of the newspaper moves toward state building through local institution building. Their proposals rested on a mixture of socialist and neocorporatist ideas.[23]

All these individuals shared one idea—the necessity for local Palestinians to actively participate in the shaping of their political fate. At the same time, they were dismayed by both their own parochialism and the considerable external obstacles that lay in their path. The inability of any of these three groups to build up a viable territorial center was demonstrated by the 1972 elections,[24] where the victors were, overwhelmingly, traditional supporters of Jordan; those supporting a Palestinian-entity had been forced out of the race by the PLO factions.

In retrospect, the supporters of the Palestinian entity hardly posed a threat to the PLO's preeminence. Their lack of diplomatic access on any level was underscored by Jamal Abdul Nasser's persistent refusal to meet with them, let alone share their ideals.[25] Moreover, they were challenging a movement whose level of institutionalization and cohesion far exceeded their own. They had all the characteristics common to precursors of nationalism rather than its realizers; they were a handful of individuals composed of journalists (such as Suni al-Bitar and Muhammad Abu Shilbaya), lawyers (such as ᶜAziz Shahada), and traditional leaders (such as ᶜAli al-Jaᶜbari). Historically, such nationalists tend to be replaced by second-generation groups whose leaders are organized according to political party or movement rather than loosely affiliated to a salon.[26] They were all the more disadvantaged in challenging an already existing organization, the PLO, which had the ability to punish opponents and also enjoyed the official blessings of Arab states.

Nor, of course, was Israeli support assured. The Israeli government's refusal to countenance a political party in the West Bank was absolute. Shlomo Hillel, then minister of police, justified this ban on the basis of comparative historical analysis. He argued that national movements that fought for either devolution of power or some form of power-sharing were inevitably replaced by more radical leaders seeking self-determination, a principle that Israel denied to the Palestinians.[27] Why, then, he queried, should Israel encourage a process that could only end in further repression and frustration?

Advocates of the Palestinian entity were men before their time. What they were offering, an essentially communal solution to a conflict that was viewed by the powers at the time as an interstate issue, simply did not appear on the international agenda as a viable solution. Israel viewed the territories as its negotiating card toward peace with its major state adversaries. Jordan and Egypt would have been forced to relinquish formerly held territory to the new state. Even Syria, who would not have renounced any territory in order to fulfill such aspirations, was hardly interested in such a solution, either because it did not want a solution at all for ideological reasons, still envisioned a Greater Syria, or simply did not want to be second in line at the negotiating table with

Israel. The United States, the last major actor, supported some form of compromise solution between Israel and Jordan. Devolution from occupation to statehood would have satisfied none of these states' wishes.

Despite the inherent weakness of the advocates of territorial devolution, the PLO went to great efforts to combat them. For while both the territorialists and the PLO agreed that the Arab Palestinian people needed to affirm its particularistic national identity, promote Palestinian institutions, and be instrumental in deciding their own political fate, this commonality of interests only intensified the conflict. It was clear that both sides sought to lead the Palestinian struggle along the course that would suit each side best. Moreover, all the major figures behind the Palestinian entity were native West Bankers satisfied at negotiating a solution that was restricted to the territories. The PLO, on the other hand, represented a constituency composed of essentially refugees who did not, for the most part, regard only the territories as their land of return.

Enmity thus prevailed between diaspora and territorially-based leaders. In the 4th PNC held in Cairo in July 1968, the Executive Committee issued a long but vociferous condemnation of the Palestinian entity idea:

> The Palestinian National Council in its resolutions warns of dubious calls to establish the fake Palestinian entity that will emerge on the basis of giving legitimacy and according persistence to Israel, something which contradicts completely the right of the Arab Palestinian people to its homeland in Palestine in its entirety. . . . The resolutions of the council pointed out that the fake Palestinian entity is in reality an Israeli colony, and it will liquidate the Palestinian problem to the benefit of the Israeli entity . . . in addition to the establishment of a quisling Arab Palestinian administration which Israel will rely upon against the Palestinian revolution. The National Council denounced in the most precise manner the idea of the fake Palestinian entity on Palestinian occupied territory after June 5, 1975, and it announces that any Arab individual or circle, Palestinian as well as non-Palestinian, who calls for such a quisling entity or who supports it, are the enemy of the Arab Palestinian people and the Arab nation.[28]

The ideological offensive became more intense as the fortunes of the PLO in Jordan ebbed. Though the PLO came under the control of Fath, the major force advocating the assertion of Palestinian identity and the preeminent role of the Palestinians in the Arab-Israeli conflict, it nevertheless began to place greater stress on pan-Arabism. This was reflected in the PNC resolutions of 1970 and 1971, which included demands for unity with Jordan.[29] The trend toward pan-Arabism served two purposes: to underline the moral obligation of Arabs to the Palestinian cause, despite the dismal fortunes of the organization representing it, and to delegitimize the Palestinian entity idea by juxtaposing regionalism (*iqlimiyya*) with loyalty to the time-honored ideal of pan-Arab unity.

The PLO, of course, won hands down. The advocates hardly left a historical echo. Nevertheless, they do reflect the logic of another path that could have been taken. Ironically, the PLO themselves ended up settling for less than they bargained for, lending weight to the notion that as intense as the struggle over the shape of the political kingdom may be, it might ultimately be less significant a question than who is to rule it.

Seeking Parity: The Palestinian National Front

Batting down its opponents on the ideological front was not the PLO's only method of preserving hegemony in the national movement. Recognizing the need for practical action, in the summer of 1973, Fath made common cause with the Jordanian Communist Party (JCP) and other, smaller political carry-overs from Jordanian times to set up a Palestinian National Front (PNF).[30] Through such mobilization, Fath hoped the PLO would be able to contend with (1) Jordan, which was willing to enter into some form of federation with the West Bank, (2) Israel, which, the PLO believed, was eager to grant the territories some form of home rule, and (3) the inhabitants of the territories, who living under an extractive and fiscally stingy military occupation, were beginning to embark on institution building on their own in order to provide services that the authorities were not providing. Through the PNF, the PLO aimed to coopt the existing potential and direct it along lines more amenable to the diaspora center.

The PNF set itself three essential tasks: (1) To politically mobilize the territories' inhabitants on behalf of the PLO; (2) to create institutions that wed political mobilization with the provision of real social services; and (3) to aid guerrilla activities. Though many of its activists were apprehended by the authorities in three large sweeps in the first four months of 1974, principally when it became involved in terrorist activities, it proved quite successful in achieving its first two objectives.[31] The expansion of the Communist-dominated Voluntary Work Committees in the Jerusalem area and other major towns, and an increase in the activities of existing leftist-dominated social service institutions such as Samiha Khalil's In^{c}ash al-Usra attested to its success.[32]

The popularity of the PNF was also reflected in a new emphasis on institution building in the press. During his tenure of office as editor of *Al-Fajr*, Communist Bashir Barghuthi transformed the PLO-controlled newspaper into a vehicle for the dissemination of state-building ideas. Special sections were devoted to parent-teacher and teacher organizations, labor unions, village federations, and worker and farmer cooperatives.[33] The newspaper called for both the proliferation of institutions as well as their territorial amalgamation.

But, as was to be expected, an ability to meet its objectives was not the criteria by which the PLO mainstream judged the PNF's efforts. The links the JCP, the dominant force within the PNF, possessed to Rakah, the Israeli Communist Party, and the Soviet Union, and the territorial framework in which it played a dominant role aroused the PLO's ire.[34] The ouster of Barghuthi as editor of *Al-Fajr* in 1977 brought the long-troubled cooperation to an end.[35] It was the last time Fath was to support a multiparty organ, institution, or party in the territories. Henceforth, centralized institution building was to be the prerogative of the diaspora center. The masses would only be mobilized in frameworks subordinate to the PLO.

State Building, Mobilization, and the Mayoral Elite

These lessons, however, were still unknown to the mayoral elite that had been elected in the 1976 elections. True, the outcome of the Rabat conference in 1974 foreclosed the possibility of openly challenging the diaspora center, but at the same time it did not preclude state-building strategies that could change the balance of power between diaspora leaders and territorialists.

Thus, the PLO became locked in a fundamental struggle with the West Bank's more radical mayors. While the PLO primarily sought to mobilize voice, the mayoral elite continued to look for ways to develop proto-state institutions (see chapter 4). Why mobilization and state building presented a trade-off and were not complementary had to do with the nature of Israeli control. Israel was willing to grant the mayors room for maneuver provided the mayors kept the peace. The PLO's mobilized resistance, on the other hand, invited Israeli repression, which hurt not only the mobilized but their institutions as well.

So strong were PLO suspicions of their territorial counterparts that they had been aired even before the 1976 municipal elections. "In my judgment," wrote one author in *Shuʾun Filastiniyya*, the PLO's academic journal, "the involvement in the PLO concerning the municipal councils represents a land mine that could boomerang against us. That is to say, it would be a big mistake if we push the establishment of a leadership framework within the occupied land, a leadership that enjoys a great deal of its legitimacy from the Israeli occupation."[36] The author later expressed fear that these mayors were containing the masses and suppressing their mobilization against the regime, an assertion that seemed to be valid enough. A notice signed by Nablus mayor Bassam al-Shakʿa and heads of the municipal council, the chamber of commerce, and labor unions that called for the cessation of protests was a good example:

> Out of our concern for our city and our citizens, and out of a desire to strengthen our steadfastness and the future of our children, and the preser-

> vation of our achievements and national unity, we call upon you to restore the life of our proud city to its regular state, to bring back the students to the schools, the workers to their places of employment and the merchants to their businesses.[37]

Though the mayors tried to allay PLO suspicions by professing loyalty to the PLO and drawing a distinction between national and municipal affairs, their actions belied their words. While the period preceding the 1976 elections was one of the most tumultuous years of Palestinian political protest, the two-year period after the elections revealed a downturn in mass protest, in large part because the mayors intervened to pacify volatile situations.[38] Nor was it difficult to assess the political dividends of such interventions. The press reported a feverish agenda of meetings between mayors and military officials revolving around development plans.[39]

Nevertheless, the PLO pressed for wide-scale mobilization, which demanded the mayors' full participation. And despite PLO fears, they responded with alacrity, and convened massive rallies denouncing the peace process. Between rallies, however, they busied themselves with the organization of the National Guidance Committee (NGC), a twenty-three-person body representing most of the organized sectors of Palestinian life.[40]

The NGC had several goals: one, it hoped to offset the possible costs of Israeli punitive action as the sole conduit of monies flowing through the Jordanian-Palestinian Joint Fund, which had been established by Arab states at the 1978 Baghdad Conference to fight the Camp David peace process.[41] It also attempted to recreate the PNF as its secret arm, primarily to represent its interests against those of Jordan in the Joint Committee, established to allocate Joint Fund resources, which Israel forbade the NGC to meet.[42] Third, the NGC had a definite state-building agenda. Through it, the radical mayors hoped to develop the municipalities as the administrative and technical nuclei for economic and social development.

So while the mayors willingly mobilized, they sought two objectives to offset its costs—the establishment of a collective and organized leadership and economic development. Once again the Zionist precedent is illuminating. In Zionist state formation, the nexus between investment in politically dominated economic activity was an important source for state formation. The Histadrut formed the basis of power for Mapai and its state-building leadership. In the late 1970s, Palestinian mayors hoped that allocations from the Jordanian-Palestinian Joint Fund would facilitate a similar process.

The PLO refused all of the NGC's requests.[43] It distributed the funds over a wider number of municipalities willing to be coopted and increasingly channeled funds to student-mobilizing frameworks rather than the municipalities and basic economic sectors.[44] Decision-making remained the prerogative of the PLO and the Jordanians. Moreover, the PLO pressed for the inclusion into the NGC of pro-Jordanian mayor Rashad al-Shawa of Gaza, whom the NGC feared would help break up its ranks.[45] His inclusion would have also violated an NGC principle that all member mayors be chosen in free elections. These moves dovetailed nicely with the PLO's implicit collusion with the Israeli authorities when it repeatedly resisted calls by leftist factions in 1980 and 1981 to honor the decision made by the 14th PNC in 1979 to renew efforts to establish the PNF after Israel had foiled their last effort by placing its leadership under strict surveillance.[46]

The NGC, Mobilization, and the Left

By the late 1970s, it became obvious to the PLO that the urban elite that effectively dominated politics in the territories resented the subordinate role the PLO had allocated to them. The PLO could only view with increasing alarm their persistent attempts to create centralized territory-wide institutions. Even more alarming was the character of the NGC. For the first time, a civil societal elite was working in tandem with organized political groups.

The role of the left was crucial in providing the NGC with popular support. Both the radical mayors and the leftist factions opposed Jordan, the common foe. But so, too, did the leftist factions oppose the mainstream PLO for its attempts to subordinate the territories.[47] These forces embarked on a major campaign in the late 1970s to fight attempts at PLO hegemony.

The earliest efforts were those of the Communists, the political movement most jealous of maintaining a measure of independence from and political parity with the PLO. They were the only political grouping from an exclusively territorial Palestinian political organ that had no direct organizational linkages with the diaspora. In the fall of 1975, after tensions between the PLO mainstream and the Communists had begun to surface in the PNF, the Communists in the territories decided, with the assent of the JCP, to form the Palestinian Communist Organization in the West Bank.[48] The organization became a full-fledged party in 1982. Ironically, the Communists, who accused the PLO of fragmenting territory-wide institutions, or "*taftit al-dakhil*" (literally "disintegrating the inside"), were the first to mobilize along strictly party lines. The appearance in 1978 of the Al-Tali^c^a newspaper weekly, edited by ousted *Al-Fajr* editor Bashir al-Barghuthi, broke the monopoly that Fath possessed in the nationalist Palestinian press, inaugurating a new era of multiparty Palestinian press.

More important, however, were their efforts of mass mobilization. As far back as the early 1970s, the Communists in the Palestinian National Front placed a premium on institution building, in contrast to the "resistance," which stressed guerrilla activities.[49] In part, this was due to Soviet policy, which opposed such activities in the territories. But it was also due to the harsh objective conditions under which the Communists operated in the Middle East. The Communist vision, particularly in the conservative Middle East, could only strive to attain long-term political goals through equally long-term socialization activities. Unlike factions in the PLO such as Fath, change in the social structure was more important than the achievement of immediate political goals, which could only result, at the present stage of local development, in a neofeudal regime. Such a regime would, in all probability, persecute the Communists. It was only natural, then, that they stressed the establishment of institutions that wedded political mobilization with the delivery of socially needed public services. Work in the social welfare field also accorded them the legitimacy they lacked as nonbelievers in a traditional religious society

The Voluntary Work Committees (Lijan al-ʿAmal al-Tatawuʿi), which appeared principally in the wealthier Jerusalem-Ramallah areas in 1972–74 despite attempts to penetrate the rural areas, were the earliest examples of Communist mobilization. These youth committees engaged in reforestation and public cleaning campaigns, took part in collecting harvests, and provided labor for integrating villages into the electric grid of the Arab Jerusalem Electric Company.[50] In July 1980, thirty committees convened at Birzeit University to establish the Federation of Voluntary Youth Committees.[51] The Communist takeover of the Nablus-based Federation of Arab Labor Unions; the spread of union activities into cities such as Hebron, Tulkarem, and Qalquilya, where such activities had been moribund since 1967; and the establishment of union branches in villages mostly in the larger Jerusalem area but around Hebron as well, should also be noted.[52] Finally, both a woman's wing, the Palestinian Federation of the Working Palestinian Woman and the first Health Aid Committee (Lajna al-Ighatha al-Tibbiyya) were established at this time.[53]

Local activists in the Democratic Front for the Liberation of Palestine (DFLP) rapidly followed suit. Of all the factions within the PLO, the DFLP was, in general, the greatest champion of territorialization and independence. Their early mobilizing efforts clearly reflected this approach. The establishment of the Women Action Committees (Lijan al-ʿAmal al-Nisaʾi) in 1979, which offered services not offered by the authorities, such as kindergartens, day care centers, and knitting and sewing training, was their most important contribution.[54] The union branch, the "Union Labor Bloc" (Kutlat al-Wahda al-ʿUmmaliyya), unionized the growing class of paraprofessionals such as nurses and electricians and attempted to protect the rights of Palestinians working in Israel.[55]

Yet despite these efforts and the prominence the left achieved in the NGC and other territorial bodies, these movements were severely constrained in their efforts at expansion. The more the left attempted to expand beyond the Jerusalem metropolitan area and into rural areas, the stronger was the resistance to the Marxism it espoused.

The Economic Basis for Fath Mobilization

Why Fath, the richest, most powerful, and most popular organization within the PLO, was the last faction to engage in mass mobilization in the territories may be due to the fact that it had the most to lose in the long term from such territorialization. Fortunately for Fath, however, new social groups emerged (students and prisoners from increasingly humble origins) that it could mobilize at a far less risk than it would working in tandem with the bourgeoisie elite represented by elected mayors.

Ironically, the dynamics of the dependent economic relationship Israel imposed on the territories provided Fath with this opportunity. How they enmeshed has to do with the way the Israeli-imposed common market impacted differently on the various social classes in the occupied territories. Basically, white-collar workers, who lacked knowledge of Hebrew and faced stiff competition from Israelis, suffered most from its consequences. Politically, they were the first to mobilize against the occupation. At the same time, they were, to Fath's advantage, weakened. By contrast, farmers who retained their markets in Jordan and the Arab world through the "open bridges" policy, the small entrepreneurial class who profited from subcontracting with Israeli firms in labor-intensive textile operations, and most of all, rural laborers who began to work in Israel, benefited from access to the Israeli market.[56] These workers were soon able to provide their children with high school and higher education. High school enrollment increased between the years 1969–75, from 17,682 students to 33,487 in the West Bank, and from 11,252 to 17,252 in Gaza.[57] The increase in postsecondary enrollment was even more dramatic: from a few hundred in teacher and vocational institutions in 1968 to 16,997 students in 1983, enrolled in twenty small Palestinian universities and junior colleges located throughout the territories. The growth in the number of inhabitants with thirteen years of schooling (as a percentage of the general population) reflects this well (see table 3.1).[58]

The geographical dispersion of these institutions was also critical. Local higher education is cheaper than education away from home, and so with the increase of institutions of higher learning, lower-status segments of the population were encouraged to attend. Indeed, the very weakness of the territorial national movement, analyzed in the next chapter, which tried to centralize education and avoid duplication when these institutions first came into being, proved to be a political boon in years to come. Had the local nationalists succeeded, they would have created more costly centralized education excluding the social segments of the population who became so important in the expansion of the national movement in the territories, particularly the type of activists that emerged in Fath institutions.

While the ranks of the newly educated swelled, the labor market's occupational structure hardly changed to absorb these newly educated cadres. This

Table 3.1. Educational Attainment in the West Bank and Gaza after Age 14 according to Years of Study

	Years of Study				
	0	1–6	7–8	9–12	13+
1970	50.1	16.8	7.2	31.5	0.5
1980	30.2	20.1	10.2	32.6	6.9
1986	23.1	19.5	10.0	36.1	11.3

was particularly true of the Israeli labor market, which (in the years 1970–84) accounted for 86.4 percent of job growth for those employed in the West Bank and all the growth in employment for workers in Gaza.[59] Throughout the period of expansion in high school and college enrollment, the Israeli labor market continued to absorb primarily blue-collar workers. Thus in 1986, two years after the increase in enrollment in higher education ceased, 97.5 percent of Palestinian workers in Israel were employed in blue-collar work. (see table 3.2). A sharp drop in wage differentials by schooling group occurred by the mid-eighties and the premium for working in Israel was eliminated.[60] It was evident that neither the Israeli nor the local economy provided employment commensurate with the expectations of graduates from high schools or institutions of higher education.

Table 3.2. Employed Residents of Judea, Samaria, and Gaza by Occupation and Place of Work, 1986 (%)

	In Israel	In Judea and Samaria	Total
	100.0	100.0	100.0
Scientific and academic workers	0.3	3.3	2.2
Other professional, technical, and related workers	0.8	8.8	5.9
Administrators and managers, clerical and related workers	0.6	5.6	3.8
Sales workers	2.6	14.6	10.3
Service workers	1.3	5.1	7.4
Agricultural workers	16.1	24.9	21.7
Skilled workers in industry, mining building, transport, and other skilled workers	27.8	27.1	27.3
Other workers in industry, transport, building, and unskilled workers	40.5	10.6	21.4

A comparison with Israeli Arabs who progressed on the occupational ladder over the years suggests that Hebrew, which the Israeli Arabs learn in the government school system, and which Arabs in the territories do not, continues to be a major hindrance to the occupational advancement of such workers in the Israeli economy (see table 3.3). But the growth that occurred in the civilian, governmental, and military-industrial complexes in Israel, all of which require, at the very least, Israeli citizenship, also ruled out the possibility of the absorption of Palestinians from the territories in higher-status jobs.

Not only did these newly educated cadres not find suitable employment, they entered the workforce after the era of prosperity in Israel came to an abrupt end in the wake of the 1973 war. After the war, GNP growth rates for the economies of the territories declined from the 13–15 percent of the early 1970s to 6 percent in the second half of the decade. In the first half of the 1980s, it shrunk further to 1.5 percent for the West Bank and a mere 0.8 percent in Gaza.[61] Wage rates for employment in Israel declined in Gaza in real terms by 4.8 percent between the years 1970–74 and 1980–84, and increased by a mere 13.5 percent over the same years in the West Bank. These developments had important political implications. If in the first years of Israeli rule, the blue-collar rural worker and farmer opposed the radicalism of the white-collar class for economic reasons, their children, graduates of the high schools and universities, joined forces with the older "white-collar" elite against the occupation also for economic reasons.

Students in Search of the Surrogate State

Typically, states with underdeveloped industrial sectors and inordinately large service sectors expand the public sectors to absorb the growing num-

Table 3.3. A Comparison between Israeli Arabs and Arabs in the Territories Employed in Israel according to Major Categories of Occupation (%)

	1969		1975		1982	
Occupational Categories	IA*	AT†	IA	AT	IA	AT
Unskilled	22.0	42.1	12.2	40.3	9.5	37.6
Semiskilled	31.3	28.9	33.4	38.4	30.4	38.2
Skilled workers	41.3	26.8	46.7	20.3	46.0	23.1
Clerical, sales	1.1	1.1	1.8	0.8	2.6	0.3

* IA = Israeli Arabs
† AT = Arabs from the territories

ber of educated unemployed and thereby avoid unrest. Most states prefer tackling the economic difficulties caused by bloated bureaucracies rather than the more arduous problem of comprehensive economic development.[62] With respect to the territories, however, the Israeli authorities chose neither alternative. Focusing increasingly on Jewish settlement and state expansion, the authorities transferred resources away from the maintenance of control over a potentially volatile population under occupation and applied a policy of fiscal austerity in the occupied territories, thereby keeping growth in government-financed public employment to a minimum. This intensified the effects of economic integration with the Israeli economy in skewing the occupational distribution of the market toward blue-collar work (see table 3.4).

Palestinian graduates were thus left with the choice to either lower their job expectations and seek employment in Israel, emigrate to the Gulf states to seek more remunerative employment (at least until the oil boom in the Arab world ended in 1983), or (the worse alternative from the Israeli point of view) petition their own charismatic "government in exile," the PLO. The same can be said of the other white-collar sectors, such as the professionals and the municipal workers, who had the most to gain from the growth of the state. Thus, particularly after the decline in emigration to the oil-rich states from 1983 onward, several social groups in the local population coalesced around a common "interest" against the occupation upon which a national movement could flourish.

If the Israelis were not ready or able to coopt the educated, the PLO was. The growth of student enrollment coincided with the Baghdad Conference of 1978, where oil states pledged $150 million annually to the PLO and Jordan to be used for political institution building in the territories. Some of these funds were used to form the mass mobilizing organizations and high-level labor-intensive institutions spawned and dominated by the various factions in the PLO.[63] Eventually, though, the expansion of the surrogate state needed to end, leaving an increasingly higher percentage of youth with only one option left—employment in Israel. The situation then became ripe for intifada. The expansion of the Shabiba youth movement and the development of a middle command assured its perpetuation.

Table 3.4. Employed Persons in White-Collar Occupations as a Percentage of Employed in Egypt, the West Bank, and Gaza, 1984

	Egypt (1983)	West Bank	Gaza
Academic, professional, and technical	11.0	8.7	7.6
Administrative	2.0	1.0	1.1
Clerical	8.5	2.7	2.4

The Emergence of The Shabiba Youth Movement

Where the Baghdad Conference presented the PLO with financial opportunities to check the urban territorial elite, the sharp growth in student enrollment in the twenty institutions of higher education supported by these funds enabled Fath to mobilize wider segments of the population and thereby bypass that elite.

The type of higher education that had emerged in the territories was ideal from the PLO perspective for several reasons. First, it involved small, intensely competitive, mostly private institutions. Thus, on the institutional level, no one institution or coalition of them could threaten the stature of the PLO outside.

Secondly, highly localized education meant cheaper education as there was less need to board away from home. Thus, a greater percentage of students from the villages and refugee camps could attend them. Unlike the urban elite (traditional, professional, or radical) that resented the subordinate role accorded by Fath to activists in the territories, these students had no such inhibitions and were hardly likely to resent the subordination Fath demanded. To the contrary, any institution building, however subordinate their own role, presented these students with avenues of social and political advancement denied them politically by the occupation, and financially by the constraints of the Israeli economy.

From the point of view of Fath, the students were the perfect cadres for political mobilization. The Israeli economy, in which most of the incremental job growth for Arabs from the territories occurred, absorbed almost exclusively blue-collar labor, leaving students dissatisfied and free to devote time to the cause. Moreover, students, as opposed to the professionals and notables who dominated the NGC, could not easily transform themselves into national leaders. They lacked seniority (in a culture that gave age its social due), elite connections, and the aspiration to challenge, on a personal level, the leadership of the PLO. Finally, students were replaceable. A leader who became too prominent could easily be challenged by the activists of the following academic year.

The establishment of the first Shabiba Youth Committees for Social Work in 1980–81 and the launching of the Shabiba Student Movement a year later reflected Fath's first major effort at coordinating mass political mobilization in the territories. Through Shabiba, political activism rapidly shed its elitist trimmings and became the concern of the educated, but common, young man.

The importance of the universities and colleges cannot be overstated. This was due not only to their numbers but also to their location, the socioeconomic background of the student they were attracting, the increasing enrollment of Muslim students and, most of all, the political socialization students received. By 1981, institutions of higher learning covered almost the entire West Bank and Gaza (under Jordanian rule, six of eight had been located in the Jerusalem-Ramallah area). Predominantly Muslim Nablus became the site of the first university outside that area. A Shariʿa college set up in 1971 in Hebron was transformed into a four-year B.A.-conferring institution a decade later. A new Shariʿa college was established in the small town of Qalquilya in 1977. Structurally, higher education became much more popularized with the establishment of private vocational junior colleges in 1983. These institutions followed the American model, offering two-year programs, and thus attracting lower-status students who could not afford a four-year university education.[64]

Ultimately, these trends of popularization, Islamicization of the student body, and geographical spread of higher education away from the Jerusalem metropolitan core aided Fath in achieving the hegemony it needed. An analysis of the 1985–86 student union election results in the major institutions of higher learning clearly indicate that with the exception of Gaza University, the more predominantly Islamic the institution's student body composition was and the greater the institution's distance from the Jerusalem area, the greater was the support for Fath's Shabiba Movement (mostly at the expense of the leftist factions) along with the Islamic Bloc. Shabiba also did best in the junior colleges, suggesting that the movement attracted poor, if not the poorest, students.[65] In Birzeit University, in which Christians accounted for approximately 25 percent of the student body, the Shabiba narrowly fended off (36.8 to 34.7 percent) a leftist coalition of PFLP, DFLP, and the Communists. The Islamic Bloc won 28.5 percent.[66] At Al-Najah University, located in the more distant but sophisticated provincial city of Nablus, the balance of forces was altogether different. The Shabiba movement won 49.3 percent of the vote and the Islamic Bloc garnered 37.7 percent, while the two leftist factions, Jabhat al-ʿAmal and the DFLP's al-Wahda al-Tullabiyya (Student Unity Bloc), received a mere 13.1 percent of the vote combined.[67] A sample poll conducted among students in that university in 1981 revealed that only 1.4 percent of the student body were Christians.[68] At Hebron University, which was almost exclusively Muslim, the Shabiba won 50 percent of the vote, the Islamic bloc 43.6 percent, and the leftist coalition garnered only 6.4 percent of the vote.[69] Only in Bethlehem University, where Christians accounted for 40 percent of the total student body, did Shabiba not win a plurality, which went to the PFLP's Jabhat al-ʿAmal al-Tullabi al-Taqaddumiyya (Progressive Front for Student Action), which won nearly every year since the late 1970s.[70]

The Shabiba thus firmly established itself as the central mass-mobilizing organ in the territories. The timing of its entry, particularly into student politics, was perfect from Fath's point of view for two reasons. First, in 1982 the Shabiba was able to lead to victory national coalitions of the Shabiba, DFLP, and PFLP blocs over the Islamic bloc in three of the major universities and thus stem the Islamic tide that took place due to the lack of a strong non-Marxist nationalist alternative in former elections.[71] Moreover, as these victories occurred after the 1982 war when the diaspora PLO was at its lowest ebb since its forced ouster from Jordan in 1971. The elections were also harbingers of things to come. For the first time, the fortunes of the nationalist movement inside the territories did not directly depend on the political strength of the PLO outside. The seeds of local assertiveness, which became prominent in the intifada, had already become evident. Fath hegemony was also important in the long term to achieve greater conflict resolution within the broader political movement, which included, as mentioned earlier, Islamic elements. A modus vivendi of sorts emerged in the mid-1980s between the nationalist camp and the Muslim Brotherhood after years of intermittent conflict that reached its climax with the November 1984 murder of ᶜIsmaᶜil al-Khatib, an instructor in English literature at Gaza University and a member of the Brotherhood. The agreement that ended the more extreme forms of violence between the two camps would have been unthinkable had Fath not been able to carry its political weight as the dominant party grouping in the local Palestinian arena. That modus vivendi made possible tacit cooperation between Islamic groups and the PLO in the early critical stages of the intifada.

The Emergence of the Middle Command

While students formed the recruiting pool for Fath mobilization, they were not themselves the founders of the first Shabiba Committees in West Bank villages, refugee camps, and urban neighborhoods in 1980/1, nor of their student wing, Harakat al-Shabiba al-Tullabiyya, first established at Birzeit University in 1982.[72] Rather, these were established by former prisoners, whose socialization within Fath ranks had begun as early as the age of fifteen and sixteen. Incarcerated in Israeli prisons—where they engaged the authorities through a political committee and its spokesman, the "shawish"—and exposed to mutual and intensive indoctrination, they were rapidly transformed into an ideal middle command. They were officers who could lead but, by the same token, were subordinate to a hierarchy. Their time in prison helps to explain why Fath waited so long to mobilize despite the weakness of the opposition; not only did it need time to cultivate a generation of students, but, even more fundamentally, it suffered from a dearth of men in the West Bank that having grown up within Fath ranks could be depended upon. Released prisoners, it could be ensured, would remain subordinate to the outside center and promote mobilization over institution building.[73]

Especially prominent in this middle command were younger prisoners incarcerated in the latter half of the 1970s and released at the end of the decade or the beginning of the 1980s.[74] As most were apprehended before they committed the acts they had planned, they received relatively short prison terms.[75] Organizational leaders such as Samir ʿAtili, ʿAdnan Damiri, Ghassan ʿAli al-Masri, and Samir Subihat shared several important features characteristic of the middle command that emerged at the time. All were arrested for attempted terrorist activities in the mid–1970s and were released in the next five to seven years. Upon their release, all became active in student politics in the key institutions of higher learning in the West Bank. And all affiliated themselves with the Shabiba movement.[76]

The rise of this middle command represented a generational change in terms of age, modus of operandi, and sociological background from the mayoral leadership in the NGC that was officially outlawed on March 11, 1982, after a series of dismissals, administrative arrests, and deportations of its members.[77] Eleven of the twelve NGC members that had been placed under administrative arrest resided in urban areas, predominantly in the Jerusalem metropolitan area,[78] and included three town mayors, two lawyers, a dentist, an engineer, the president of the Jerusalem Federation of Charitable Organizations, and three newspaper editors. All of them were high-level professionals who combined political with professional pursuits.

The new organizational command, just like the students they led, originated from more geographically dispersed areas, principally from small towns, villages, and refugee camps. Half were of lowly rural and camp backgrounds and they were all nearly twenty years younger than the most prominent members of the NGC. While the main NGC members were white-collar professionals, the careers of the activists were almost totally linked to popular mobilization within the organizations as students, labor unionists, or teachers. Among those placed under area confinement in 1984, of the 37 whose occupation is known, 22 were students, 5 were workers, 5 were rank-and-file journalists, 2 were shop owners, and 1 was a teacher. Only one, a lawyer, formally belonged to the higher ranks of the white-collar class.[79] Thus, while the leaders of the NGC represented a professional elite in the major towns, the emergent organizational command was of humbler social origins and occupations.

Above all, these men accepted hierarchy, organization, and ideology. They knew how to act but not to speak, to be followers not leaders, and to respect the basic ground rules in the relationship between the PLO and the territories. They represented a middle command rather than a leadership, even a local one, as the NGC was often called.

An insularity from outside influences was another characteristic that distinguished the new middle command from the charismatic leadership it replaced. The PLO preferred "in-bred" organization men rather than known and socially privileged leaders. ʿAdnan Damiri's biography is telling. The fact that he was unknown to many observers even after he had been active for ten years in the territories is reflective of how command patterns changed. The mayors, on the other hand, headed municipalities that were intimately connected with, and ultimately dependent on both Jordan and Israel. Bassam al-Shakᶜa, who assumed the mayorship of Nablus in the 1976 municipal elections, was an internationally known personality soon after being elected. His charisma contributed to the tensions that prevailed between the PLO and many of the mayors.[80]

Marginalizing Deportees in the Diaspora Center: The Bifurcation of Leadership

As the PLO sought to undermine the emergence of a local political leadership, the emergence of an unknown middle command was preferable to rule by notables such as al-Jaᶜbari and Kanᶜan, or even the second generation of leadership led by men who emerged in the 1976 municipal elections, such as Nablus mayor Bassam al-Shakᶜa and Ramallah mayor Karim Khalaf. However, Israel's removal of the NGC leadership and their replacement by a loyal middle command that respected the PLO's monopoly on strategic decision making did not completely allay fears of the possibility that an alternative leadership would emerge. Extra safeguards were therefore necessary.

Therefore, the PLO even sought to restrict the power of territorial leaders who, deported by the Israelis, joined them in diaspora. In the 12th Palestinian National Council held in 1974, four West Bankers were included in the fifteen-member Executive Committee of the organization for the first time since Arafat took over the PLO in 1969.[81] Yet despite the rise since then of pro-PLO political mobilization in the territories, the number of deportees in the Executive Committee decreased rather than increased. In the 15th PNC held in Algiers in 1981, the number of "West Bankers" was reduced to two out of fifteen. Their number increased to three in the following PNC in 1987. But this new member, Sulayman al-Najjab, was included not to represent the territories per se but the Palestinian Communist Party, which was joining the PLO fold for the first time.[82] Significantly, the PLO Executive Committee did not include any of the thirty-three activists that were deported in the period between the intifada's outbreak and the 19th PNC session held in November 1988. Neither did it designate any of the deportees on the Executive Committee to participate, let alone lead, the first round of negotiations over the future of the territories, which were held between the PLO and the United States in December 1988.[83] The Executive Committee continued to reflect the prevailing diaspora-centered communal structure even after nearly two years of intifada forced the realization that the battlefield and arena of sacrifice had almost completely shifted from the diaspora to the territories.

Removal and rotation of deported members in the PLO Executive Committee further marginalized the role of territorialists in the diaspora center. By the 1981 PNC, only one member, ᶜAbd al-Muhsin Abu Mayzar, remained of the four that had been included in 1974. The second representative chosen in 1981, Hanna Nasr, ex-president of Birzeit University, served for only three years, from 1981 to 1984, temporarily replacing Iliya Khuri for the "Christian" seat in the PLO Executive until the latter returned to his seat in the 17th PNC held in Jordan in 1984. The politically more active, and critical, ʿAbd al-Jawad Salih was forced to vacate his seat in 1981. Abu Mayzar eventually withdrew of his own accord, after siding with Fath rebels against Arafat in 1983. Such rotation and change contrasted markedly with the stability of the top leadership in the Executive Committee. In 1992, only one truly politically active deportee from the territories, Muhammad Milhim, the mayor of the small town of Halhul near Hebron, sat on the Executive Committee, but he did not command any position of power within the organization.

The same marginalization of the territorialist middle command and leadership prevailed in Fath circles. Despite the deportation of thirty Fath and Shabiba members by the time of the 5th Fath congress in August 1989, none of them were among the nine newly elected members to the twenty-one-member Fath Central Committee.[84] Only three seats were allotted to unnamed activists from within the territories, even though the assembly decided to increase the membership of the Central Committee from 15 to 21 members. Similarly, only three deportees were elected to the fifty-member Revolutionary Council. Only one of these was an intifada deportee, Marwan al-Barghuthi, the former president of the Birzeit Student Council and, presumably, a member of the Intifada Unified National Command. The other two, Abu ʿAli Shahin and Akram Haniya, were from the pre-intifada era.[85] Even the Democratic Front for the Liberation of Palestine (DFLP), a faction that prided itself in particular for its early focus on mobilization efforts in the territories, saw fit to allocate only three places out of thirteen in its highest organ, the Political Bureau, to unnamed members within the territories in February 1990.[86]

The PLO preference for the development of a professional officer corps that stuck to the organization of resistance to the Israeli authorities and refrained from engaging in broader Palestinian politics is best reflected by the "independence document" episode of early August 1988.[87] The Israeli General Security Services (the secret service) found a document declaring the independence of the Palestinian state in the offices of Faysal al-Husayni's Arab Studies Society. Husayni was reputedly the head of Fath operations in the territories (and indeed formally designated as such after the Cairo agreement of May 4, 1993).[88] The document listed 144 members from the territories in the proposed provisional council, a similar complement of diaspora members to be designated by the PLO.[89] Of all of these, only 2 of 53 deportees or those designated to be deported—a Birzeit University professor who was a leader of the Palestinian Communist Party and a DFLP labor unionist—appeared on the list.[90] The deportees, those who organized the intifada, were middle command and, as such, not regarded as prime candidates for political leadership.

An additional safeguard to the marginalization of deportees was the bifurcation of leadership functions in the territories, which, under the mayoral elite, had been combined into one leadership. While Damiri and his colleagues built up the Shabiba organization, Fath elevated "spokesmen," such as Hanna Siniora, the editor of *Al-Fajr*, and Faʾiz Abu Rahma, the head of the Lawyers Association in Gaza, who enjoyed neither widespread popularity nor strong connections with mass organizations such as the Shabiba organization. To make sure that Siniora remained no more than a "spokesman," the PLO supported magazines such as *Al-Bayadir Al-Siyasi* and *al-ʿAwda* to add competing voices that served to curtail his local influence. The adoption in 1987 of a pro-PLO stance by *Al-Quds*, by far the most widely read newspaper in the territories, further reduced the local influence of both *Al-Fajr* and its editor.[91] "Spokesmen" were also replaced with relative frequency.

The bifurcation between political spokesmen and the intifada's middle command might have reflected institutionalization in an orderly polity. For the Palestinians, this state of affairs only further reflected the internal fragmentation of territorial Palestinians and their subordination to the outside center.

Conclusion

The marginalization of the territorial Palestinians in the decision-making forums of the PLO contrasts sharply with the situation that prevailed in the Zionist movement, where the territorial leadership dominated the WZO and the territorial rank-and-file were accorded a "double vote" in organizational elections, compared to diaspora voters. In the Palestinian case, instead of a diaspora leadership being replaced by a territorial leadership, one finds increasing subordination to the outside center. The extent of such subordination proved to be a function of PLO penetration. When the PLO and its factions possessed few political connections within the West Bank, one could still find aspiring state-builders operating independently of the PLO. By the mid-1970s, however, they were either thoroughly defeated or coopted.

By 1976, the mayoral elite, allying with the territorialist Palestinian Communist Organization, had effectively lowered their sights to seeking parity within the PLO, though they might have still harbored aspirations to eventually replace the PLO's diaspora focus. The NGC's readiness to play a mobilizing role and incur the wrath of Israel effectively led to their demise and deinstitutionalization. But so, too, did direct efforts at mobilization enable the PLO, and especially Fath, to bypass the NGC by "jumping over" the urban elite to mobilize the growing student population. At the same time, the PLO cultivated a spokesmen leadership. The mayoral elite, the only strata in the West Bank that could effectively organize civil society politically and institutionally, became a distant memory. Territorial center-building gave way to politicized factionalism and diffusion as the goal of mobilization overrode concern for state formation. While the Zionists abroad subsidized political parties in Palestine out of which the new leadership of the Zionist movement emerged, the Palestinians outside built up mass movements in the territories that subordinated the inside to the outside.

4

Education and State Building

The Palestinians in the territories, living under an occupation rather than a Mandate, were never able to create the quasi-state institutions that characterized the Yishuv. Instead, in order to address pressing social needs, foster national identity, and pave the way for future state building, they had to build legitimate functional institutions that the Israeli authorities would have difficulty opposing. No sector of life engaged the attention of Palestinian institution-builders as much as that of higher education. This chapter analyzes the interplay between the PLO, local politics, and civil society in the creation of a Palestinian system of higher education in the territories. It examines two major territory-wide projects, and finally, the way the diaspora-territorial conflict was played out within al-Najah National University, one of the most important institutions of higher learning in the territories in the late 1970s and early 1980s.

The Arab Palestinian University Scheme of 1972

Having failed in their call for a Palestinian entity, its advocates focused instead on the creation of a Palestinian Arab university as a form of long-term institution building. The idea dated back to the first year of occupation when Aziz Shahada, a Christian lawyer who represented Palestinian refugees at the 1949 Lusanne Conference, presented a draft proposal to Moshe Dayan, Israel minister of defense, at the beginning of 1968. A year later, Shahada asked his friend, Dr. Muhammad Nashif, the director of the government-controlled Teachers' Training College in Tulqarem, to sound out the Jordanian authorities on the possibility of establishing such an institution under the aegis of the University of Jordan, which had been founded in Amman six years previously.[1] Presumably, the request was a technical matter, but political considerations demanded it. As a prominent advocate of the Palestinian entity, Azis Shahada was suspect in Jordanian eyes, thus making it imperative to get their assent on the matter. Besides this, however, Jordanian consent was necessary as Jordan could prevent the university's accreditation, without which its graduates would likely not be employable in the Arab world.[2]

Despite these early proposals, the real push for the project came only three to four years later and was timed to take advantage of the weakness of the two forces that were likely to oppose it, Jordan and the PLO. In the years 1971–72, the Palestinian resistance movement was in a political and military abyss, having been decisively defeated and ousted from Jordan. The evacuation to Lebanon had not yet been completed, and the air was poisoned by recriminations between the factions over who was responsible for the fiasco. The almost total absence of guerrilla activity in the territories reduced the threat of retaliation against those who considered taking a different course of action than that taken by the PLO. Jordan, meanwhile, was isolated in the Arab world for its crackdown on the Palestinians.

Nevertheless, there was also Israeli opposition to consider. Israeli policy, at least as it was formulated by David Farchi, Dayan's special adviser on the territories, supported local institution building when it was part of the process of normalizing life, but not as a means of creating a new political process. This became clear in the spring of 1971, when the Israeli authorities notified Shahada that they would only agree to a meeting to choose a preparatory committee for the university provided that the committee was limited to professionals in the field of education.[3] Unfortunately, the personalities behind the request were pronouncedly political. All of them—Shaykh al-Ja^c^bari, Hamdi Kan^c^an, Elias Bandak (the mayor of Bethlehem who, at one time, had proposed the incorporation of Bethlehem into the state of Israel), and, of course, Shahada himself—were identified as supporters of the Palestinian entity.

Shahada had no choice but to meet Israel's dictate. The meeting that he organized was attended by persons directly involved in education, most of whom, as members of the educational bureaucracy in the West Bank, were still receiving supplementary salaries from the Jordanian government. This may well explain their timidity; to Shahada's regret, those attending the meeting changed its subject from the proposed university to the more innocuous theme of coping with problems faced by students who completed the Jordanian matriculations (imtihanat al-tawjihi).[4] This, however, did not prevent the foreign minister of Jordan from branding those seeking to establish the university as traitors and agents of Israel. Al-Ja^c^bari, who was also the former minister of education of Jordan timidly denied that any linkage between the two topics was made at the meeting.[5]

Efforts to establish the university persisted nevertheless. In July 1971, it was al-Ja^c^bari's turn to approach Dayan on the matter. The response he received was more problematic than that given to Shahada. Though Dayan assented to the idea, in principle, he suggested that al-Ja^c^bari approach the Israeli Ministry of Education to discuss its realization. Such a course of action posed two serious problems. First, it ran contrary to the principle of complete independence of the project, without which it would lose credibility among Palestinians. After all, its supposed goal was devolution from Israeli occupation, not integration into the Jewish state. Second, no Arab government would recognize the degrees such an institution would confer.[6]

More intensive efforts to establish the university were made soon after the West Bank municipal elections of spring 1972. This time, the initial moves were shrouded in secrecy. On September 1, 1972, *Al-Quds* reported that a preparatory committee for an Arab Palestinian university had been established but did not mention the date of its establishment nor the names involved. It did, however, announce that the committee had sought government authorization, that it intended to widen membership to include mayors and members of chambers of commerce, and, perhaps most importantly, that it had received Jordanian assent. Two weeks later, *Al-Anba*, the Israeli General Federation of Labor's Arabic daily, reported that Israeli authorization was granted on the request of mayors and education officials and that Anwar Nusseibeh, a former defense minister of Jordan, felt that Jordanian assent was forthcoming.[7]

Moreover, it was announced that the Ramallah municipality, under the mayoralty of Karim Khalaf, had already authorized municipal land for the university's purpose.[8] Khalaf, who was later a leading figure in the NGC, was known to the authorities by that time as an opposition leader. In a meeting between himself, al-Bireh mayor ᶜAbd al-Jawad Salih, and Dayan, the minister of defense cautioned both against turning their cities into centers of demonstration against the occupation, for otherwise he "would send the paratroopers in."[9] The authorities were also miffed by Khalaf's opposition to Israeli representation on the board of the Jerusalem District Electric Company, the largest Arab economic institution in the territories. He shared this view with Salih, the most radical of the mayors in the West Bank, who was later deported for his presumed role in the Palestinian National Front. The two mayors viewed acquiescence to the presence of two Israeli representatives on the board both as a tacit agreement to a unified Jerusalem as the capital of the state of Israel, as well as the beginnings of Israeli takeover of this key Arab institution.

Several days later, *Al-Quds* announced that Harb al-Harb, a Communist known for his close links to the Palestinian resistance, was to serve on the preparatory committee as the Ramallah representative. His inclusion suggests that those behind the university project were deliberately trying to win over representatives of the PLO factions that were inimical to central institution building and to downplay the fact that so many of its initiators were advocates of the Palestinian entity. Nevertheless, Harb was not one of the men comprising the preparatory committee who met the following day at the Ramallah municipality.[10] Theirs were more familiar faces, including Al-Jaᶜbari, the chairman, Shahada, the assistant chairman and the moving force behind the project; and Hamdi Kanᶜan, who "represented" Nablus. All were known advocates of both the Palestinian entity and the university. A fourth member, ᶜAbd al-Nur Janho, a Ramallah businessman and land dealer who prospered under Israeli rule, was included to ensure Israeli support. (Janho was later assassinated by a member of the PFLP).[11] Another member, the district head of education, was a longstanding official in the Jordanian bureaucracy. Two professionals, a physician and a lawyer (both from Ramallah), were also included. Only Khalaf, as the sole "radical," broke the committee's homogeneity.[12]

One man missing from the list was Nihad Abu-Gharbiyya, the founder of al-Ibrahimiyya College in Jerusalem and a member of the Islamic Higher Council, who, in an *Al-Fajr* interview two months previously, had announced that he was a candidate for membership. In that interview, Abu-Gharbiyya bitterly attacked Jordan for hypocritically rejecting Shahada's proposals on the grounds that there could be no academic freedom under Israeli occupation, for it had not existed in Jordan either. He also expressed doubt regarding Israeli intentions. Ultimately, he proposed the establishment of a technical-vocational university rather than the traditional liberal arts school in order to better meet the needs of the labor market. A liberal arts education would only promote emigration, while an emphasis on technical subjects could fill the need for high-quality technicians.[13] Abu-Gharbiyya's absence from the committee was deliberate. Shahada and his friends had still not resolved the thorny issue of Jerusalem representation, which Israel would adamantly oppose. As far as Israel was concerned, the divorce between Jerusalem and the West Bank had to be as complete as possible.

But this was only one of several problems facing the committee. More important was the question of how to achieve recognition for the university. This involved pan-Arab acceptance, particularly from the Federation of Arab Universities (FAU) and, to a lesser extent, the Arab League. Though in the past, the FAU had agreed that higher education in the territories was a necessity, it never gave its assent to a central university. Instead, it preferred that a system of higher education emerge from existing institutions. At a FAU conference in May 1972, the president of Cairo University proposed that five colleges spread across the territories should serve as the nucleus for such a university.[14] At the conference, it was decided that each college would specialize in one field. Theological and Islamic jurisprudence would be studied at al-Azhar College in Gaza; medicine would be taught in the al-Maqasid Hospital; agriculture in Tulkarem Government College; engineering in al-Najah College; and humanities and pure sciences at Birzeit College.[15]

The federation's proposal raised an important point—the need to capitalize on existing institutions in order to reduce start-up costs. Indeed, Hafiz Tuqan, the former mayor of Nablus, sharply criticized the committee, pointing out that more adequate forums already existed. Tuqan proposed that the Professional Union Forum (Majma^{c} al-Niqabat al-Mihniyya) should undertake the project, and that it should only be pursued on condition that it receive prior authorization by the FAU. Along with many others, he questioned the intentions of the men heading the project, who were known for their pro-independence proclivities.[16]

Finally, the composition of the committee, most of whom were from Ramallah, exacerbated regional animosities. *Al-Quds* inveighed against this:

> The idea [of the university] is a lofty idea, especially as it solves a practical problem facing thousands of students. The public was pleased in principle at the idea, realized its goodness, and awaited its beneficial effects. But this attempt began to be plagued with imperfections . . . which cast the idea into the wind and the beautiful dream began to fade. The more heated the ideas, the more heated became our passions which were directed by the desire for publicity. . . . The subject of the university is not connected with specific notables nor is it related to specific towns, and it is not right that it become a point of controversy between notables and municipalities. The sacrifice of those with wherewithal, be they notables or institutions, will resuscitate it and protect it along the path it must sooner or later inevitably take.[17]

The newspaper also regarded prior acceptance by the FAU as a necessary prerequisite for pursuing the project. It stressed the importance of imbuing the university with an Arab "personality," consistent with its stance that continuing to pursue the Palestinian entity idea was futile: "The desire to absorb the students is an important objective, but the consecration of the Arab intellectual tradition and Arab culture, the defence of the Arab and his development through academic scientific research are the conditions necessary in order to intensify the connection and steadfastness of the professional and academic cadres."[18] *Al-Quds*'s reservations and those of its readers, which were expressed in numerous articles on the subject, had a clear impact on the committee. On September 28, 1972, it agreed to include representatives from Jerusalem, and by doing so, risk Israeli opprobrium. The committee emphasized that the university would be "Arab in terms of its financing, staffing, programming and direction."[19] According to *Al-Quds*, the positions taken by the committee won the approval of several towns and Chambers of Commerce.

Yet despite these declarations, committee members met three days later with Yigal Allon, the deputy prime minister and acting minister of education of Israel. It was the first publicized meeting between an organized body from the territories with an Israeli minister commanding a civilian ministry.[20] The assent to meet with him decisively contributed to the project's end. Two weeks after the meeting, Khalaf resigned from the committee. In a detailed letter of resignation, Khalaf argued that both the meeting with Allon and the issue of representation over Jerusalem had led him to resign. Employing pan-Arab terms, he accused Shahada and the others of "breaking the ranks of our people's national unity and acting to promote "communal (ta$^{\supset}$ifiyya) and racial (^{c}unsuriyya) feelings." This attack echoed similar Fath and Jordanian denunciations that accused them of "regionalism" (iqlimiyya).[21] Taken literally the charge was ridiculous: Shahada was a Protestant, al-Ja^{c}bari was a devout Muslim, and both were natives of the area. Khalaf was really taking a stand against the idea behind the university—using the institution to promote the establishment of a Palestinian state. He supported the idea of a university, but only on functional grounds. Like Tuqan, he believed that such a program should be placed under the jurisdiction of existing institutions, such as the labor unions, the municipalities, the Chambers of Commerce, and, most importantly, the various already-existing colleges. What Khalaf failed to mention in his letter was the pressure Jordan was placing on him for successfully contesting the April municipal elections, after the previous mayor, Nadim Zaru, was deported in 1971. As far as Jordan was concerned, Zaru was still the official mayor while Khalaf's participation was both illegal and disloyal, and a move clearly serving Israeli interests. The Jordanian authorities, in retaliation, had decided to sever all links with his municipality.[22]

Attacked from all sides, prospects were fading fast for a central Arab Palestinian university that would be located close to Jerusalem and that could serve as an important building block in the development of the Palestinian state. Jordan, rather than the PLO factions, struck the final blow. On October 22, 1972, Dr. Ishaq Farhan, the Jordanian minister of education and long-time member of the Muslim Brotherhood, bitterly denounced the plan and insisted that "severe damage will be caused to the students studying in the [West] Bank."[23] He claimed that not only would such an education increase emigration for lack of suitable employment opportunities, but that it would end in the "Judaicization" of the inhabitants of the West Bank.

But while the thought of Palestinizing the project was seen as an attempt to sever links with Arab-Islamic culture, the Jordanian opposition was also overtly political. Farhan claimed that "the Israeli authorities were trying to create the basis of the Palestinian state through the creation of an autonomous system of education."[24] *Al-Quds*, in its editorial on the very same day, lamented the desires of such external forces to maintain the West Bank as a periphery. "The fear of the Palestinian entity or the Palestinian state continues to be the ideological basis for any discussion on public affairs outside the territories, especially in Amman."[25]

Farhan's denunciations served as the project's death sentence. A draft constitution for the "Arab Palestinian University" was published at the end of October, in which the "focus on Arab and Islamic civilization and the propagation of Arab culture" appeared as one of its principle goals, but the project never emerged in the public eye again, despite occasional discussions on the subject.[26]

While letting the university die quietly, the PLO did not stand on the sidelines.[27] On the contrary, the organization declared its intention to create its own popular university in the diaspora.[28] The PLO thus affirmed what was to become standard practice: that centralized institution building had to be the monopoly of the diaspora lest it become a vehicle for political devolution and the establishment of a rival Palestinian political center in the territories.[29]

The CHE and the Nationalization of Higher Education[30]

Five years after the demise of the Palestinian university, local Palestinians once again attempted to achieve political goals via an educational route—this time through the creation of a Council for Higher Education (CHE). Instead of developing a central university to compete with the PLO, however, this group attempted to transform existing institutions of higher learning into a unified territory-wide system of higher education in order to achieve some kind of parity with the outside center.

The CHE was a far more ambitious and successful project than Shahada's, certainly in terms of the diversity and prominence of its founders. The driving force was Ibrahim Daqqaq, a Communist who had been known in the PNF for his critical attitude toward the PLO.[31] Aiding him was Nablus mayor Bassam al-Shakᶜa, elected in 1976 from the nationalist pro-PLO list, and Karim Khalaf, the mayor of Ramallah.

A novel feature of the CHE was its territorial scope. It was the first autonomous local public institution in the territories since 1948 that included representatives from both the West Bank and Gaza (though the latter's representation in the council was never proportionate to Gaza's share in the total population).

In addition to being a territory-wide body, the CHE sought to include representatives of all the major public institutions in the territories at the time, with the exception of religious organizations linked to Jordan. The first general council included ten elected mayors (including Fahd al-Qawasmi, the recently elected mayor of Hebron), prominent specialists in the field of education, representatives of the Jordanian bureaucracy, representatives of the professional unions, intellectuals, and academics representing the three existing universities—Birzeit, al-Najah National, and Bethlehem.[32] In addition, the general council included two major social organizations, the Jerusalem Federation of Charitable Organizations, which comprised nearly 100 charitable societies under the presidency of Amin al-Khatib, and the Inᶜash al-Usra society of al-Bireh, represented by its president, Samiha al-Khalil. Also, the CHE, rather than being the creation of individuals as the Palestinian university had been, emerged out of an existing organization, the Majmaᶜ al-Niqabat al-Mihniyya (the Forum of Professional Unions) in Bayt Hanina, established in 1972 by the five professional associations that existed in the West Bank at the time.[33] The CHE seemed to aspire to represent the West Bank on matters far wider than those of its stated goals of improving coordination and long-term planning of institutions of higher education. The ten mayors elected in

1976 that headed the list of the general council's founding members were listed with the word "elected" prominently placed by the side of each name. The CHE was evidently trying to emphasize its representation not only in terms of the breadth of its membership and organizational scope, but by virtue of its inclusion of the only group of truly elected politicians in the Palestinian community inside or outside the territories.[34]

The Diversity of Institutions of Higher Learning

The transformation of the highly diverse institutions of higher learning in the territories was no easy task. Almost all twenty institutions that existed represented a power base for some segment of the population. Family or religious interests served as the basis of their organizational frameworks. Birzeit University, the most veteran, was founded by the Nasr family under Quaker influence in 1953 as a two–year college and permitted by the authorities to expand into a four-year degree-conferring university in 1972.

Bethlehem University (founded by the La Salle order under the supervision of the Apostolic See) reflected another dimension of social parochialism. The university's major goal, according to the public relations material it distributed in English, was to foster the Christian presence in the Holy Land. It was run by foreign clergy who regularly filled the two top senior positions of president and vice-chancellor until 1981.[35]

The establishment of the Shari^ca College in Hebron (founded by Hebron mayor, Muhammad ʿAli al-Ja^cbari) was even more parochial.[36] The involvement of the al-Ja^cbaris remained considerable even after the college grew into a university; the incumbent president of the institution, Muhammad Nabil al-Ja^cbari, is the founder's son. CHE founders were convinced that permission for the college's establishment was part and parcel of al-Ja^cbari's collusion with the military government regarding the Palestinian entity idea.

The establishment of the "Polytechnic," a vocational community college renamed the Engineering and Vocational College in 1983, and technically the handiwork of the Hebron Graduate Union (an organization founded in 1953 to foster education in Hebron and beyond) was linked to the Qawasmi family. Nabil al-Qawasmi was one of the leading founders and its first college president. Al-Qawasmi is the brother of murdered mayor Fahd al-Qawasmi, who was one of the founders of the CHE.

Even more blatantly familial were the private, for-profit institutions. Marwan ʿAbd al-Hadi, of a large landowning family based in Nablus, established the al-Rawda Teaching College in 1970.[37] Four years later, the same institute created a paramedical center that became a full-fledged community college in 1983.[38] His brother Salih inherited the head position.

Of greatest concern to the CHE was the control wielded by the wealthy al-Masri family in al-Najah National University in Nablus, after its transformation from a high school and teachers' college in 1977. The al-Masris competed locally with the al-Shaka^{c}as, the family of Nablus mayor and CHE secretary, Bassam al-Shak^{c}a. The founding board of governors did not include Bassam, making it the only university board to not include the local mayor.

Diffusion rather than nepotism characterized the colleges of Al-Quds University, presumably supported by Jordan. The staff of the oldest, the College of Medical Sciences, a paramedical vocational college established in Ramallah in 1978, was the most radical. The College of Propagation and Religious Principles (Kulliyat al-Da^{c}wa wa-Usul al-Din) in the northern suburb of Jerusalem, while formally affiliated to the same organization, was a men's college dominated by the Jordanian-controlled Muslim Affairs and Religious Endowment Administration (Idarat al-Shuʾun al-Islamiyya wal-Awqaf), with a student body controlled by the Muslim Brotherhood. The other two colleges, the College for the Arts for Women and the College of Sciences and Technology in the Jerusalem suburb of Abu Dis were independent nationalist-oriented institutions.

Two small junior colleges teaching the basics of the Shari^{c}a, in Abu Dis, and Qalquilya, added to an already rich mosaic. Both were supervised and financed directly by the Muslim Affairs and Religious Endowment Administration. The United Nations Relief Works Administration's two teacher colleges in Ramallah and Gaza and a vocational community college in Kalandia on the northern outskirts of Jerusalem completed the picture.

Transforming this mosaic into a uniformly structured system of higher education, in which institutions would be governed by similar constitutions delineating similar governing bodies and the relationships between them, was no easy task, even in the best of circumstances.[39]

Partisan Politics

Like many potential reformers, the CHE elite represented men and women of the left whose ethos, ideology, and political affiliations differed considerably from the vast majority of even the educated strata of Palestinian society in the occupied territories. Their numerical insignificance contrasted sharply with the representation they sought to achieve in the CHE. This is a dilemma that has been analyzed cogently by political scientist Samuel Huntington as the trade-off between representation, which in traditional societies often breeds stagnation, with the desire to reform, which generally requires some form of absolutism. One has to centralize power in order to reform and one has to exercise such power autocratically to push the reforms through.[40] Reform becomes both a means and an end. The elite in the CHE, however, could neither centralize power nor wield it effectively.

Thus, the founders of the CHE attempted to promote individuals and institutions that would cooperate most with their attempts at weakening nepotistic and traditional elements and facilitate the transformation of this heterogeneous mosaic into a rational system of higher education. The allotment of positions in the secretariat and membership in the forty-one-member founding General Council clearly reflected their bias. The most striking example was the exclusion of Rashad al-Shawa, the mayor of Gaza, which was the most populated city in the territories. The founders justified it on the grounds that he was nominated to office rather than elected.[41] Narrower considerations also prevailed, however. Al-Shawa was the leading pro-Jordanian political figure in the territories, and thus not liked by the principal founders of the CHE. This may also explain why no representative of the Muslim Affairs and Religious Endowment Administration was invited, despite its involvement in both secondary and higher education.[42]

The CHE's anti-Jordanian bias was matched by an antireligious sentiment. The exclusion of Shaykh Muhammad ʿAwad, the president of the Islamic Court of Appeals and the founder and president of al-Azhar College in Gaza, contrasted sharply with the inclusion of a representative of an even smaller institution from Gaza, the "national college," headed by Wadiʿ Tarzi, a participant in the founding congress of the PLO in 1964.

The founders of the CHE clearly favored leftist institutions, both for their political leanings and the political autonomy they enjoyed. Thus, the small Arab Thought Forum (Al-Multaqa al-Fikri al-ʿArabi), founded by prominent leftists, received representation equal to that received by the entire Jerusalem Federation of Charitable Organizations—an umbrella organization of over 100 charitable organizations—and the president of the Arab Thought Forum, Mahdi ʿAbd al-Hadi, was elected secretary of the council. Moreover, Samiha Khalil's Inʿash al-ʾUsra organization, dedicated to the promotion of Palestinian folklore and self-help, was accorded representation, while two pro-Jordanian regional federations of charitable organizations in Hebron and Nablus, consisting of over eighty charitable societies in all, were excluded.[43]

The bias extended down to representation of the educational institutions themselves. Four considerations prevailed in allotting representation on the general council: (1) The degree of nationalism permeating the institution (2) the degree of independence the institute enjoyed from outside power centers or their territorial branches (3) their potential for future growth and (4) the degree of public control and accountability over them.

With these guidelines, the CHE accorded the three universities of Birzeit, al-Najah, and Bethlehem greatest representation. All possessed high potential for growth and were institutions open to public scrutiny. Nevertheless, even these universities were accorded representation differentially on the basis of other considerations.

Birzeit University clearly ranked higher than the other two, not so much because it was the first university established in the territories, but for its nationalist credentials. An active policy of Arabizing the curriculum, the participation of its student body in demonstrations against the Israeli administration, and the subsequent deportation of Hana Nasr, its president, in 1973 had already given Birzeit University a reputation for being a champion of the national cause.[44] Also, the university was an independent institution with a board of governors drawn from prominent members of Palestinian civil society. Dr. Gabi Baramki, Birzeit's acting president, was elected president of the CHE Executive Committee. An additional member represented its faculty.

Al-Najah University, which was the largest university from its inception, was also accorded two representatives. However, unlike Birzeit University, neither the chairman of the board of governors nor the president of the university was included; instead, a member of the board and an academic took their place. Bethlehem University, headed by a foreigner, was represented by one faculty member only, Anton Sansur. Its student body had proven its national credentials by organizing its first Palestinian folklore festival in 1974.[45]

Least represented were the three UNRWA institutions, which only received one representative for all three. But at least they fared better than the two colleges belonging to the Jordanian-controlled Muslim Affairs and Religious Endowment Administration, and the Shari^{c}a college of Hebron, which were excluded altogether from membership in the CHE. (The Polytechnic and the institutions belonging to Al-Quds University had not yet been founded.)

Politics and Education: the Quest for Parity

Ostensibly, the CHE's aims were limited strictly to educational concerns. Its founding charter cited as its major objectives interuniversity coordination, the establishment of new universities, colleges, and research libraries wherever necessary or financially possible, the development of existing institutions of higher learning according to a CHE-developed plan, and coordinating with Arab states the enrollment of Palestinian students into their educational institutions.[46] A closer look, however, reveals that its objectives were thoroughly political.

The political dimension of the CHE first manifested itself when the CHE decided to send a delegation to meet ministers of education and heads of Arab universities, officials from UNESCO, and the Arab League.[47] The news item that reported this made no mention of meeting Palestinian institutions abroad, except to identify the PLO as the sole representative of the Palestinian people. The council was evidently willing to acknowledge the PLO's legitimacy, while at the same time developing its own autonomy as much as possible. This was also reflected by the success of the CHE in extracting recognition from the Federation of Arab Universities "as the ultimate national institution responsible for educational and cultural matters in the area," despite the formation by the PLO of the al-Majlis al-Aᶜala lil-Tarbiyya, lil-Thaqafa, wa lil-ᶜUlum (the Higher Council of Education, Culture and Sciences) in the very same year.[48] Also, the council received $41,000 from the Federation of Arab Engineers.[49] Until that time, the CHE had only managed to collect from its members a total of 1,500 Jordanian dinars (less than $5,000).[50]

The CHE continued on its independent course the following year when it invited Professor Norman Hunt of Edinburgh University, an expert on higher and vocational education in developing countries, to evaluate the needs and problems of higher education in the Occupied Territories and present policy suggestions to meet them.[51] Hunt called for marked expansion of technical colleges on the "junior college" level so that within ten years only one-third of the students would study in the four-year universities and two-thirds would be channeled to technical and paraprofessional education, a situation similar to the one then prevailing in Jordan.[52] He reasoned that such changes would reduce emigration—a serious problem in 1979, the climax of the oil boom years. The CHE accepted his proposal, although only one college at the time, the Hebron Polytechnic, provided technical education.[53]

More ambitious still was the drafting of the "Charter of Higher Education." The charter called for the unionization of faculty and students and the participation of both groups in policy-making forums in the universities; it also obligated universities to abide by CHE decisions.[54] The CHE had been emboldened by a prolonged five-week student strike from early March to April 10, 1979, at Bethlehem University, which forced the university administration to concede to some of the CHE's demands. The Popular Action Front, the newly established student movement affiliated to the PFLP that dominated the student union, led the strike. The CHE pressed the university authorities to accept all the students' demands, including the formation of a local board of governors to replace the existing consultative board, the right of the student council to collect and distribute scholarships freely, and the introduction of a course on Palestinian politics.[55]

This victory could not, however, offset the challenges and setbacks the CHE faced at the time. The establishment in 1978 of the College of Propagation and the Foundations of the Faith, the first four-year religious college in the West Bank, and the Islamic University in Gaza, were probably the most serious. Both had been formed without prior coordination with or authorization from the CHE, thus challenging the CHE's claim to monopolize the authorization of new institutions of higher learning and strengthening opposition to the CHE's secular nature.[56] Even worse, the universities under CHE supervision themselves did not abide by CHE decisions: both Birzeit and al-Najah Universities set up engineering departments without prior CHE authorization.[57]

The PLO Response

Only by monopolizing most of the monies flowing to higher education and increasing those flows considerably could the CHE hope to play a centralizing and coordinating role in forging a national system of education, overcome the opposition of individual institutions, and promote technical education. Unfortunately for the CHE, only the Jordanian Palestinian Joint Committee, established in the spring of 1979, possessed such funds. On October 17, 1979, Gabi Baramki, the president of the CHE, addressed a letter to the Joint Committee requesting aid in order to meet the CHE's objectives. Baramki asked for a small sum of 50,000 J.D. to meet immediate expenses as well as to clear past debts.[58]

Shortly after the call for aid was made, the PLO, in collusion with Jordan, exerted pressure to reduce the stature and mandate of the CHE. It was especially concerned about reducing the influence of leftists and radicals and removing from the CHE men prominent in the recently formed NGC. The two leading politicians influential in both institutions, al-Shakᶜa and Khalaf, were then at the height of their popularity. The emergence of a charismatic "elected" leadership wearing two hats—leaders of a territorial body in the form of the NGC, and a neofunctional tool such as the CHE—was bound to threaten political forces outside the territories. Changing both the institutional and personal composition of the CHE was a useful first step in depoliticizing the council and reducing its autonomy.

According to ᶜAbd al-Jawad Salih, a January 1980 meeting in Lebanon between three of the presidents of the member universities and PLO representatives initiated the process. Baramki was one of those present at the meeting. The discussion focused on ways to reduce the political clout of the CHE and bring the institution under the wing of the "Higher Council" set up by the PLO.[59] The Higher Council would then decide on the changes that would eliminate politicians from the council and reduce the CHE to a body composed solely of academics. Soon after the alleged meeting, reports appeared in the pro-Jordanian *Al-Quds* that personnel changes were going to take place in the CHE in a meeting of the general council scheduled for February 27, 1980.[60] Meanwhile, the Joint Committee met in the final week of February in Amman. It recognized the CHE and decided to allot one million J.D. to its budget.[61] The victory, however, was inconsequential, for it decided to simultaneously direct 100,000 J.D. to each university directly, including to the Islamic University of Gaza, and 150,000 J.D. to the small medical sciences college set up in al-Bireh.[62] The latter was a member institution of the Jordanian-sponsored

Al-Quds University. The message of the Joint Committee was clear: the money was there to bolster the CHE should it institute the necessary changes, but it could also be used to increase the autonomy of the universities at the expense of the CHE.

Changes were made by the CHE, as spelled out by Baramki at the February 27 meeting. He proposed widening membership from 38 to 43, with a future option of increasing it to 60 members.[63] Most of the new members included institutions that were pro-Jordanian, pro-PLO, or under one or the other's influence. The inclusion of Rashad al-Shawa and Muhammad Milhim, the mayor of Halhul, were the most important. Al-Shawa was pro-Jordanian, while Milhim was known as a Fath supporter. According representation to the president, a member of the board of governors, and a representative of the faculty of the Islamic University in Gaza also prejudiced the standing of the leftist founders. For the first time, the Muslim Affairs and Religious Endowment Administration was accorded one representative. In addition, three colleges that made up Al-Quds University, the College of Sciences at Abu-Dis, the College of Medical Sciences at al-Bireh, and the College of Propagation and the Principles of the Faith (Kulliyat al-Da^cwa wal-Usul al-Din) were accorded another representative, as was the Hebron Polytechnic. The inclusion of a representative of the Chambers of Commerce, a traditional pro-Jordanian stronghold, had much the same effect. There was no doubt that Baramki's proposal seemed, at least at face value, to enhance the representative nature of the council, which, by necessity, tilted the balance against the wishes of many of the founders.

Judging by the responses in *Al-Quds*, the changes were not sufficiently far-reaching: a proposal that appeared in the newspaper on February 25 tilted much more in Jordan and Fath's favor. It called for a forty-nine-person council in which representatives of educational institutions were to be a clear majority (32 of 49), compared to 20 out of 43 in Baramki's proposal. The proposal in *Al-Quds* increased representation to the institutions of al-Quds University from three to five, the extra two to represent the university as a whole. Three more slots were accorded to the three shariʿa colleges, including the Hebron Shariʿa college that Baramki's proposal continued to disregard. Finally, the religious pro-Jordanian proposal omitted reference, and thus representation, to the key leftist institutions in the West Bank and Gaza—the Red Crescent Society in Gaza under the presidency of Dr. Haydar ʿAbd Al-Shafi, the Inʿash al-ʾUsra, and the Arab Thought Forum.

Tensions between the secular and religious were manifested principally in Gaza. In an open letter in *Al-Fajr*, Sami Abu Shaʿban, a well-known educator from Gaza, echoed the feelings of discrimination felt by Gazans in the original CHE. He suggested that this could be remedied by the inclusion of religious dignitaries from the area.[64] Nevertheless, on February 25, as the various proposals concerning the composition of the CHE were circulated, an agreement disadvantageous to the religious establishment was signed in the home of Rashad al-Shawa between ʿAbd al-Shafi and Shaykh Muhammad ʿAwad, the founder and chairman of the board of governors of the Islamic University. The agreement defined the Islamic University as a "scientific" institution of higher learning that granted representation on its board to the professional institutions in Gaza, all of whom were controlled by nationalists.[65] These included the Union of Engineers, the Union of Lawyers, the Arab Medical Society (which ran the Blood Bank of Gaza), and the Red Crescent Society. The existing board, composed primarily of religious dignitaries and figures, was declared temporary.[66]

The agreement encountered stiff opposition from Islamic groups in Gaza. A mob led by the Muslim Brotherhood damaged the Red Crescent society and set fire to its library.[67] Muslim institutions (controlled by the Muslim Brotherhood), including the Al-Jamʿiyya al-Islamiyya, denounced the agreement for failing to accord representation to Islamic groups or to all towns situated in Gaza, and for according to all religious dignitaries—ʿulama, judges, and the teachers in al-Azhar College combined—one representative only, the same representation accorded to the small al-Kulliya al-Wataniyya in Gaza.[68] Such an explosive response was bound to be detrimental to the CHE's authority.

On another front, pro-Jordanians such as ʿUthman Khalak and Muslim dignitaries in the West Bank such as Shaykh Jamal al-Qaʾid joined together to protest the "presumed" undermining of diaspora decision making that they perceived the council had usurped for itself.[69] To ensure civic space for their activities they were ready to enlist the outside center against a rival local power. Just how important it was for local dignitaries to defend local institution building from local coercion was reflected by an editorial against politicization of social institutions that appeared in *Al-Quds*:

> Our region is showing a noble positive movement toward the establishment of public and charitable humanitarian institutions, as well as the creation of an educational infrastructure through the establishment of sport and social clubs. All these institutions share one common goal—protecting society from disintegration and the provision of as many services as possible in all areas and on all levels. Suddenly a small coterie of people saw fit, much to our regret, to bombard these institutions with abhorrent partisan politics (*hizbi*). In their need to politicize (*tasyyis*) these institutions . . . [they] are causing their atrophy. . . [T]heir attrition by stratagems and divisiveness [causes the institutions to] lose their raison d'être and increases divisiveness among the people.[70]

The efforts of the religious and the pro-Jordanians, together with mayors of towns who sought additional representation in the council, soon bore fruit. On March 19, the Forum of Professional Unions rejected the Baramki proposal, presumably in favor of the Jordanian draft.[71] An *Al-Quds* editorial explained the professional unions' retreat from previously radical positions on the basis of the "opposition of men who realize their responsibilities in maintaining the independence of higher education by demanding that the CHE be composed of men of education only and by removing politicization and politicians from its midst."[72] In reality, these professional groups placed their material interests—ties to both Jordan and the PLO—above ideological considerations. On April 9, that opposition was practically translated into a boycott when an insufficient quorum of members (23 of 43) appeared at a meeting. On the following day, Dr. Kaʾid ʿAbd al-Haqq, Elias Freij, and Baramki were called to Amman to meet with the Joint Committee.

From that point on, the institution began to flounder. Israeli harassment of CHE officials prominent in the NGC and their placement under town arrests, as well as the maiming of al-Qawasmi and Milhim by the Jewish underground, not only prevented meetings but seemed to press home the vulnerability of centralized political institution building. In October 1979, the CHE elected Kaʾid ʿAbd al-Haqq, the newly instated pro-Jordanian president of al-Najah University, its president, replacing Baramki. Elias Freij, the mayor of Bethlehem, called for the transformation of the CHE into a forum of educators.[73] In May 1981, the Joint Committee provided the CHE with 50,000 dinars, a sum that allowed the CHE to be no more than a conduit of funds whose apportionment would take place outside the territories.[74] The PLO continued to support universities individually, even the Islamic University in Gaza which did not abide by CHE policy and had ousted its acting president, identified with the PLO, and replaced him with Dr. Muhammad Saqr, a man known for his strong links with the Muslim Brotherhood and who subsequently transformed the university administration into a stronghold of the movement.[75]

No "nationalization" of the system of higher education took place despite the support of both the student movements affiliated to PLO factions, and the al-Najah and Birzeit Faculty Unions.[76] The charter became a dead letter. The administrations in these institutions remained in control of the Islamists, the pro-Jordanians, and pro-PLO notables. The transformers who had hoped to dictate their terms to civil society failed.

The CHE had not only tried to impress upon the PLO the importance of long-term functional state formation but also to shape the form and character it would take. The men behind the CHE sought to forge institutions within civil society that would promote excellence, be governed by rational secular procedures, promote internal democracy wherever possible, and interact with other organizations within civil society. They opposed foreign tutelage, nepotism, parochialism, and patrimonialism.

Like many reformers, they sought to standardize society as a means of reforming it and create the centralized state apparatus through partisan politics. They failed to realize, however, that standardizing diversity was also autocratic. Many segments of civil society made common cause with outside forces, principally Jordan and the PLO, in combating such attempts. The PLO championed the mosaic and found many vested interests within the territories that were willing to collaborate with them in maintaining it.

The pluralism that was victorious characterized not only the system as a whole but the individual university as well. Often, it was deliberately constructed by the outside center. This is examined in the following section, on politics at al-Najah National University from 1977 to 1984.

The CHE and al-Najah National University

While all the institutions of higher learning interested the founders of the CHE, al-Najah National University in Nablus was the one that attracted their attention the most. One reason was its size. From its inception, it was the West Bank's largest university, enrolling in the 1977–78 academic year 924 students, compared to 827 in Birzeit University, the second-largest institution of higher learning. This gap increased, so that by 1981–82 there were 2,822 students in al-Najah compared to Birzeit's 1,882.[77]

Al-Najah was also important for a variety of geographic and social reasons. Under Jordanian and Israeli rule, institutions of higher learning were located primarily in the greater Jerusalem area extending from Bethlehem in the south to Ramallah in the north. In contrast, al-Najah National University, established in 1919 as a high school and extended into a teachers training institute in 1965, was located in Nablus, a citadel of nationalism and Palestinian Arab opposition in the Mandate, Jordanian, and Israeli periods. The city reflected the continuity of Arab Palestinian history in contrast to the fragmentation experienced elsewhere. Al-Najah shared some of the town's historical prominence: ᶜIzzat Darwaza, a leading pan-Arab thinker and activist during the Arab rebellion of 1936–39, was its second principal when it was still a secondary school.[78] Moreover, al-Najah was the first university that was almost wholly Muslim. In the 1981 academic year, Christians comprised only 2 percent of the student body compared to around 25 percent in Birzeit University and 40 percent in Bethlehem University. The university, however, was neither religious nor focused on Islamic subjects.

The founders of the CHE also concentrated on al-Najah because of the nepotistic control the al-Masri family exercised over it. The al-Masris, one of the five most prominent families in Nablus and probably the wealthiest, were closely linked to the transformation of al-Najah into a university in 1977. In a delegation that was sent to receive the local military governor's assent to the move, three of its nine members were al-Masris: Hikmat, a former member of the Jordanian senate and chairman of al-Najah University's board of governors; his son-in-law Zhafir, assistant mayor and chairman of the local

Chamber of Commerce; and Maʿzuz, a wealthy benefactor. In line with its conservative president and board of governors, al-Najah was decisively pro-Jordanian and sympathetic to Islamic tradition. The delegation itself was clearly pro-Jordanian, including as it did Ibrahim Sanubar, the chairman of the General Committee of (Matriculation) Exams (Al-Lajna al-ʿAmma Lil-Imtihanat al-Tawjihi), Khafiz Tuqan, a former mayor, and ʿAbd al-Raʾuf al-Faris, a wealthy farmer who later established the pro-Jordanian Agricultural Cooperative Society supported by the Joint Committee.[79]

The appointment of Dr. Kaʾid ʿAbd al-Haqq as the president of the university in September 1977, a month before the first academic year began, confirmed the close relationship between the institution and Jordan. Al-Haqq, a native of the region, was formerly the head of the Teachers Training and Curriculum Development Department in the Jordanian Ministry of Education and former rector of ʿAbd al-ʿAziz Ibn Saʿud University in Saudi Arabia. Both positions placed him squarely in the conservative pro-Jordanian and Islamic camp.[80]

From the outset, the university was well connected in the Arab world. Its first fund-raising campaign began with a meeting between King Hussein and Hikmat al-Masri.[81] Funds were plentiful and varied, flowing in from such diverse sources as the Jordanian Council of Higher Education and Libya. The links to Jordan were also academic: the rector of the engineering college of the University of Jordan and the head of the Engineering Department of the Royal Scientific Association traveled to Nablus to help plan the establishment of an engineering school at al-Najah.[82]

In addition to its close links to Jordan, the university was unique among the three universities at the time in cultivating close ties with the two existing Shariʿa institutions in the West Bank and the Islamic University in Gaza. To the latter, al-Najah University sent Dr. Yusuf al-Haqq, a lecturer in Arabic language and the son of the president, to bolster its Arabic studies department.[83]

In the university's first year, there was little to suggest that al-Najah University would become one of the major arenas of political contestation in the occupied territories. Despite Mayor al-Shakʿa's exclusion from the board of governors, he seemed more than willing to place national objectives above matters of personal honor, expressing his willingness to engage the aid of the engineering department of the municipality on behalf of the university, for example.[84] On the university's side, Hikmat al-Masri met with Dr. Anton Sansur, Bethlehem University's representative in the CHE, even though he personally had been excluded from the council. Most importantly, the university hosted one of the founding meetings of the NGC.[85]

The Elements of Conflict

The emergence within the university of two organizations controlled by opposing political forces set the basis for the conflict. In June 1979, the al-Qutla al-Islamiyya al-Mustaqilla (the Independent Islamic Bloc), most of whom were affiliated to the Muslim Brotherhood, replaced a politically neutral student federation and council established a year earlier.[86] The Iranian revolution no doubt influenced the elections, but the issues were primarily local. In the previous year, for instance, Islamic fundamentalists had demanded the separation of the sexes in lecture halls, but the student council and the university refused to comply.[87] The newly elected council expended considerable effort in promoting ties with the Islamic colleges in Jerusalem and Hebron.[88]

Meanwhile, the faculty and the administration began to organize a faculty and employee union. Its pompous name, "The Union of Employees and Teachers of the Universities and Private Institutes in the Occupied Territories—The al-Najah National University Branch" (Niqabat Muwazifi wa Mudarisi al-Jamiᶜat wal-Maᶜahid al-Khassa fi al-Manatiq al-Muhtalla, henceforth the faculty union) reflected the intentions of its leftist founders—to establish one translocal professional union that would represent the teachers and the administrative staff in all universities and private colleges throughout the territories.[89]

It was obvious, however, that the founders of the union aimed at much more than a monopoly on collective bargaining. In April 1980, Dr. Salah Abu-Tin spelled out the objectives of the faculty union in a working paper, which clearly indicated the faculty union's preference for an alliance with the CHE. "We see the need to make every kind of effort to forget our personal differences and controversies, and mobilize our resources on behalf of the CHE, in order that it will be able to realize all the ambitions of our people and its hopes, and that its appearance in the right form will enable the resolution of many problems, so that it [the CHE] will be able to mould these institutions into one unified national academic unit."[90] While the CHE was to nationalize the system from the top, the faculty union clearly envisaged itself as a tool to nationalize educational institutions from below.

A necessary first step was to ensure the prerogatives of the faculty in university academic affairs. The modest nature of the demands reflected the monopoly of power in the hands of the board of governors and the president. The faculty union sought the participation of the faculty in deciding the structure of the curriculum, the right to research problems pertaining to the university itself, and the promotion of faculty members on the basis of academic ability alone. Above all, the faculty union sought the revision of the university charter to reduce the prerogatives of the board of governors and institute a university council in which the faculty, not the governors, would have the upper hand.[91]

Professional and salary issues were also aired in the working paper. The faculty union sought greater equality between the administrative staff and the faculty, expansion of grant disbursements for study abroad (an important item, given the high proportion of teachers without doctorates), reduction of teaching loads in order to pursue studies and engage in research, and the university's financial participation in the health and pension schemes of its employees.

These radical demands were made in equally radical times. On May 3, the Israeli authorities arrested Muhammad Sawalha, a member of the faculty union's secretariat and one of its founding members, for engaging in "subversive activities."[92] Nine days later, in one of the most intensely contested elections, the National Student Unity Bloc (Qutlat al-Wahda al-Wataniyya al-Tullabiyya, henceforth al-Wahda), a coalition of all PLO-affiliated student groups, narrowly defeated the al-Qutla.[93] Al-Wahda gained six seats compared to al-Kutla's five, a balance of power that hardly facilitated the restoration of calm to the campus, which had become the scene of violence between nationalists and fundamentalists. Tumultuous as these events were, they paled before the maiming by Jewish terrorists in June of al-Shak^{c}a and Khalaf, the two leaders of the NGC and staunch supporters of the CHE's efforts to nationalize the universities. It was at this point that the faculty union formally linked up with the CHE, as two of its faculty members finally took their place as representatives in the CHE council. One of the representatives was Dr. Abu-Tin.[94]

Maintaining Notable Control

For the board of governors, the institutionalization of the faculty union, the nature of its demands, its link with the CHE, and the growing politicization of academic life posed a serious threat. It not only refused to negotiate, but was bent on breaking up the union entirely. In a general meeting of the faculty union, the authorities were accused of trying to set up a duplicate union with the help of 500,000 J.D., allegedly provided by the Jordanian-Palestinian Joint Fund.[95]

This accusation was indeed justified. Responsible for the creation of the duplicate union was Dr. Kamal al-Saigh, the new rector of the Engineering College. From the wide coverage given to him and his wife, Nawwal, in *Al-Quds*, and the absence of such coverage in the nationalist press, one can assume that these Harvard-trained academics were charged with the task of pacifying the situation from within, utilizing their academic prestige to do so. Nawwal, a lecturer in urban planning, was appointed the head of the Social Sciences Department. Both came out strongly in support of distancing al-Najah from politics in the territories.[96] On June 22, al-Saigh announced the chief officers of his new faculty union on the basis of elections conducted the day before. His union was limited to the academic staff and focused solely on internal university affairs, in sharp contrast to the original union and its intentions to integrate with other institutions of higher learning. Attempting to woo less ideologically motivated faculty members still loyal to the renegade union, al-Saigh announced that the new union was inaugurating a faculty housing scheme.[97]

Moreover, the board of governors refused to renew the contracts of four activists in the faculty union: its chairman Adnan Idris, Muhammad Sawalha, Yihya Hadir, and Haifa Irshid, on the grounds that they failed to meet acceptable academic standards.[98] All four were identified with leftist factions of the PLO. The faculty union called a strike ten days later, with the participation of many of the students of the al-Wahda.[99] Soon thereafter the faculty union demanded to know why, if these four had been dismissed for low academic performance, the matter had not been raised by the heads of their departments in the three to four years these lecturers had been teaching. And why did their departmental heads remain silent over the matter? According to the faculty union, the dismissals had been announced without prior warning and not through the president's office, as was stipulated by the university charter.[100] The union argued that the board of governors had no business deciding the fate of academic staff.

Instead of responding to these allegations, the administration appealed to the public's reluctance to bear the costs of a shorter academic term incurred as a result of the faculty union-led strike. The call was permeated with religious symbols that appealed to the paternal authority of the heads of the students' families.[101] Both sides also asked the municipal council to persuade the other to meet its wishes. The union appealed to the "national institutions," the labor unions and municipalities, the CHE, and the other universities to intervene on its behalf. An emergency meeting of the faculty union on July 2 was attended by 130 staff and faculty members, an overwhelming majority of university employees. This turnout attested to a failure on the part of al-Saigh to create a viable alternative.[102] Notably, al-Saigh's union felt compelled to support the union's strike.[103]

The response of the national institutions was encouraging. The strike generated front-page headlines in the local press, which was generally supportive and recognized the larger issues behind the strike. The Nablus-based General Federation of Labor even sent members to participate. The professional union branches in the city made due with large announcements supporting the union.[104]

An Ephemeral Victory

In an agreement reached on July 7 under the auspices of the municipality, neither side came out a clear winner. Nevertheless, the union appeared to have gained the upper hand. Although the drafting of the university charter was to remain the prerogative of the board of governors, the fourth clause stated that the board "would assess anew the university charter with the aim of revising these by-laws in a manner appropriate to the quick growth of the university, and the development of our national (*wataniyya*) hopes and national legacy."[105] The revised charter, much to the delight of the faculty union, had to meet the approval of the university council. Most importantly, it stipulated a short deadline for revising the charter, no later than the eve of the new academic year. Clause 2 guaranteed the right to unionize, thus conferring complete legitimacy on the existing union. As for the issue of the dismissals, it was to be discussed in the university council, though with the all-important proviso that the decision had to receive the approval of the board of governors. A week later, the board of governors decided on the basis of the findings of a faculty committee to renew the contracts of the four faculty members who were dismissed.[106]

Less heartening for the faculty union was the fact that the agreement had been reached through the local municipality rather than under the aegis of the CHE, as, for example, had occurred during the Bethlehem University student strike in April 1979. But the relationship between the board of governors and the CHE was too tense, their positions too much at loggerheads, for the CHE to be an arbitrator. Furthermore, these were hectic times. The NGC's campaign against the Camp David accords was in full gear, as was the backlash against it. In this state of affairs, conflict resolution had to be as local as possible without the intervention of an institution seeking to impose a centralizing influence. Nevertheless, the agreement appeared to set in motion a gradual shift in power from the board to the faculty, which, given the growth of the university's enrollment, could only grow more numerous and stronger.

The Alliance Between the Board and the Islamic Fundamentalists

Such a shift was contingent, however, upon the faculty union maintaining university support against the board on its issue of contention. Thus, the growing tension within the student body between fundamentalists and nationalists not only robbed the faculty union and its agenda of center stage in the local political arena but presented the board with opportunities to forge a new alliance with the opposition. Instead of emerging as the champion of institutional progress, the faculty union was relegated to the sidelines of a conflict that greatly threatened al-Najah University's stability.

While the faculty union was struggling to achieve practical successes—the purchase of lands for faculty and employee housing, operationalizing medical health care services, and ensuring free education at the university for their offspring,[107] the conflict between the two major student coalitions was taking a violent turn. Some of it was directed against the faculty. At a meeting of the faculty union on July 21, members pressed for more guards on campus in order to protect faculty.[108]

To make matters worse, the Israeli authorities were beginning to make common cause with Hikmat al-Masri against the faculty and the CHE. Israel refused to license new construction at the university, presumably because of the political agitation at the university, issued an ordinance subjecting all faculty nominations throughout the territories to the approval of the authorities, and refused to extend the visa of union activist and Geography Department head Dr. Walid Mustafa, forcing him to leave that summer.[109] Mustafa, a member of the Palestinian Communist Organization (in 1982 renamed the Palestinian Communist Party), became a representative of the party in the 18th PNC in 1987 held in Algeria). His forced departure came at a time of rapid growth in student enrollment and a pressing need for more, not less, faculty. The move aimed to both intimidate the faculty and to press home to a wider public the point that politicization of the university would not be tolerated by the Israeli authorities. Under the circumstances, the board of governors reneged on their promise of a new charter.

While the faculty union forged a close alliance with the nationalist-controlled student union, it remained quiet for most of the year. This low profile might have been due to a belief that the coalition among the students, the faculty, and the radical political elite, and the gradual recovery of al-Shakᶜa,would in due time tip the scales in its favor.

The Fundamentalist Election Victory

The student election results of May 1981 were certainly a setback for change. The nationalist students, divided by factional differences, split into a pro-Fath "National Student Movement" and the National Student Unity Bloc (NSUB), a coalition of PFLP and DFLP supporters. This paved the way for the Islamist al-Qutla to regain control of the council. As the new council promised to be decidedly more hostile to its aims, the union decided to immediately renew its efforts to nationalize the university while the present student union remained in office.

Dr. ᶜAbd al-Haqq's resignation as president on May 19, 1981, one week after the student elections were held, provided the necessary crisis to renew the campaign. Objecting to the resignation, the faculty union argued that the decision was made under the pressure of the board of governors.[110] Its members were convinced that the board was trying to encourage job rotation among senior faculty and administration in order to prevent the emergence of independent power centers within the university.

Faithful to the broad alliance between the nationalist student formations, the faculty, and the CHE, the student union proposed the establishment of a joint committee composed of two members of the faculty union, two neutral members, and two members of the board of governors to discuss the president's resignation. In a more bellicose tone, it demanded the cessation of all dismissals of faculty, administration, or students until the implementation of a new charter as stipulated by the agreement of the year before. It demanded, moreover, that these revisions be made no later than the beginning of the following school year.[111] Supporting the nationalists was the Professional Union Center at Bayt Hanina, which recognized that the resignation crisis was linked with the wider problem of the university charter and extensive structural reform.

Meanwhile, the fundamentalist violence continued. According to nationalist sources, the violence began on June 23, 1981, when nationalist students challenged, in academic fashion, an antinationalist address by Sabri Abu Dhiab, a prominent member of the al-Qutla and incoming student council member, which was entitled: "Nationalism: Its Meaning, Its Origins, and Its Evaluation."[112] Islamists in the meeting hall reacted to their queries with violence, attacking the nationalists with clubs and ejecting them from the lecture hall. Seven nationalist students were severely injured in the incident. The nationalists claimed that the fundamentalists had deliberately placed the clubs in the hall for anticipated use.

The Union Takes Sides

While in the past the faculty union had attempted to maintain neutrality in the face of fundamentalist violence, this time it explicitly supported the injured students and identified itself as a nationalist organ defending its interests. It not only called for the punishment of the fifteen culprits who owned up to their participation in the violence but issued warnings to the Islamist camp as well. "We in the union," explained its secretary, Wa'il al-Qadi, in an interview in the Communist *Al-Tali ͨa*, "are part of the national movement within the university and outside it, and every slur against it is a slur against the national movement as a whole."[113] Its message to the national forces both inside and outside the territories, however, continued to stress the need to resolve the conflict by addressing the issue of the university's by-laws, in sharp contrast to the PLO's position that insisted on treating the issue as a conflict between rival forces rather than a problem of institution building. An investigative committee set up the day after the attack was ordered to present its findings in three weeks' time.[114]

Those findings were never aired. To pressure the authorities, the nationalist students and faculty, in conjunction with their Birzeit counterparts, convened, on July 10, an open conference on the theme of freedom of expression and democratic procedure. The conference was attacked by hundreds of fundamentalist students with violence spreading to all parts of the city. The university authorities, despite the objections of the faculty union, decided to close down the university for an indefinite period, a move unprecedented in its history.[115] The faculty union preferred that the university remain open so that it could emphasize not only its wish for change and reform but its commitment to providing uninterrupted education. A dormant university inevitably meant sharing the blame for failing to provide such a service. Nevertheless, it was a prudent move, for street violence between the opposing student groups continued for three days throughout the city.

Nationalization Aborted

An escalation of conflict took place on all sides. The Islamic fundamentalists spread rumors that the nationalist students desecrated mosques after having shown intolerance against religious ceremonies on campus. In return, the nationalist student groups decided to go underground with the establishment of the National Unity Student Committee (NUSC).[116] Together with the faculty union, the CHE, and other national institutions, the NUSC coordinated a campaign against the administration and the fundamentalists.

The faculty union also hardened its position. A follow-up committee set up by the faculty union on July 14 demanded that the board take concrete steps within a week toward drafting the new university charter and the punishment of the fifteen major offenders implicated in the violence of June 23. If it failed to do so, the faculty union threatened to "convene a general assembly which would elect a board of governors, due to the fact that the present board does not work to the benefit of the university."[117]

Could such a revolutionary position by the faculty union be explained only in light of the violence at al-Najah University? Overall circumstances could not have generated such optimism for so bold a move. Though the Professional Union Center had come out in clear support of the faculty union, both the CHE and the radical mayors, two traditional bases of support, were surprisingly docile. And then, of course, the faculty union was still struggling against a hostile but legitimate student council controlled by fundamentalists. Its new attitude probably had more to do with a report released on July 6 by Dr. Naʾif Nimr Khirma, a Palestinian lecturer at the University of Kuwait, and representative of a Gulf state society that disbursed funds to Palestinian universities. Sympathetic to the nationalists, he was invited by a reluctant Hikmat al-Masri, more for his financial clout than his political leanings, to investigate the outstanding issues at al-Najah University.

Khirma's report read as if it were written by the faculty union. Khirma belabored two points: the need for a new university charter and the need to establish internal university organs that would ensure joint democratic activity between all levels of the university, including the student body. There was also an implicit attack on al-Masri himself: "The running of higher scientific institutions is based on teamwork within the framework of clear laws and procedures. That is to say, the university is administered by internal organs, each one specializing in its allocated role in a manner that does not leave any important matter of interest to the university in the hands of one man, no matter how exalted."[118]

But when push came to shove, the position of the faculty union crumbled while that of the board stood firm. The follow-up committee set up to apportion blame and punish those who took part in the violence was the weak link. Set up after the board closed the university, it had consisted of senior faculty, including deans, as well as more junior faculty active in the faculty union. The closer the deadline, the greater were the number of defections among the senior staff, until the committee finally dissolved altogether on July 20.

Once again, the board, having overcome a crisis, decided to take the offensive. On September 27, 1981, four days before the opening of the 1981–82 school year, the university dismissed four teachers, all of whom were activists in the faculty union.[119] Two of them, Sawalha and Idris, had been two of the four dismissed but returned to their posts the previous year. The other two, Muhammad ʿAfiz Nabulsi and Mahir Abu Hilal, were the secretary and treasurer of the faculty union, respectively. All four were members of the leftist faction that had contested union elections earlier that year that had been won by Fath supporters. Al-Masri was obviously attempting to neutralize Fath opposition in his bid to maintain power.

The formal reason the board gave for the dismissals was the need to improve academic levels at the university. None of the four possessed a Ph.D. The faculty union responded by pointing out that only four days before the decision to dismiss Mahir Abu Hilal was made, the deans' committee turned down a request he submitted to continue his doctoral studies abroad because of his department's pressing need for good teachers. The committee, moreover, had not contested his research abilities.[120]

Following the bard, the Israeli authorities once again moved to hinder the faculty union.[121] Forbidding travel to all faculty in Palestinian universities killed two birds with one stone. First, it prevented faculty union members from traveling abroad to present their case to the PLO and Palestinian communities and demand more effective intervention on behalf of the faculty union. After all, a Fath-dominated union had adopted the basic CHE position. Second, the move was made in conjunction with the provisions of Israeli Order 854, which stipulated that all transfers of faculty as well as new appointments had to meet the approval of the authorities. One can safely assume that the occupation authorities would never give their approval to the four dismissed by al-Masri. The point was clear—opposition to al-Masri meant, in all probability, academic joblessness.

On the other hand, the severity of the authorities was matched by nationalist fervor. For the first time, Palestinian prisoners in the Beer-Sheba penitentiary sent a petition denouncing the board of governors.[122] Prisoners from the Jenin prison-camp soon followed suit.[123] Thirty-one national institutions called upon the university to revoke the decision.[124] The crisis became a major issue, if not the key one, in the local political arena.

The faculty union first took a conciliatory posture by avoiding a strike. Instead, it appealed to the municipal council to come to its aid. In a comprehensive statement on the crisis publicized two weeks later, the municipal council completely backed the faculty union position. "We were astonished by your decision," wrote the council to the board of governors. "None of the academic or administrative organs participated in the step taken, collective punishment was exercised, and there was infringement of the right of employees to unionize."[125] The declaration then went on to support the basic position of the faculty union by linking the dismissals with the clear need to modify the university charter.

The real importance, however, lay in the document's ending. For the first time, events at al-Najah were placed in the broadest political setting: "The decision was made at a time when our eyes were cast in the hopes of a united Arab stance in face of the plot manifested on the local plane of executing a policy of self-government: on the Lebanese and Arab plane, by the concentration [of Israeli forces] in southern Lebanon, and internationally in American and international moves in implementing the Camp David document . . . and at a time Military Order 854 is continuing to take control over the sector of higher education."[126]

Elite Responses to the Crisis

The faculty union's conciliatory attitude ended when Muslim fundamentalist violence broke out once again on October 18, 1981. The faculty union and the NUSC responded by calling for a joint strike. This time, the faculty union faced a more sympathetic president, Dr. Mundhir Salah, who had replaced al-Haqq, and somewhat braver deans. While previously, the senior faculty refrained from taking any stand, in this crisis they emphasized that they had nothing to do with the decision to dismiss the four.[127] Though the statement clearly stopped short of denouncing the board's decision, it nevertheless highlighted the move's illegality.

Disappointing news, however, came from unexpected quarters—the PLO. A front-page headline in *Al-Fajr* read "The Palestinian leadership calls for a resolution to the problem at al-Najah University." But to the union's disappointment, the PLO merely called for the return to the status quo ante: "We are witnessing how the enemy is attempting to strike at the unity of the student body. We call upon every body to rise to the occasion so that a clear decision can be reached regarding the return to the previous situation."[128] Worse still, the PLO viewed the problem as a local political problem limited to the student body alone rather than a structural problem with much wider ramifications.

It took a territorialist keen on promoting local institution building to place the problem in the proper context. Bassam al-Shakᶜa's full-page article that appeared on the front page of the newspaper was more forceful, though hardly as supportive and concrete as the faculty union would have liked: "It is the obligation of officials to foster dialogue between students, employees, and the administration in a democratic framework, despite differences in opinions, streams of thought, and inclinations. Were such behavior to aspire to the unity of all sectors of the university . . . then the university would be able to live up to its academic and social mission to its people and country and participate in a practiced and realistic manner in the resolution of its problems, whether it be regarding the issue of our people and its unity and struggle within the framework of the Palestine Liberation Organization, or in the implementation of a unified policy of higher education of our people."[129] The future of al-Najah University, according to al-Shakᶜa, was intimately tied to increasing the power of the territorialists within the PLO as well as institutionalizing a national system of higher education. The importance of al-Najah University stemmed from the peculiarities of the political situation: "In the absence of national government and the diversity of views and opinions, there is no alternative but to place trust in the institution and its mission as a critical factor and a starting point from which all obligate themselves to leap forward . . . ; a democratic framework in relations between personnel, through joint efforts and through joint interaction for the good of the university, will be a basis for the resolution of problems [facing it]." Nevertheless, he refrained from presenting concrete proposals as "a man from the outside" who did not wish to "arouse sensitivities (itharat al-ihsasat)." His ardor he left to higher politics as he stated that resolution of the crisis would "benefit us all so that we could state with resolve, No to the new or old Civil Administration . . . No to Military Ordinances 418, 873, and 854 [all of which were directed at Palestinian institutions in the territories] . . . and Yes to our universities and their nationalist direction . . . Yes to the unity of our people within the framework and leadership of the Palestine Liberation Organization." An article by Karim Khalaf seconded his call for democratization but was more explicit about the need for structural reform.

Now that the elite was openly debating the issue, it was the turn of Hikmat al-Masri to state his views. In a statement consisting of several points, he accused the faculty union of expressing its views concerning al-Haqq's dismissal in the form of graffiti on the university's walls instead of discussing the issue with the board of governors. He added that "I did not see the mayor of the city protest," in obvious allusion to al-Shakᶜa. Al-Masri censured the faculty union's moves against all those employees opposing it. He deplored the faculty union's delegitimization of the legal student council and "the establishment of another student bloc by the name of 'al-Wahda student bloc'." This last point was an ingenious but blatant distortion of the facts, for al-Wahda, which represented the DFLP and the Communists, existed as a legitimate electoral bloc. The alternative to the Student Council was the NUSC, whose correct name al-Masri surely knew. Through the distortion, al-Masri attempted to identify the NUSC with a small Marxist grouping that was a political pariah to most of Palestinian society rather than with an organization led by the Fath-affiliated student group. Through this distortion, he might also have been trying to wrest the Fath-affiliated students away from the NUSC. Finally, al-Masri pointed out that the faculty union had defied the authority of the CHE when it refused the latter's proposal to set up a committee to investigate the crisis, a committee composed of the president of the university, a member of the board, and a member of the faculty who would be nominated by the board.[130] The refusal to concede to the proposal was less a reflection of the faculty union's defiance than how subverted the CHE had become by late 1981. The union had clearly lost its institutional patron, though the university charter prototype remained on record.

The fact that, for the first time, articles began appearing that directly challenged al-Masri's authority offered cold, though timely, comfort to the faculty union. Dr. Ahmad al-Ghawl reminded al-Masri "that history collects the facts of man with compassion . . . his illustrious deeds in one's youth for when he is old." He reminded the reader of al-Masri's illustrious national past when he was one of the leaders of the National Constitutional Party in the early 1950s that challenged absolute monarchical rule in Jordan and championed Arab nationalism. Al-Ghawl also noted his economic achievements which had benefited Nablus as a whole. "Why then allow history to collect the unsavory facts now?" he asked.[131] Dr. ʿAbd al-Sitar Qasim, the head of the follow-up committee set up by the faculty union during the first crisis in July 1980, was more blatant and academic. Al-Masri's paternalism was juxtaposed to objective organizational behavior, a reflection of a problem that existed far beyond the confines of al-Najah University: "The Arab world continues to suffer from a struggle between two types of thinking: a pattern of thought that emanates from benevolent paternalism and that monitors the public interest according to its will, and the other pattern of thought that views progress through the principle of objective administrative thought, especially the impersonal manner of coping with problems that arise. This struggle is taking place on all levels, formal and informal."[132] Another reader perceived the struggle between al-Masri and the faculty union as revolving around the former's desire to "Jordanize the university" (*ardanat al-jamiʿa*). She urged that the university be placed under self-rule.[133]

Violence: The Third Round

All this took place while the latest strike was quickly becoming the longest of its kind in the territories. It began on October 18, a mere twelve days after the beginning of the semester (which had already been postponed for ten days because of the crisis over the dismissals). A hunger strike called by the NUSC on November 14 in which 120 local students and 20 more from Birzeit participated added an element of human drama, particularly with the hospitalization of six of them.[134] The hunger strike must have been effective, for, four days later, the board agreed to discuss the four dismissals.[135]

An agreement was reached between the municipal council and the board of governors with the close cooperation of a transformed and tamed CHE. The agreement stipulated the establishment of a committee to seek a comprehensive settlement of the problem of reform at al-Najah and specifically to decide on the final status of the four dismissed. It consisted of the new president, Mundhir Salah, a member of the board of governors, and Dr. ʿAwni Badr, the chairman of the faculty union who also headed the pro-Fath electoral list.[136] Once again the two organs, the faculty union and the NUSC, welcomed the agreement but reiterated their determination to pursue the struggle until matters were resolved to their satisfaction: "the gist of the problem revolves around who hold the keys to power and control. There is only one solution to this problem: Putting an end to the complete concentration of power in the hands of the board of governors. This has to be done with utmost speed by ratification of democratic laws and by-laws that distribute authority and responsibility among the [various] organs within the university."[137] The faculty union nevertheless decided to call off the strike, "in response to national organs and institutions inside and outside, especially the Palestine Liberation Organization." In addition, a committee consisting of two members of the board and a representative of the CHE was set up to look into the dismissals.[138]

At long last, a university council was set up composed of heads of the colleges and headed by the president to draw up a new charter.[139] At the end of November, the faculty union publicized the fact that the four dismissed teachers had received their salaries in full, and finally on January 8, 1982, the board of governors decided to reinstate them.[140]

The optimism generated by this success was quickly dashed by serious violence that broke out the day after the decision was made. A procession to the university administrative offices organized by fundamentalists opposed to the professors' reinstatement turned violent when fundamentalist students began attacking students identified with the opposition, damaged university buildings, and threw Muhammad Sawalha out of a second-floor window, badly hurting him.[141] Forty students and faculty members, mostly belonging to the nationalist camp, were injured. Violence spread to other parts of the city and broke out in the Polytechnic College in Hebron and as far away as the city of Gaza, where fundamentalists burnt the offices and library of the Red Crescent Society offices in Gaza (for the third time).[142] The Red Crescent society was headed by Dr. Haydar ʿAbd al-Shafi and symbolized the institutional power of the secular left in Gaza. The nationalists claimed that outsiders had reinforced fundamentalist ranks in al-Najah University itself.[143] Little wonder that the university was once again closed for two weeks.

Aborting the Univeristy Council through Traditional Conciliation

For the NUSC and the faculty union, this series of events formed a worrisome pattern. There was, however, one small ray of hope. The university council had become a reality. It was now up to the nationalists to make sure that it could live up to its task. Breaking up the pattern of violence by punishing the culprits seemed to be the most important first step. As long as the university authorities did not mete out punishment, structural transformation would be postponed indefinitely.

The university authorities' first moves—to dismantle the fundamentalist-controlled student council and obligate itself to publish the findings concerning the latest act of violence within twelve days—seemed promising enough.[144] The next move, however, seriously undermined the faculty union. The university council, rather than acting as a tribunal and punishing the culprits itself, turned the case over to an external ad hoc "committee of conciliation."[145] How could traditional conciliation work between two sides that long ago evinced no willingness to come to any agreement? Worse still, the committee of conciliation threatened to split the nationalists. For this "tribal mechanism," as the NUSC so deprecatingly called it, consisted not only of notables and dignitaries in the Jordanian-controlled Muslim Affairs Religious Endowment Administration, but also mayors Hilmi Hanun of Tulkarem, Wahid Hamadallah of ʿAnabta, and Amin al-Nasr of Qalquilya, all of whom were members of the NGC, with credentials sufficiently nationalist to justify their removal from office by the Israeli authorities two months later.[146]

The committee of conciliation's findings, which they issued in January 26, 1982, spelled disaster for the nationalist forces within the university.[147] Apportioning blame equally on both sides, the committee advised the university council to close the case. They failed to identify the offenders and did not recommend individual sanctions. The committee completely disregarded the fact that the dissolved student council had refused to cooperate with the committee's investigation, in sharp contrast to the NUSC. The university council's verdict conformed to the committee of conciliation's findings. No sanctions were imposed on the fundamentalists.[148] The lesson was clear: notables of any hue were more likely to remain loyal to their social circle than to their ideology. Like the PLO, these mayors approved of political mobilization against the Camp David accords which did not threaten their social space, but not the development of local institutions, like the union, which could replace them or pose a threat to their power.

While the PLO's *Filastin al-Thawra* continued to urge patience and understanding, the leftist factions seethed over developments at al-Najah. According to *Al-Hurriyya*, the official organ of the DFLP, al-Masri was directly responsible for the violence. As early as December, he had sent his "bullies" to tame the nationalist students who objected to his meeting with Menachem Milson, the recently instated head of the Civil Administration, who had vowed to use the resources of his newly formed bureaucracy to fight the power of the PLO in the territories. As far as *Al-Hurriyya* was concerned, al-Masri's behavior "not only threatens the status of a national and academic university, but threatens to a great extent the position of the popular nationalist movement and its role in the struggle against Israeli occupation, and its attempt to implement self-rule."[149] The DFLP was convinced that al-Masri and the authorities struck a deal in which special treatment would be meted out to al-Najah University by the authorities in return for suppressing student and faculty union power. According to *Al-Hurriyya*, al-Masri was also in league with Jordan.

In general, the weekly implied that the PLO was neither aiding the effort nor cooperating with the masses.[150] A report the following week clearly stated its disappointment in the PLO position: "The PLO and its institutions, such as the Committee of the Occupied Territories and the Department of Higher Education, are requested more than any other organ to discard their ambiguous and noncommittal stances and to play a major role in revealing the stratagems of the Jordanian regime in its attempts at extending its control over the teachers of the institutions of higher education . . . and to extend material and national aid which will enable these institutions to stop Israel's crushing onslaught."[151] The left also utilized the opportunity to condemn the fundamentalists. The "prisoners of the Palestinian revolution" in Israeli jails specifically denounced the Muslim Brotherhood for the role it played in the events at al-Najah University.

Attempts at Cooptation

In addition to violence and the loss of wider political support, the nationalists within the university also had to contend with al-Masri's astute political moves. He cooperated closely with the president in establishing a documentation and research center focusing on Palestinian studies and folklore and, more importantly, coopted some key opponents in the process.[152] Dr. ʿAbd al-Sitar Qasim, a prominent activist in the union, was appointed rector of the College of Economics, the largest faculty in the university. Another activist, Dr. Ahmad Bakr, was appointed the head of the Research and Documentation Center. Both moves might have been inspired by the cordial relations between al-Masri and President Salah.

The victory of a coalition under Shabiba leadership in the student elections on November 29, 1982, set the stage for a nationalist resurgence.[153] In early February, discontent resurfaced, this time from the senior ranks of the university. Five deans resigned over irregularities in the running of the university, although they returned to their posts soon afterward.[154] At the end of February, Dr. ʿAbd al- Sitar Qasim resigned from his post as rector.[155] Again, irregularities ranging from appointments and dismissals to misappropriation of building funds precipitated the crisis and, once again, all conceded that the lack of an appropriate charter was the core problem. A committee was formed yet again to change the university's by-laws. Only this time it was no longer part of a broader political drive to transform local Palestinian institutions into one unified university system. Too many of the key sister institutions in the occupied territories had been humbled by that time—an appointed mayor rather than an elected one sat in the town hall of Nablus, Israel had forcefully removed Shakʿa and his associates from politics, the NGC had disappeared, and the CHE, a mere vestige of its former self, could not come to the aid of reformers.

When the next scandal erupted, the issue of structural reform was never even raised. The scandal revolved around a wall that had been pulled down on university grounds after it had been in danger of crumbling and then rebuilt by the same contractor who built the first. It turned out that he was a former engineer of the university and secretary of its building committee that was, in fact, the board of governors wearing a different hat.[156] Both the faculty union and the student council wondered how the defendant could be his own judge. They claimed that, at the very least, the board should include representatives from the student body, the faculty, and members from independent but knowledgeable bodies such as the local branch of the Lawyers Guild and Engineering Union. ʿAdnan Damiri, the president of the student council and founder of the Fath-affiliated Shabiba student movement at the university, tied the crisis to other political issues—punishment of nationalist students and the scuttling of a vice-presidency for academic affairs, a post that served to disperse administrative power in the university. The pro-PFLP biweekly *Al-Shirʿa* was even more blunt: "Public monies were being stolen in broad daylight, and the thief was still maintaining his leadership, surrounding himself with the halo of bourgeois notability."[157] As Qasim noted, this was just another example of failed structural reform that was so prevalent in the Arab world.[158]

Conclusion

The PLO clearly profited from the consistent pattern of events at al-Najah University. Crisis deepened politicization of Palestinian society. By adopting a noncommittal stance, the PLO helped maintain the consensus on political mobilization while local rivalries within institutions curtailed institution building. Thus, the PLO achieved hegemony in al-Najah University through the Shabiba student movement, which enjoyed an absolute majority in student councils from 1983 through 1987, and transformed the institution into one of the leading centers of opposition to Israeli rule.

Yet PLO control brought al-Najah University no closer to structural reform, even though by 1982 Fath controlled the student council and the faculty employee union. Meanwhile, the board of governors, opposed to reform, had allied itself with the Islamic fundamentalists.

The maintenance of pluralism within the institution and Fath hegemony within the student and professional unions at al-Najah conformed to a pattern of promoting diaspora-inspired mobilization of opposition in the territories while assuring weak institution building. As mobilization increased and the prospects of some form of self-government became more realistic, the PLO increasingly fragmented the institutions created within civil society. In the trade-off between control and functional efficiency, the latter was sacrificed to the former at al-Najah University. This order of preference reflected the larger relationship between the PLO and the occupied territories. The stronger territorial movements become, the weaker and smaller scale the public institutions in the territory must be.

5

The Intifada and State Building

"We shall burn the land under the conqueror's feet. Let the whole world know that the volcano of resistance that the Palestinian people ignited will not stop until the Palestinian state—with Jerusalem its capital—is achieved."[1] Having linked revolutionary violence to independence so forcefully in its first communiqué, did the Unified National Command of the intifada (UNC) place equal emphasis on state building? Is it indeed true that the ideological shift from "liberation" to "independence" signaled, as one scholar claimed, "a new strategy for the PLO inside the Occupied Territories: building embryonic institutions of power" for the future state?[2] And did such "embryonic institutions" of power actually take shape during the years of intifada?

Ibrahim Abu Lughod has written that "unless the intifada is placed in comparative perspective and set up against the backdrop of the historical quest for Palestinian statehood, it is difficult to appreciate."[3] This chapter analyzes, specifically, the relationship between the intifada and the *evolution* of the state, rather than that between the intifada and the attainment of statehood. By examining the series of communiqués issued by the UNC during the intifada, we can analyze the PLO's impact on the formulation of strategy during the intifada, the shaping of territorial institutions, leadership patterns, and conflict-resolution mechanisms.

Strategy and State Formation

Before trying to analyze the empirical impact of the intifada on Palestinian state formation, it is important to first look at the relationship between intifada *strategy* and the formation of the state. The UNC communiqués focused much more on national liberation than the academic literature, which concentrated on its revolutionary aspects, would lead us to believe. The assumption of the literature was that the participants in the intifada—the "insiders"—sought to destroy the old social order in order to build the new.[4] A focus on national liberation, however, involves diplomacy, usually achieved best by the outside. The discrepancy between the communiqués and the academic literature has much to do with the authors' sympathies, but it also has to do with the fact that the PLO could more easily put pressure on the drafters of the communiqués than upon scholars. Indeed, initial communiqués were more revolutionary and emphasized the ability of the inside to beget the state. A notable example is the UNC's tenth communiqué, which announced its intention to "continue the popular and armed revolution until the [establishment] of the Palestinian state."[5]

However, as the population's ability to participate in mass demonstrations wore thin over time and PLO pressure on the inside increased, the communiqués started to inform the Palestinian population that their sacrifices would facilitate independence, not through revolution, but rather through the convening of an international conference where the PLO would, like the FLN had for Algeria, capture the state: "Behold our glorious leadership registering, by way of intensive political activity, the most wondrous achievements . . . on the path toward the international conference with full powers and Palestinian representation which will express the legitimate rights of our people: return, self-determination, and the establishment of the Palestinian state, rights recognized by most of the states of the world."[6]

Amid calls of violence and diplomacy, the state-building project of establishing a national authority proved to be a minor theme in the UNC communiqués. Nor did the communiqués ever spell out how localized popular committees, through which the intifada was to be organized, would be transformed into a national authority.

Concepts like "national authority" and "people's authority" have never amounted to much in revolutionary contexts, still less in a national liberation movement split in two and facing the repression of a powerful state. Consider, for example, the first time a UNC communiqué mentioned the national authority: "The popular committees have spread all over the occupied homeland. Our people have begun to erect a new national life and to increase its national authority."[7] Obviously, the reference is to the development of a countergovernmental structure whose dispersion would facilitate the eradication and replacement of the occupation regime. Similarly, Communiqué 55 two years later noted that civil insubordination and institution building were two sides of the same coin.[8]

Yet such calls were in no way an exhortation to the "inside" to actually create a national authority. Rather, while the role of the inside was to wear down the enemy by perpetuating mobilization, only diplomatic efforts could lead to the creation of the state. Salim Tamari, probably the most astute analyst of the intifada, hoped that Palestinian populism based on the popular committees would be used to "constitute *not* the embryonic foundations of a new society but the nascent organs of an alternative power base," by undermining the basis of Israeli rule until the PLO established itself as a state power in the occupied territories.[9] The populist revolutionary rhetoric of the communiqués concealed the fact that institution building was to play second fiddle to mobilization. In other words, the inside was to focus its efforts on assisting the PLO in "state creation," rather than state building. The latter they were able to leave alone until the PLO was able to territorialize and control the process itself.

Diplomacy Rather Than Devolution

More than any other single issue, the conflict over local elections epitomized the struggle between the evolutionary state-building approach favored by the territorial Palestinians in the initial stages of the intifada and the international diplomatic approach favored by the diaspora-based leadership.

The right to hold municipal council elections was a prominent feature of the UNC's early communiqués.[10] These communiqués, heeded by the inhabitants in the territories, established the newly emergent UNC as the leading force behind the intifada. Yet as time passed, the UNC, under PLO pressure, became increasingly lukewarm regarding elections. While in January 1988 the UNC demanded elections with no preconditions (except that they would be "free"), by May and June calls for elections included the proviso that they be held under international, preferably, United Nations supervision.[11] By October, the request for elections was omitted altogether[12] and by February 1989, the PLO had rejected local elections as long as the Israeli occupation persisted (Communiqué 34 in February 1989). This rejection took place two months before the Shamir plan calling for territory-wide elections was announced on April 14. Palestinians regarded his plan as a deliberate Israeli attempt to foster the emergence of a local leadership in order to negotiate a settlement with Israel based on nonterritorial autonomy.[13] Following the PLO's declaration of the Palestinian state on November 14, 1988, based on UN Resolution 181, which partitioned Palestine into two states, one Arab, one Jewish, and Arafat's subsequent recognition of the existence of the state of Israel, it would have seemed that the PLO would readily agree to free local elections in the territories. The PLO, as early as 1976, had scored, almost by default, a sweeping victory in West Bank municipal elections. How much more it would win in 1988 or 1989, when the UNC, "the fighting arm of the PLO in the territories," had proven so loyal and dominant a political factor in the territories?[14] It was the success of elections, not their failure, that the PLO feared—a fear that came all to naturally to a diaspora-based national movement that sought resolution to the Palestinian problem solely through their own diplomatic efforts, not in conjunction with a territorial evolutionary process. The elections could serve no other purpose than to facilitate the emergence of a local leadership that would be ready to negotiate an evolutionary path to Palestinian statehood. The PLO, by contrast, wished to keep the resolution of the conflict confined to outside diplomatic channels only. The PLO's November policy changes enabled the organization to maintain its high diplomatic profile and ensured that the international peace conference continued to be a viable option. These concessions maintained the "functional" gap between the diaspora center, which monopolized diplomacy, and its territorial periphery, which carried out the intifada. By the time the territorialists gained access to the international arena in fall 1991 with the inauguration of the Madrid peace process, their elite was vulnerably exposed to an organized hard core affiliated with the factions on the outside, and with a much stronger Islamic fundamentalist opposition.

Diaspora State Building Rather Than Territorial Center Building

The events surrounding King Hussein's decision in July 1988 to sever Jordanian ties with the West Bank serve as one indication of PLO reticence in territorial institution building. King Hussein's move—which began with the scuttling of a grandiose Jordanian-sponsored five-year development plan and the decision to dismiss the 21,000 employees of Jordanian institutions in the territories—left a vacuum that the territorialists were eager to fill.[15] While the PLO wavered in its response to Jordan's actions, the local press responded with alacrity by publishing editorials exhorting the chambers of commerce, the professional unions, and the municipalities to sever all links with Jordan and become "complete and independent Palestinian institutions."[16] More importantly, it was at this time that Israeli security forces found the independence document in Faysal Husayni's Arab Studies Association that envisioned the emergence of a Palestinian National Council, half of whose 180 members would be representatives from the territories.

Instead of responding to the demands for institution building, UNC Communiqué 24 emphasized the diplomatic track:

> To our valiant people and glorious masses. The UNC emphasizes that the steps taken by Jordan to sever its legal and administrative ties is an important political move, one of the achievements of the intifada that has restored to itself a Palestinian right that has been stolen during forty years of guardianship and annexation. We emphasize that there is no reality to what is called the political vacuum, because our people in the occupied territories have always seen the PLO as their sole legitimate representative, its political leader, and the undisputed leader of its struggle. . . . We emphasize that the PLO, comprising its central command institutions, expresses politically the aspirations of our people, and that the just solution to our Palestinian problem will come through the international community reflected by an international conference in which the PLO will cooperate as an equal partner with the other sides.[17]

Subsequent communiqués of the UNC upheld the proliferation of popular committees that the institution-builders in *Al-Fajr* intuitively understood were leading to diffusion and fragmentation rather than toward a process of state formation. "Independence will be achieved by more and more popular committees," assured the writers of Communiqué 28. Only in Communiqué 32, after the declaration of independence and the official proclamation of the State of Palestine, did the PLO see fit to respond to local calls for the Palestinianization of translocal institutions "provided it does not harm the bonds of amity and brotherhood . . . with the fraternal Jordanian people in particular and the Arab people in general."[18] (The UNC was referring to the "white-collar" professional organizations that maintained formal ties to Jordanian parent organizations.)

In the first year of the intifada, there was no serious attempt to create translocal institutions. The closest was the UNC's demand for the establishment of national export and marketing institutions to export Palestinian produce independently of Agrexco, the Israeli export-marketing board.[19] Nevertheless, the communiqué called for the creation of more than one institution. In any case, there was no indication that the PLO was even ready to finance such a project.

In the second year, the Higher Student Council was the only translocal institution that the UNC formed "as the final authority in all student affairs in the state of Palestine."[20] It urged that all educational institutions cooperate with the council.

The PLO also made no effort to create their own Palestinian examination system that would be accredited by Arab states, in order to replace the Jordanian and Egyptian matriculation exam systems operating in the West Bank and Gaza.[21] This may be due, however, to the inability to create an alternative educational system. As early as the fall of 1988, several communiqués urged the reopening of the established school system in the West Bank.[22] Where schools remained in session, the UNC called upon the population "to keep the schools open and not give the occupation authorities pretext to close them again."[23] Nevertheless, Palestinians both inside and outside the territories voiced disappointment over the pace of institution building, noting the absence of such basic institutional mechanisms such as a territory-wide committee of general education and a health board that would coordinate the activities of the various health organizations.[24]

Instead of focusing on specific institutional projects, the UNC, with PLO support, adopted a vague and unrealistic policy of economic disengagement from the Israeli economy. An Israeli decision in the summer of 1989 to replace identity papers in Gaza with magnetic cards that could be monitored by computers located at checkpoints out of Gaza clearly reflected the weakness of UNC policy.[25] The authorities hoped that limited access to employment could act as an incentive for collaboration, a sanction against potential activists, and a means for denying security suspects employment in Israel. The UNC turned the issue into a test case, calling upon workers to refuse their cards or burn them, if they possessed them already. The work boycott lasted three weeks, followed by several months during which the strike forces confiscated the magnetic cards from Arab workers. But by the end of the year, it was clear that the authorities had won out. No political reality could alter the fact that Palestinian workers depended inordinately upon the Israeli market, while Israel could afford restricting access (over 40 percent of the Gazan labor force was employed in Israel, while they comprised only 4 percent of the total workforce there). By the end of the intifada's third year, Palestinian labor union leaders were desperately seeking ways to ensure Arab employment in the Israeli market in the face of competition of thousands of Russian Jewish immigrants who were arriving in the country monthly.[26]

Leadership Subordination

The intifada presented the PLO with a major dilemma. Since the emergence of the NGC, the PLO had striven consistently to prevent the consolidation of a unified territorial leadership. On the other hand, the persistence of the intifada—vital for meeting the PLO's political objectives—called for local centralized direction. The mainstream's vacillation in creating a territorial leadership seemed to be confirmed by the key role the DFLP played in initiating the organization of the intifada, despite its minuscule size compared to Fath.[27]

There are also indications that the PLO set its "spokesmen" and notables against attempts by the intifada's organizational leadership to cluster around the UNC. On January 6, 1988, just as attempts to form the UNC were moving at high gear, a group of these spokesmen and notables, led by Hanna Siniora and Mubarak ʿAwad, dramatically announced a radical campaign of civil disobedience against the occupation. They called for the burning of identity cards issued by the authorities and the boycotting of Israeli goods produced by local Arab producers.[28] These demands were far more radical than those that had appeared in earlier communiqués issued by PLO factions. In the fifth communiqué, issued by the UNC in late January, the leftist organizations attacked these demands for being premature, although this did not prevent the UNC from adopting civil disobedience as a basic strategy, indicating that the struggle revolved around leadership rather than policy.[29]

Another attempt to disunite the local leadership took a different form. On January 14, 1988, Sari Nusseibeh, acting Birzeit University President Gabi Baramki, and other leading pro-PLO figures called upon Israel to permit political activity and contact with the PLO, abolish the VAT, and cease exploitation of water sources in the territories.[30] This significantly milder approach can be linked to shifting PLO objectives. On January 6, the PLO sought to prevent the emergence of the UNC. After that failed, the PLO sought access to political activity that could challenge the new UNC. By late February, a modus vivendi emerged between the diaspora center and the UNC's local leadership. While the UNC dropped its demand for local elections, the diaspora center agreed to cease attempts to circumvent the UNC's sole leadership in the territories, provided it be the arm that executed PLO policy rather than a participant in its formulation. Only after this agreement, did *Filastin al-Thawra*, the official organ of the PLO, first mention the UNC, (three weeks after the journals of the PFLP and DFLP had done so). The frequency with which Arafat's name was mentioned in the UNC communiqués in the first year of the intifada reflected its increasing subordination to the PLO (see table 5.1). In the first ten communiqués, he was not mentioned a single time; in the second batch of ten he was mentioned twice; in the third, seven times. The communiqués also mentioned the PLO with increasing frequency: 41 references in communiqués 1–10, 48 in 11–20, and 52 in communiqués 21 to 30. While the PLO only appeared in the signature 6 out of the first 10 times, it signed off on all of the following ten (and 9 out of the third 10).

Diffusion at the Top—A Look at the UNC

While sanctioning the UNC, the PLO made sure that it could not become an effective operational command. Instead, it developed into a "moral leadership," comprising representatives of Fath, the DFLP, the PFLP, the Palestinian Communist Party, and a few independents. Its major task was paperwork—drafting the communiqués (*nidaʾat*) of the intifada—rather than giving orders to a defined network of activists.[31] The UNC's general task was not so much to mobilize support itself, as the NGC had attempted to do, but to oversee the intifada and emphasize the goals that would make the inhabitants' self-directed sacrifice worthwhile.

Table 5.1. References to the PLO in the UNC Communiqués of 1988

Communiqués	1–10	11–20	21–30
PLO signature	6	10	9
Reference to PLO in body of text	41	48	52
Reference to Arafat	0	2	7

Source: Shaul Mishal with Reuven Aharoni, *Avanim ze lo hakol* (Tel Aviv: Hakibutz HaMeuchad, 1989), 47.

As a mere "moral" leadership, the UNC was ill-equipped to deal with the political and organizational fragmentation. Small-scale, diffuse institution building had been the norm in order to reduce the vulnerability of the intifada to Israeli reprisal; but proliferation could also intensify conflict, duplicate scarce resources, and create confusion that, in the long term, could reduce mass participation.

The UNC, aware of these dangers, attempted to project an image of unity by avoiding any reference to the factions that made up the UNC in the intifada's first year. By the beginning of the second year, however, UNC communiqués began commemorating their founding anniversaries,[32] and by August 1989, the UNC was content with standardizing the slogans and directives that appeared on leaflets and on walls, and did not demand that the organizations and factions responsible for writing them sign off as the UNC (Communiqué 44, August 18, 1989).

Indeed, at least three parallel but separate structures had emerged. The dominant political forces, which included Fath and the affiliated Shabiba movement; the Palestinian Communist Party; the DFLP and its affiliated al-Wahda movement; and the PFLP and its affiliated Jabhat al-ʿAmal movement all provided the organizational link between the UNC and the organizational modes further below.[33] The Israeli authorities directed most of their blows at this level of organizational command by deporting its activists, placing others under extensive and prolonged administrative arrests, and by declaring the political organizations illegal.[34]

The service wings of the political forces, which wedded the provision of social services with political mobilization, formed another network of institutions. These movements included the Shabiba Movement for Social Work, and the various women's organizations such as the PFLP's Committees of Palestinian Women, the DFLP's Women's Action Committees, and the Communist Committees of the Palestinian Working Woman. Israeli authorities curtailed the activities of this structure and one organization, the Shabiba movement, was outlawed completely in March 1988.[35]

Popular and other ad hoc committees, an innovation of the intifada, represented the third and major structure. It was on this level that the architects of the intifada not only adopted the small local unit as its basic organ, but sought its continued multiplication. Communiqué 6, issued at the beginning of February 1988, two months after the outbreak of the intifada, was typical: "Let us develop various forms of appropriate organizational structures such as committees and task forces, in every place, village, and [refugee] camp so that we can reach every neighborhood and every street on the path of comprehensive civil rebellion." Communiqués 55 (April 20, 1990) and 56 (May 13, 1990), two and a half years later, voiced the same requests. The organizational structure of the intifada thus seemed to focus on increasing participation of all segments of society, generating ever-expanding circles of small-unit organization. Better, the UNC believed, that such organization be rudimentary and widespread than tight-knit but limited, and that it be loosely organized rather than pyramidically structured and vulnerable to blows by the Israeli authorities.

While the nationalist groups in the territories failed to create a cohesive organizational center for directing the intifada, at least two outside political forces also contributed to political balkanization. Neither the al-Jihad al-Islami, a group that advocated and practiced armed struggle throughout the intifada, nor Hamas, the Islamic Resistance Movement that had emerged out of the Muslim Brotherhood and enjoyed a much wider popular base and support, joined the UNC despite pleas to do so by the PLO factions. All three vied for the symbols of governance and leadership in the UNC's calls, the strike days commemorating the outbreak of the intifada, and the popular committees and strike forces. Hamas even went so far as to ratify and disseminate a constitution in obvious imitation of the PLO. While the PLO factions concluded periodic agreements with Hamas over specific issues of contention, thereby managing to avoid open violence for the most part, they failed to cooperate on functional and organizational matters at any level.

The Popular Committee's Noninstitutionalization

While the popular committee was supposed to be the basic coordinating unit in the intifada, the communiqués of the UNC failed to suggest how they should be constituted. They did not define the functional jurisdiction of the various committees, delineate a hierarchy between the popular committee and other specialized committees, or point to ways that would foster institutional amalgamation.

The Absence of Functional Jurisdictions

The communiqués never outlined a clear division of labor between the various organs operating at the grassroots level of the intifada. Essentially, there were three major problems: First, it was unclear what ought to have been the relationship between the popular committees and the "national committees" that were mentioned frequently in the communiqués in the first year of the intifada. The national committees were composed of the local representatives of the factions, while the popular committees were made up of both independents and professional activists. Thus, the national committees should have possessed some supervisory role over the popular committees. Yet Communiqué 9 (March 8, 1988), for example, asserted that both shared a supervisory role over fund-raising campaigns along with other pre-intifada institutions: "We call upon the people in the cities, villages, and camps to set up agencies to raise financial donations and donations in kind under the supervision of the national and popular committees in the neighborhoods, the villages, and the camps . . . with the warning that one should not meet requests for aid from outside the committees you yourself established." Both also shared the task of forming vigilance and defense committees to guard shops forcefully pried open by the military and that had to be protected from looting.[36] Finally, both organs were entrusted with "drawing up the necessary plans to promote the intifada" (Communiqué 23, August 5, 1988). No mention was made of who should comprise these various organs or the procedures necessary in choosing them.

Second, the relationship between the popular committees and other strike committees remained undefined. In Communiqué 2 (actually the first communiqué of the UNC), the popular committees were called upon to punish strikebreakers, indicating that the there was no functional specialization between the popular committees and the strike forces.[37] Only in Communiqué 10 were strike forces made responsible for making sure that the police hired by the military administration resign in accordance with previous UNC directives.[38] The UNC regarded the resignation of police as the first stage to full civil revolt. While strike forces were designated "the fighting arm" of the UNC in Communiqué 18,[39] Communiqué 27 demanded that both the strike forces and the popular committees escalate the number of strikes and intensity of rock throwing at the occupation forces.[40] Similarly, the relationship between the popular committees and the functional organs that proliferated in the first year of the intifada, such as the surveillance, food, and medical relief committees, were never defined.

The Absence of Hierarchy and Linkage

Despite jurisdictional confusion between the national and popular committees, the latter clearly possessed more functions. UNC communiqués called on popular committees to market local produce through local marketing boards,[41] establish agricultural cooperatives, explore ways to extend aid to industry, ensure worker rights, and find employment for workers.[42]

At the same time, the UNC communiqués did not define the hierarchical structure between the two. The fact that the UNC gave both kinds of committees some of the same functions implies the absence of any hierarchical linkage between the national and popular committees. The persistence of the national committees, however, indicated that the higher leadership was reluctant to accord power to the popular committees. It may also have indicated a lack of popular mobilization in certain areas and the need of a professional hard core to step in.

Nor were the popular committees themselves placed in any kind of hierarchical relationship to larger structures, with one exception: in early February, Communiqué 5 stated that "the regional committees of the UNC were in the process of making contact with popular committees in order to coordinate activities." The fact that this is the only time such an arrangement was mentioned would seem to indicate that both the regional committees of the UNC and subsequent coordination ceased to exist. And while it is true that two months later, the UNC urged "every area" to take over local government and UNRWA schools and force their reopening, the area in this case was a geographical referent rather than a specific institution.[43]

Hierarchy and Diffusion

In contrast to its approach to internal organization, the UNC frequently invoked the hierarchy principle between factions inside and outside the territory, particularly over issues of internecine strife within or between factions and the killing of suspected collaborators.[44] The PLO obviously adopted a two-track policy to intifada-related activities: it sought to diffuse territorial institution building while maintaining distinct subordination of the factions that were linked hierarchically to the outside. As late as 1990, the PLO was calling to proliferate grassroots organization—"to continue forming, building, and developing popular committees and their specialized committees that constitute the alternative popular authority to the occupation's collapsing organs and departments."[45] Yet they wanted to make sure that "popular authority" did not evolve into a state formation.

The popular committees' amorphousness and its duality of function with the national committees was not merely coincidence, as a debate between Fath and the Communists suggests. While Fath perceived the popular committees as another instrument for mobilizing resistance subordinate to the outside, the Communists, the only territorial party, viewed them as the apex of the institution-building process.[46] In the leftist view, the other committees, especially the strike forces, were to be the offshoots of the popular committees.[47] Fath, by contrast, viewed the popular committees as extensions of party control.

The official UNC position reflected, ironically enough, the position of the Communists. Communiqué 25, written after Israeli Minister of Defense Moshe Arens outlawed the popular committees and announced the exile of the first group of twenty-five activists, stated under the heading "popular committees" that "the UNC emphasizes the continuation of the establishment of the independent authority of the people on the path towards freedom and independence."[48]

In any event, it is doubtful whether the popular committees could have lived up to the civil society role that was prescribed for them by the Communists (an ironic turn to the right given the party's ideological orthodoxy and Leninist structure). As long as the popular committees were associated with confrontation and violence, they inevitably invited state repression, which increased the costs of resistance. The PLO might have hoped that aid from Arab countries would equal and perhaps exceed what workers earned while employed in Israel, thus facilitating mass participation. But as this never materialized and at best financial incentives remained constant, the number of participants declined. The intifada became increasingly characterized by a subsidized hard core who could afford to continue challenging Israeli authority.[49]

The Demise of Intifida Institution Building

By September 1988, it was clear that Fath had won the battle in ensuring fragmentation. Israel's onslaught on Fath-based popular committees in Gaza in July 1988, the proliferation of popular committees linked to the DFLP and PFLP,[50] and the formation of partisan strike forces[51] indicated the demise of coalition-structured institutions. Fath's decision to establish the "Palestinian Popular Army" on a single-party basis in the fall of 1988, rather than consolidate a fighting organization coalescing all organizations and unaffiliated activists, basically foreclosed any possibility that an independent and autonomous supraparty territorial power base would emerge.[52]

UNC communiqués indicate that attempts to cope with fragmentation failed miserably. In 1990, UNC committees composed of local faction representatives were supposed to replace the moribund popular committees and serve as the nucleus of reform. The UNC hoped that these committees would bring members of the factions together with independents, "to ensure the broadest popular participation."[53] Alas, restructuring proved no more successful than had the early efforts to develop the popular committees. Eight months later, the term "national committees" reappeared, replacing the stillborn UNC committees. The new committees' task was "to deepen Palestinian democracy and to broaden participation of the masses in national decision making.[54] The nomenclature changed once again four months later when, in Communiqué 78 the UNC sought the reorganization and enlargement of "people's" committees (*lijan al-sha*ᶜ*b*), instead of UNC, national, or popular committees.[55] Clearly, this confusion diverted attention and resources from either mobilization or institution building.

So ephemeral did intifada-generated institutionalization prove to be that when widespread cheating on the *tawjihi* exams engendered a sense of severe social crisis, it was organizational modes rooted in civil society from pre-intifada days—such as popular meetings and the punitive measures taken by the political factions—that effectively came to grips with the problem rather than the institutions associated with the intifada.[56] This was acknowledged in Communiqué 82, in which the UNC called upon "institutions" and "mass structures" (the second tier of mass movements formed in the decade preceding the intifada) to form "national" institutions to combat widespread cheating in the matriculation exams,[57] thus ignoring the strike forces or popular committees, if, that is, they still existed.

Mobilization of Violence and Institution Building

Before the intifada, the outside center preferred the mobilization of violence and political protest to institution building.

An analysis of the UNC calls in the first year of the intifada indicates that this trend continued. As the PLO solidified its control over the UNC, the call to violence increased dramatically over time, from 10 directives in the first 10 communiqués, to 45 directives in communiqués 21–30 (see table 5.2). By contrast, the directives associated with severing economic ties with the authorities and institution building[58] proportionately and absolutely decreased from 19 directives in the first 10 communiqués, to 15 in the third. In the first 10 communiqués, directives associated with severing economic ties and institution building outnumbered communiqués related to violence almost two to one. The data for communiqués 21–30 shows a dramatic reversal: directives to violence outnumbered the institution-building category three to one. The emphasis on violence went hand in hand with the growing subordination to the PLO. Division of labor between the "inside" and "outside," along the lines of brawn and brain, increased during the intifada to the detriment of attempts at territorial state-in-the-making.

The Intifida and Diffuse Institution Building

In spite of the PLO's strategy of promoting diffusion and political competition, "insider" institution building actually accelerated during the intifada. This bolsters our assertion that the lack of Palestinian state building cannot

Table 5.2. Types of Directives that Appeared in UNC Communiqués in the First Year of the Intifada

Communiqués	1–10	11–20	21–30
Category			
Violence	10	32	45
Severance of Ties	19	21	15
Civil Disobedience	18	22	27

Source: Mishal with Reuveni, *Avanim ze lo hakol*, 46.

altogether be blamed on Israeli occupation. An analysis of *Al-Quds* reveals both the dimensions this process reached as well as its rate of acceleration. (*Al-Quds*, in contrast to other newspapers such as *Al-Sha^{c}b* and *Al-Fajr*, was never a party newspaper, and therefore less apt to exaggerate institution-building activities the way mobilizing party organs typically do.)

Seven consecutive issues of the newspaper were analyzed for the last week of June for the years 1972, 1986, and 1992. The years chosen are not arbitrary: 1972 represents the period before an organized political institution, the PNF, made institution building a major political priority; 1986 stands almost on the eve of the intifada; and 1992 was chosen to see the effect of sustained mass violence and repression on institution building. Analyzed were news items generated locally regardless of their scope (local, regional, or international), placement, and style (dry news vs. commentary and analysis).

The findings strikingly demonstrate the growth of territorialism under Israeli rule. Between June 23 and June 30, 1972, 41 news items concerning events generated locally appeared on 40 pages of the *Al-Quds* newspaper for that week. By 1986, *Al-Quds* reported 123 local events in a total of 72 pages, a threefold increase in the number of events compared to 1972. In 1992, four and one half years after the outbreak intifada, the focus on internal society continued to increase. In the last week of June, the newspaper reported or advertised a total of 192 news items focusing on news generated locally, a 56 percent increase compared to 1986 and an almost fivefold increase since 1972. If one were to measure column inches or to count words, the increases over time would be even more striking.

Some of the difference in spatial magnitude is captured by the distinction between local news items appearing on the front page and local items relegated to the remaining pages. This measure also includes a qualitative dimension, however. In June 1972, no local news item made the front page, a small indication of the territories' thorough peripheralization at the time. News was made anywhere but at home. By 1986, that had changed noticeably, as *Al-Quds* reported on its front page thirteen news items reflecting political or economic life in the occupied territories. Of the thirteen items, five concerned Jordanian involvement in West Bank affairs, as the newspaper had a pro-Jordanian orientation until the summer of 1987, when it switched to a more pro-PLO orientation. Four more were related to matters of Israeli suppression. Of the rest, one was an article on Gaza City by former mayor Rashad al-Shawwa, one headline reported *tawjihi* results, and two were related to economic matters. Thus, the change from 1972, as dramatic as it was, still reflected a dependency on the outside, as 9 of the 13 local items reported on the impact of Israel and Jordan on the territories.

By 1992, *Al-Quds* headlines reflected the activities of a highly self-conscious, albeit fragmented, territorial society. Not only did the number of news items or announcements on the front page of the newspaper concerning local events increase from 13 to 24, but local personalities in the peace delegation and local institutions were making headlines (three and eight, respectively). The news items relating to institutions included an announcement from the West Bank Federation of Chambers of Commerce, a proposal for the establishment of a Palestinian television network, and the schedule of the first Palestinian film festival organized under the aegis of the Palestinian National Theater in East Jerusalem.

The back pages of *Al-Quds* reflected increasing institutional richness and diversity as well. In 1972, municipal functions performed by the West Bank municipalities, formal institutions linked both to the military government and Jordan, accounted for five of six new items that reported on local civic or political institutions. The sixth news item reported the founding of a new journal. By 1986, news regarding local institutions appeared in forty-eight news items. Municipalities, the "official" public organizations in the West Bank, remained prominent amongst the list, but ten items also involved political groups, labor unions, and charitable organizations. Most of the latter institutions were created since 1972 and were affiliated or linked to Palestinian organizations only. By 1992, the municipalities' activities, which, for the most part, had been taken over by the military authorities since 1982, accounted for only 10 of 72 news items dealing with local institutions. Political institutions linked to the surrogate state and movements within civil society such as the Palestinian Federation of Writers and Zakat committees predominated.

Perhaps the most dramatic evidence reflected in *Al-Quds* of local Palestinian territorialism is the formation of a territorial academic and public policy elite concerned with local institution building. Whereas in 1972, *Al-Quds* reported local affairs in brief technical terms, by 1992 local educators and others with particular expertise in public affairs, as well as political personalities, were analyzing and commenting on local affairs extensively in long articles, some of it within a state-formation paradigm. The data in this regard reflects dramatic change. Only one such article appeared in the period under investigation in 1972, five in 1986, and a full sixteen in 1992. In the last week of June 1992, long articles appeared on the problems wrought by intifada violence, the need to combat cheating in the *tawjihi* high school exams, a second in a series of three articles on the relationship between a liberal educational philosophy and the problems facing the educational system in Gaza schools written by Dr. Ihsan al-Agha, the dean of the Educational College of the Islamic University, an article by a social worker on the local drug problem, extensive articles on labor unions, the local economy, marketing, the prospects of industrialization in the future Palestinian state, and an article on the national health project. Despite both the violence directed against the occupation and internal violence, most of the focus was on constructive building and reforming civil society rather than critiques of the occupation.

It goes without saying that most of the writing emanated from a Palestinian nationalist perspective.

Thus, despite massive mobilization in the intifada, institution building continued to increase rapidly. Furthermore, it was not a matter solely of magnitude. The articles in *Al-Quds* in 1992 increasingly reflected the ideological, if not the programmatic, message of the UNC communiqués—the quest for statehood, even if many of the articles centered around themes of social deterioration.

The marked growth in organizations rooted in civil society contrasted sharply with the deterioration of the social fabric and political tensions generated by the mobilization of violence. It suggests that a different balance between functional institution building and the mobilization of violence might have been more beneficial to state formation in the long run. More importantly, it suggests that there were possibilities for the formation of macro-institutions even under Israeli occupation. In any event, if Palestinian civil society was unable to form or integrate into an emerging national authority, at least it grew and remained vibrant. Whether this will prove sufficient to curb a Palestinian state's future power and influence it toward taking a democratic course is another question altogether.

Conclusion

To answer this chapter's opening question, it cannot be said that the PLO created embryonic state institutions of power during the intifada. By enhancing the visibility and role of the inside over the outside, the uprising merely exacerbated the dilemma of territorialization faced by the PLO. It was only natural then that the PLO continued and even intensified policies of coping with the dilemma inherited from the pre-intifada era. It promoted political mobilization at the expense of institution building, subordinated local leadership rather than incorporate them into the decision-making process, promoted international diplomacy rather than political devolution, and fragmented the institution-building process rather than centralizing it. Tragically, the diaspora center sought to ensure that as the prospects of independence increased, there would be less, rather than more, territorial state building. A national authority composed of popular committees and aspiring to popular government resonated with romantic echoes of the Paris Commune but masked a reality of fragmentation and diffusion. While perhaps accelerating the pace toward political independence, the intifada hardly reflected progression in the way of state formation.

6

The Madrid Peace Process and the Challenge of the Inside

No other event since 1967 potentially threatened the historic relationship between inside and outside like the 1991 Madrid and Washington peace talks, which convened partly on terms dictated by Israel. For the first time, the PLO was forced to give its assent to a situation in which territorial Palestinians, albeit within a joint Jordanian-Palestinian delegation, became negotiating partners with Israel in an international forum, from which the PLO itself was formally excluded.[1] Even more noteworthy, the terms of the peace process spoke of a mandatory interim stage of three to five years of self-government (depending on the length of negotiations over final settlement beginning in the third year), in which territorial Palestinians would govern themselves, again to the exclusion of the PLO. It seemed, then, that the twenty-five-year-old dream of the advocates of the Palestinian entity was finally to bear fruit in a state-building process that conformed to the Zionist pattern before Israeli independence.

Did the territorial Palestinians take advantage of this opportunity, or did they prove once again that they were politicians in search of leadership, as Sahliyeh claimed, rather than assuming leadership themselves? This chapter assesses the impact of the Madrid and Washington peace talks on the quality of state making and links the weakness of state formation with the inability of the territorialists to transform the diaspora-center–territorial-periphery framework into a territorially centered national movement.

The PLO and the Palestinian Delegation

If Israel's intent was either to divide Palestinians or to place the territorialists in a favored position compared to the PLO, the Palestinian delegation and the PLO responded in assuring each other of the bonds of hierarchical unity that traditionally held them together. The outside expressed these sentiments in the political statement that concluded the PNC meeting a month before the Madrid peace talks: "The upcoming stage, with all its obstacles, requires that all the institutions and personalities inside and outside the homeland coordinate with the political leadership of the PLO."[2] Haydar ʿAbd al-Shafi, the head of the fourteen-strong Palestinian delegation, duly acknowledged his delegation's obeisance to the PLO in his opening address to the conference: "We have been denied the right to publicly acknowledge our loyalty to our leadership and system of government. . . . Our acknowledged leadership is more than a justly and democratically chosen leadership of all the Palestinian people."[3] In his closing remarks, he even invoked the leader of the PLO himself: "In the words of Chairman Arafat in 1974 before the United Nations General Assembly, "Let not the olive branch fall from our hands. Let not the olive branch fall from the hands of the Palestinian people'." Nabil Shaᶜth, Arafat's close advisor and confidant, was equally insistent on championing the prerogatives of the outside: "There was one Palestinian delegation, representing one single Palestinian people in all places, whether under occupation or in exile."[4]

Naturally, the PLO sought ways to ensure that the delegation would not act independently of its leadership. The nomination of seventy-two-year-old Haydar ᶜAbd al-Shafi to head the delegation rather than a younger politician such as Faysal Husayni served this purpose well. Though ᶜAbd al-Shafi was former president of the Palestinian legislative council formed under Egyptian rule, a founding member of the PLO and its first Executive Committee, and a publically acknowledged symbol of selfless long-term dedication to both the Palestinian cause and society, he also had some liabilities: he was a man of the left, of advanced age, whose relations with the Muslim Brotherhood in Gaza had been tempestuous in the past. A weak figurehead, politically unaffiliated, he made an ideal choice from the perspective of the diaspora.

To offset the collective leadership potential of the group and to advise the negotiating team, the PLO divided the inside by setting up a seven-strong advisory committee headed by al-Husayni, two other territorial Palestinians, Zahira Kamal and Hanan ᶜAshrawi (who doubled as spokeswoman for both the delegation and the advisory committee in which she was member), and three particularly gifted members from the diaspora, Kamil Mansur, a jurist and publicist residing in France, Anis al-Qasim, an attorney residing in Great Britain, and Rashid Khalidi, a Palestinian American academic.[5] This was shortly replaced effectively by a larger and misnamed leadership committee, headed by Nabil Shaᶜth and deputized by his "foil" Akram Haniya, that maintained roughly the same proportions between inside and outside.[6] It was misnamed both because above it stood the follow-up committee, headed by Mahmud ᶜAbbas (Abu Mazen), who would later undermine the delegation in heading the secret Oslo negotiations, and because Arafat's neopatrimonial practices kept him so firmly in charge of affairs.

The techniques Arafat employed were relatively simple. Every person of consequence in the negotiation process had his double or foil; every organ, its twin, every channel of communication had its duplicate; and for every person on the inside there was a person on the outside. For example, Husayni and sometimes Nabil Shaʿth, was ʿAbd al-Shafi's foil, and Akram Haniya, the deported *Al-Shaʿb* editor and Arafat's close confidant, Nabil Shaʿth's.[7] And while Nabil Shaʿth, the head of the leadership committee, formally reported to Abu Mazen of the follow-up committee, the inside reported to Akram Haniya, who in turn reported directly to Arafat.[8]

Solving the problem the interim period posed for the PLO was more difficult. On the one hand, an interim arrangement would almost certainly lead to an elected government and the creation of an alternative leadership. On the other hand, it was obvious that what could be achieved during the interim period was likely to have an important impact in the final stage of negotiations regarding both the extent of Palestinian sovereignty and the geographical dimensions of the future Palestinian entity. The tension is reflected best in the proposal for the Palestinian Interim Self-Governing Authority (PISGA) announced on March 3, 1992, the most important document produced in the first year of negotiations. The proposal stressed both the powers and jurisdiction of the proposed legislative assembly and election methods. According to the Palestinian plan, the PISGA's 180-strong legislative assembly "should have legislative powers," the government's jurisdiction "should extend to all of the occupied territories, including its land, natural resources, water, sub-soil, territorial sea, exclusive economic zone and air space," and the assembly "should be elected by the people for the people."[9] But there were limitations the PLO placed on the interim government as well. These appeared in the introductory part of the document:

> The Palestinian people have agreed to negotiate interim self-government arrangements, in a phased approach that would allow them, in the second and final phase, the free exercise of their legitimate right to self-determination. Moreover, the Palestinians in the OPT [the occupied Palestinian territories] and in exile are one people, and the interim self-government arrangements should facilitate the exercise of the legitimate rights of those in exile, who will participate in the second phase of the negotiations to determine the final status of the OPT and achieve a comprehensive settlement of the Palestine question in all its aspects.[10]

Nor could the number of delegates of the legislative assembly be overlooked. The PNC in exile was assumed to consist of 400 members, excluding 180 or so members reputedly in the occupied territories.[11] The number 180, identical to the number of representatives of the legislative assembly that appeared in the document discovered in the summer of 1988 in the Arab Studies Association, symbolized the attachment of the territorialist component to the Palestinian parliament at large, but it also emphasized that they were a minority of a much larger whole. Obviously the drafters of the document could not freely delineate the relationship between the interim government and the PLO. According to the preconditions Israel set, and to which the Palestinian delegation was bound, there was to be no relationship between the PLO and any organs created during the interim period. However, the text that appeared in the introduction of the document and the stipulated size of the proposed assembly were easily interpreted. Not only would the outside participate, but the PNC would presumably predominate in the relationship over the territorial institutions.

Israel had preceded the Palestinian proposal with its own version, which envisioned an autonomy related to people rather than territory by delegating twelve strictly enumerated spheres of government while Israel remained the source of authority and in complete control of all land and natural resources.[12] This was totally unacceptable to almost all Palestinians. No Palestinian interlocutor could accept the Likud position that crystallized during the Camp David peace talks thirteen years previously, which offered functional rather than territorial autonomy. The conception ran counter to prevailing norms of international diplomacy in which solutions to problems between the state and a people residing in a nonsovereign area are almost always territorial.

But if the Palestinian delegation was totally opposed to Likud policies, they were hardly going to accept blindly the hegemony of the outside over the inside. Instead, they challenged the PLO in three basic ways:

1. They perceived themselves as a leadership rather than as functionaries.
2. They sought to institutionalize the PLO (to which they remained loyal) in a manner that would enhance their share of power and their control over state building.
3. They attempted to promote institution building in anticipation of an interim government.

Leaders Rather Than Functionaries

As in the past, the territorialists demanded an equal relationship with the decision-makers of the PLO. While the members of the delegation remained loyal to the organization, tensions arose over its nature, was it a leadership or a symbolic institution? For the diaspora, the PLO was primarily a leadership located outside the territories. As a statement by a PLO official on the eve of the Madrid conference put it: "Our leaders agreed in Algiers [in reference to the 20th PNC held in the final week of September] to attend a peace conference. We don't want to allow Israel a free hand."[13] For territorialists such as Husayni, by contrast, the PLO was a symbol, or an entity, that legitimated Palestinian nationalism. Immediately after the end of the Gulf crisis he emphasized his belief "in the PLO as the body that confirms the existence of the Palestinian people." When asked whether he could conceive of a provisional government under his leadership, he remarked that "under our Palestinian democracy we have a National Council. It could meet soon and could confirm the current leadership or change it in the interest of the Palestinians both inside and outside the territories."[14] Sari Nusseibeh's remarks in an interview in *Al-Hayat* on the eve of the Madrid Conference is another good example of the territorialist perception of the PLO:

> The PLO is and will remain the founder or the common denominator for all Palestinians everywhere. It represents the united identity of the Palestinian people. Because our aim is to consolidate that unity and to struggle for the rights of our people as one integral unit, there is no fear for the continuous survival of the PLO. It is the only umbrella we have managed to form through our efforts at home or abroad to demonstrate that unity. The reference to the PLO as being a primarily military organization may change but that is inevitable because there is no military option today. In the course of history, some things in the PLO will change yet the organization will remain.[15]

Nusseibeh basically argued that all Palestinians indeed belong to the PLO but that there was no fixed locus of leadership within it. He wished to change the organization from within rather than replace it, as the advocates of the Palestinian entity had desired in their day (see chapter 3).

The same question of leadership arose with respect to the territorial delegation in negotiations. ʿAbd al-Shafi, in an interview in August 1992 in which he was asked whether the delegation operates under the PLO's remote control, replied: "Absolutely not. This was never the case. We are very sensitive about the role we play, even though we greatly respect our political point of reference. Moreover, we feel that we are accountable to the Palestinian street and to the Palestinian people."[16] A more interesting point is the answer to a question the interviewer never raised, the source of the delegation's legitimacy, which, for its head, was no longer derived solely from the PLO. The delegation had every right to share in formulating strategy: "In conducting the negotiations, our point of reference is both the PLO and our own political vision as a negotiating team."[17]

The independence that ʿAbd al-Shafi sought for the delegation was radically different from Nabil Shaʿth's perception of the relationship between the PLO and the delegation in an interview one month earlier:

> The PLO is leading these negotiations, both on the scene and from Tunis. The leadership group, in the field, though not at the table, was appointed by the PLO, and a special committee in Tunis follows the talks and our deliberations here hour by hour. All important decisions are referred to Tunis, faxes go back and forth, delegation members and advisors are constantly shuttling between Washington and Tunis. That is how things have been

> working ever since the opening session in Madrid, where on several occasions our entire delegation was flown to Tunis at night for consultation and brought back to Madrid the next morning at dawn. The PLO is in full control of the team.[18]

Sha^cth conceived the relationship between inside and outside as strictly hierarchical. His description of the delegation's overnight flights between Washington and Tunis emphasized the Palestinian delegation's servility to the outside leadership.

Finally, tension between inside and outside characterized the territorialists' perceptions of the relationship between the PLO and the governing body that was to be set up during the interim period. According to Sha^cth:

> The PLO will remain the real sovereign authority, if you will, of the interim Palestinian government. It will retain all decisions pertaining to a state. It will retain all the political and foreign relations, and all its embassies in the 120 countries around the world. It will retain its economic planning and economic control capability, particularly since the inside will depend so much on the outside for financing , either through Palestinian, Arab, or international means. . . . And so I do not see the PLO during the transitional stage other than as the quasi-sovereign state running the interim self-governing authority in the occupied territories. . . . When the state is formed, for the first time the center of government, both for diaspora and inside Palestinians, will move from the outside to the inside.[19]

^cAbd al-Shafi, on the other hand, emphasized the independence of the future interim government, at least with respect to the welfare of the Palestinians living within the territories:

> It is difficult to define the future relationship between the legislative council and the PLO. I do not think it would be appropriate for the PLO to impose restrictions on an elected council that legislates for Palestinian society inside the territories. I do not anticipate a conflict between the council and the PLO. On the contrary, I think that there will be harmony between them. This means that the PLO will maintain its position as the collective leadership of the Palestinian people inside and outside the territories. It is the symbol of the unity of the Palestinian people. The exceptional conditions of the interim period stage do not negate the unity of the Palestinians.
>
> However, it is only natural for the Palestinians living in the territories to have a democratic institution in the form of a legislative council with authority to pass the laws necessary for their everyday life.[20]

In an interview conducted half a year earlier, Husayni expressed similar views concerning the interim government: "It is a stage in which power will be transferred from the Israelis to the Palestinians, in which our infrastructure will be built and which will permit us to decide on our future."[21]

The argument, however, must not be overstated: inside and outside did agree over the final goal and were thus partners to an alliance rather than contestants on two sides of a divide: ʿAbd al-Shafi agreed with Shaʿth that "when we reach the stage of national independence there will be no inside and no outside. I do not know how things will look at that point in time. Perhaps the legislative council will be dissolved and general elections will take place inside and outside the territories, elections that will result in the formation of a parliament that will represent all the Palestinians regardless of their place of residence."[22] Nor did the territorial Palestinians immediately contest the size of the future interim legislative organ in the PISGA proposal, which symbolized the diaspora's ascendancy over the territorial component of the Palestinian polity.[23]

Institutionalizing the PLO

It would be difficult, if not impossible, to divorce the struggle between territorialists and the diaspora leadership during this period from the problem of institutionalization within the PLO. Strictly speaking, the issue did not pit inside against outside. The absence of institutionalization "almost as old as the founding of the PLO itself" was noted in *Al-Hurriyya*, published in Damascus rather than in the territories.[24] Nevertheless there were substantial differences between the factions on the left and the territorialists regarding the proper remedies to the problem and these in turn reflected different goals. For the PFLP and DFLP abroad, a collective leadership in the decision-making process was the ideal basis of reform.[25] The remedies the territorialists suggested, in comparison, conformed more closely to liberal democratic ideals; they sought the institutionalization of elections within the PLO's PNC, the emergence of an executive accountable to it as specified by the official founding documents of the organization, elections to the PNC in the West Bank and Gaza under United Nations supervision, and the establishment of a transitional government that would include the representatives from the territories to supervise all national institutions in the West Bank and Gaza. The latter in particular could be an important mechanism for state building before the territorialization of the PLO leadership.[26] As long as the PLO remained noninstitutionalized, there could be little increase in the input of territorialists to the decision-making process, and the outlines of a government bureaucracy could not be forged nor some rules of the game between civil society and an emerging government bureaucracy established. The most important element was timing, the desire to institutionalize *before* the peace process and the exercise of some form of sovereign power. Thus, the leftist factions were more concerned with defining the contours of the Palestinian solution; the territorialists were more concerned with strengthening a state-formation process that would enhance their power relative to the leadership abroad. Both were nevertheless at loggerheads with the diaspora mainstream, which maintained its hegemony over the inside, the power of Fath over the left, and Arafat over his lieutenants, by preventing institutionalization of the PLO.

State Building, the Negotiation Process, and Fragmentation

The idea that state building was intimately related to the negotiation process dated back to the first year of the intifada. According to Sari Nusseibeh, the key concept wedding the two was the unilateral creation of an autonomy in practice that would preempt Israeli offers of autonomy, and thereby force Israel to offer even more: "The Palestinians must render obsolete potential Israeli 'offerings' which fall far short of Palestinian national aspirations."[27] Having a state-in-the-making, he argued, would improve rather than compromise the Palestinian position in negotiations. The more effective, bureaucratized, and centralized Palestinian authority was on the ground, the more political space would negotiators be able to demand on the international bargaining table. Nusseibeh perceived power not so much in terms of territorial control as in functional terms.

Nusseibeh's opponents (principally in the diaspora) argued that state-in-the-making, divorced from the concept of a liberated area, facilitated the Israeli objective of realizing functional rather than territorial autonomy. This minimized the chances of securing so valuable a national asset as Jerusalem.[28] The problem with this position, however, lay in its duplicity. When push came to shove, the outside was just as ready to negotiate on the basis of an interim agreement that excluded Jerusalem, provided of course that Israel was ready to conclude the agreement with the outside rather than the inside.

While Husayni and ʿAbd al-Shafi called for elections both locally and within the PLO as a means of preempting the Israelis at the negotiating table,[29] Nusseibeh and Ziyad Abu Zayyad attempted to generate a state-in-the-making process by organizing twelve political committees throughout the territories.[30] Abu Zayyad first argued that these committees were to play no political role but merely provide technical expertise to the negotiators. One week later, however, he revealed that they were to perform two other functions with major political ramifications: they were both to form transition teams that would take over the functions of the vacating Israeli administration and mobilize support for the peace process and the Palestinian delegation.[31]

Husayni viewed these committees in an even broader sense. Responding to a question whether these committees would be semigovernmental, akin to the Jewish Agency in prestate days, he responded: "They do not cover all the political branches, but in the future the planning will be more sophisticated and you will see we have two goals: first to help the peace, and second to establish a Palestinian government that will aid the establishment of a Palestinian state alongside Israel."[32] The following day, Israeli sources claimed that a proposal had been drawn up suggesting the establishment of management committees composed of Arabs employed in the military administration who would then prepare for the transition period.[33] These would be supervised by a Supreme Coordinating Committee for the Assumption of Power.[34] Riad al-Maliki, a Birzeit engineering professor and PFLP supporter, confirmed these reports but downgraded the proposal's importance, claiming that Nusseibeh was only recycling a draft disseminated in the territories two years previously. He also claimed that Nusseibeh was setting up these committees to offset the growing prominence of ʿAshrawi and Husayni, an interesting idea, but one which did not accord with the facts.[35] Both ʿAshrawi and Husayni at the time called upon prominent Palestinians to join the committees headed by Nusseibeh and Ahmad Shraym, a Fath activist released in the 1985 prison exchange between the PFLP-General Command and Israel, after a long prison term.[36]

Yet no sooner had they been formed than members in the committees began to resign. Bassam al-Saʾih and ʿImad Yaʿish's resignations represented the first blow. Al-Saʾih was the son of PNC president and former mufti of Jerusalem, Shaykh ʿAbd al-Hamid al-Saʾih, while Yaʿish was a well-known Fath activist released in the Jibril exchange after serving a lengthy prison term. Both were from Nablus, a fact of considerable importance given that the Jerusalemites who initiated the formation of the committees were desperate to ensure representation from other regions, particularly Nablus and Jenin, centers of intifada violence and therefore of nationalist sacrifice.[37]

Their resignations might have had something to do with the PLO's displeasure at the quick pace of territorial institution building. An Israeli newspaper reported that Fath distributed leaflets calling for their disbandment because they hurt the strike committees "bought in blood."[38] The political underground, perhaps goaded by the outside, were obviously concerned about the political committees as possible rivals. Husayni, in an interview with an Israeli newspaper chided Fath, without specifically naming it, for adhering to the principle of collective decision making as an excuse for curtailing two political committees: "In all Palestinian institutions such as the PNC, decision-making is made by majority vote. The UNC must use that system."[39]

In the diffused political situation prevailing in the occupied territories, opposition did not emanate from clandestine organizations alone. ʿAbd al-Shafi, concerned with enhancing the stature of the negotiating team, objected to committees whose politicization would divert attention away from the peace process.[40]

But the worse opposition came from Israeli quarters. Senior military officials reportedly warned activists of the long-standing ban on political activity.[41] The following day, three mainstream and veteran politicians who had formed a central political committee in Gaza, were ordered to disband it.[42]

The establishment of three functional pan-territorial councils, on culture and public relations, housing, and the Supreme Economic Council attempted at least to fulfill the bureaucratic goal of the defunct political committees.[43] These councils had the backing of the EEC Commission, which gave the housing and economic councils the mandate to distribute $61 million of aid from the European Community.[44] They were therefore shielded from Israeli policies of deinstitutionalization.

The political action committees reappeared in July 1992 following the Israeli general elections that brought Yitzhak Rabin's Labor government to power. However, they were only assigned the role of preparing for subsequent stages in the peace process rather than taking on functions exercised by the military authorities. Thus, they only gave birth to technical committees, not nascent ministries.[45]

Once more, both the PLO and Israeli authorities had stood in the way of a state-building process, bringing to light the structural weakness of the "inside." The political committees, composed essentially of thinkers and spokesmen, had been undermined by the organs of violence. There is no better indication of how little the territorialists achieved than Sari Nusseibeh's advocacy of a strategy of preemption published in October 1992:

> In my personal opinion, and in line with the intifada's main strategies that were forged at the beginning of the intifada, the Palestinians should take unilateral steps at state-building that go side-by-side with the negotiations. Not only must we complain about the unilateral steps that Israel is taking while it negotiates with us, we must employ an equal method of taking unilateral steps building the state step by step as we begin to negotiate.[46]

As it read little differently than his 1988 article on a similar theme, this article seemed to indicate that scant preemptive institution building had occurred in the four years that had elapsed.

Rabin's Challenge to the PLO

As long as the Likud was in power, the PLO hardly perceived the Palestinian delegation to be a serious threat since the gap between Likud perceptions and Palestinian aspirations was too great to allow the consummation of an agreement. The situation changed after the Rabin-led Labor government replaced Likud in July 1992. Unlike the Likud, Rabin was interested in achieving a settlement, and, acting under the assumption that the Palestinian delegation living under occupation would be more predisposed to make concessions, Rabin had decided to promote territorial Palestinians at the expense of the diaspora. In a speech to Israeli newspaper editors on the forty-fifth anniversary of the United Nations Partition Resolution in November 1992, Rabin compared the relationship between the "PLO-Tunis" and Palestinians in the West Bank and Gaza to the historical relationship between the WZO and the Jewish Yishuv.[47] If one follows the analogy correctly, Rabin, while not implying that the territorialists should reject the PLO outright, intended for Israel to help transform the Palestinian movement from a diaspora to a territorially centered movement as in the Zionist case. While he belabored the term "Ashaf [the Hebrew acronym for the PLO]-Tunis" and "Ashaf Yerushalayim," both were Ashaf.

Placing financial resources in the hands of the delegation seemed the most propitious way to bolster the inside at the expense of the outside, especially in light of the PLO's growing financial straits. In an April 1993 interview with *Haʾaretz*, Rabin stated that "the money we will invest in the territories will pass through the Palestinian delegation. The delegation will be the address and the money will be in its hands. This will give it [the delegation] strength and power. He who has money to build schools and hospitals is in possession of power."[48] Rabin also wanted to institutionalize the Palestinian delegation's political power relative to the PLO outside when he urged carrying out territorial elections independent of progress in the peace talks.[49] Simultaneously, he overlooked Israeli-dictated conditions forbidding the inclusion of East Jerusalem residents in the delegation and permitted East Jerusalemite Faysal Husayni (considered to be the most influential nationalist personality in the occupied territories) to join the peace talks as a regular member.[50]

Repression and Diplomacy

Paradoxically, while Rabin was bolstering the Palestinians inside in relation to the PLO, he was undermining popular support for the delegation by intensifying the suppression of its constituents—the inhabitants of the occupied territories. Suppression reached a new level of intensity with the deportation of 415 activists from the Hamas and the al-Jihad al-Islami on December 17, 1992, even though only a few of them were actually members in its military wings.[51] This was the largest single wave of deportations since 1967 and more than a sixfold increase in the number of deportations since the outbreak of the intifada. Another wave of violence, culminating in the murder of fifteen Israelis in March alone, resulted for the first time in the wholesale prohibition of working in Israel for an indefinite period on March 29.[52] One-third of the labor force in the occupied territories thus became unemployed overnight;

this effective exclusion of the Palestinian labor force from the Israeli economy was, by far, the harshest single measure taken against the inhabitants of the occupied territories since the inception of Israeli rule.

The Palestinian delegation suffered the brunt of this paradoxical situation. On the one hand, Labor was supposed to be more diplomatically flexible, accepting, for example, Husayni's participation in negotiations. On the other hand, the Rabin government's policies in the occupied territories were the most repressive ever. It was the Palestinian delegation rather than the leadership outside who were vulnerable to the consequence of potential violence on the part of a public living under an increasingly harsh occupation.

The delegation reacted to its predicament by hardening its position on both procedural and substantive matters in the negotiations. Thus, the bulk of the delegation participated in the ninth round of the peace talks in Washington in April only after the PLO ordered them to do so.[53] While two of twelve delegates resigned, as they were members of the Communist Popular People's Party which had decided to boycott the talks, the remainder who did comply made no secret of their displeasure in attending the talks.[54] In the tenth round two months later, this displeasure became even more pronounced. Faysal al-Husayni did not attend the first two sessions due to meetings in Tunis and Haydar ʿAbd al-Shafi attended only the first. [55]

The hardened stance of the delegation, particularly on Jerusalem, was undermining Rabin's basic assumption, namely, that the territorialists would be more pliable on issues than the outside. As a result, unknown to the delegation, the more strident a stand they took, the more accelerated was the pace of negotiations in the secret Oslo channel. At Oslo, Rabin basically abandoned the Zionist strategy of building up the inside, preferring instead the FLN model of negotiating with the outside. Rabin upgraded the Oslo talks by replacing Mahmud ʿAbbas's counterpart, Israeli academic Yair Hirschfeld, with Uri Savir, the director general of the Israeli Foreign Ministry and Yoel Zinger, its ministry's legal adviser, who had played a role in the Camp David peace agreement. He also instructed them to sign a declaration of principles based on the Gaza first option.[56] Rabin had long ago considered the merits of abandoning Gaza and living with the consequences. Now, he began to consider ceding it to the PLO.

Rabin was changing course but was hardly a complete convert to the direct approach with the PLO. In May, he was able to test PLO-Tunis pliancy compared to that of the Jerusalem-based delegation. The United States drafted a declaration of principles entitled an "Israeli-Palestinian Joint Statement," offering early empowerment over functions "which should give Palestinians greater control over the decisions that affect their lives and fates" during the negotiating of the conditions for interim self-government, and agreeing to an elected interim self-government authority through direct and free elections.[57] Both points acted as bait to win over the territorialists participating in the

Washington talks; empowerment extended the time frame for effective state building without direct PLO interference, while the elections would strengthen the governing authority during the interim period. The PLO rejected the American initiative because it omitted reference to jurisdiction over Jerusalem, failed to commit Israel to a freeze in settlements during negotiations for the interim stage, and viewed the interim self-governing authority as having only functional, not territorial jurisdiction. The Palestinian delegation soon followed suit in a ten-point statement made by Husayni and addressed to Warren Christopher, the newly appointed secretary of state.[58] This statement reiterated substantively the same demands as the previous PLO statement and repeated a call to the United States to enter directly into negotiations with the PLO rather than the "appointed delegation." Another U.S.-written draft that gave the inhabitants in East Jerusalem the right to vote in the elections met with a similar response.[59]

Little did the inside realize how much Rabin was considering acting upon their advice of negotiating solely with the PLO particularly as PLO-Tunis began showing greater flexibility while the delegation remained obdurate. This trend became all the more apparent in early July when the delegation decided to boycott a meeting with Dennis Ross, the special Middle East coordinator of the State Department, but was compelled once more by the PLO to attend.[60] By then, the Americans had been promoting territorial empowerment in Gaza and Jericho as compensation to the PLO for relinquishing the issue of Jerusalem's inclusion in the proposed Palestinian autonomy. Sari Nusseibeh expressed the position of the Palestinian delegation in a clever play on words: "If for Israel "the Gaza first" solution is the way into negotiations, then for the Palestinians the "Jerusalem first" solution is the only way."[61] Unfortunately, for the inside, however, it was not only Israel but now the PLO as well who felt that Gaza-Jericho should indeed be first. Thus, the time was ripe, the Israelis felt, to exchange negotiating partners.

For Rabin, the moment of truth occurred three weeks later when, on August 3, the Palestinian delegation refused to hand a PLO-dictated memo drafted by United States, Egyptian, and PLO delegates in Egypt to Secretary of State Christopher because it contained neither the demand to include Jerusalem nor jurisdiction over the settlements.[62]

From Diplomacy to Power Struggle

Ironically, the inside, totally ignorant of the secret Oslo track, felt they were ready to openly challenge the leadership of the PLO. On August 5, the Palestinian delegation presented a modified declaration of its own that reinstated the demand to include Jerusalem under the jurisdiction of the Palestinian interim government, but accepted the principle of "Gaza-Jericho first" as "a form of disengagement that would constitute a real breakthrough both in negotiations and on the ground," provided that it was based on a clearly demarcated territorial base.[63] These two demands combined fit perfectly with an inside strategy simultaneously promoting legitimacy for the delegation and enhancing the opportunity to engage in territorial state building.

Fearing that the PLO would bow to Israeli pressures to omit Jerusalem from the interim agreement and miffed by their exclusion from the decision-making process, ʿAshrawi, Husayni, and another delegate, Dr. Saʾib ʿAriqat, flew to Tunis on August 9 to hand in their resignations to Arafat.[64] Only after ʿAshrawi and six other colleagues from the delegation were assured membership in the newly formed Higher Committee in Administering the Negotiations (al-Lajna al-ʿUlya li-Idarat al-Mufawadat) did she rescind her decision.[65] ʿAshrawi described the new organ as "a special steering committee that combines both the leadership from the occupied territories and the follow-up committee that used to supervise the talks from Tunis. So in a sense it is a merged committee that contains the leadership of both."[66] To confirm that the crisis was over from her point of view, ʿAshrawi emphasized that the new institution reflected the indivisibility of the Palestinians under occupation and those in exile.[67] This was a momentous occasion. For the first time, personalities from the territories, acting from within the territories, had been accepted into a policy-making forum within the PLO. ʿAshrawi hoped that the formation of this new committee would be a prelude to the integration of local institutions into the PLO organizational structure abroad.[68] The concession, however, addressed only one issue, the division of political power between the inside and outside leadership, leaving the problems of PLO institutionalization and local state building untouched.

While ʿAshrawi might have been appeased, Husayni certainly did not feel that the concession addressed the problematic relationship between PLO leadership and institutionalization. After all, what good did participation in a policy-making forum do when the members of the organization's institutions possessed no information, had no clear mandates, and that decisions had little effect on final outcomes? Husayni's attack on the PLO leadership in a special edition of *Al-Katib*, a leftist journal published in Ramallah, addressed the issue forcefully:

> In 1948, there was a Palestinian leadership leading the people that was based on a particular social hierarchy connected to land and landowners. Though this social hierarchy was destroyed in 1948, the Palestinian leadership nevertheless attempted to lead the people based on the same infrastructure that was destroyed during war and did not realize that the structure changed . . . so that eventually the people turned their back on it. The Palestinian revolution confronted, and today confronts, a similar situation. This formation, the National Council and the PLO, was built on a particular

> pyramidal structure and impregnated by the atmosphere of Karameh in Jordan, the Fakahani in Lebanon, and the armed factions, producing a particular type of Palestinian leadership. As a result of the Israeli invasion of Lebanon in 1982 and the war, that institutional edifice was destroyed. We dispersed from Lebanon and attempted to reestablish ourselves over there paying dearly for it. . . . Perhaps this fourth Palestinian revolution was fated to come to an end at the time and the Palestinian people would have turned their back to it had it not been for the fact that it was this very act [the invasion] and this very result that pushed the people in the occupied territories to the eruption of the intifada, which in itself is the result of an accumulation of resistance activities the PLO realized. Yet during this period we did not perceive what was spoken about a little while ago, namely that we tried to lead using the same formats that we employed in Fakahani and in southern Lebanon. The result was that . . . we moved from an intifada in which a people resisted and confronted an army of occupation, into an army of the people confronting an army of occupation, and then armies of the people confronting an army of occupation, into armies confronting one another.[69]

Husayni did not mince words, suggesting that venerable leadership must give way to new ones when the historical conditions that facilitated their emergence no longer applied. Otherwise, they visit disaster upon their people, who quickly spurn them. Soon after the interview, in a meeting with Fath supporters in Hebron, he dramatically proposed the establishment of a national salvation government to cope with the disintegration of institutions in the territories, implying Arafat's failure to maintain the institutional infrastructure[70] (he later denied the call for such a government).[71]

Husayni found ready allies outside the territories as well. ʿAbdullah Hurani had publicized in last week of August that the executive committee had no knowledge of the organization's worsening financial plight and was inactive in the peace process.[72] Both revelations reflected Arafat's monopolization of power within the PLO at the expense of its formal institutions.

The delegation had its detractors too, however. One commentator in *Al-Quds* was particularly blunt: "The delegation problem which ended with the expansion of the Higher Committee for Overseeing the Negotiations, consisting of the inside and the outside, revealed a fact that must be given great importance in order to avoid future problems. . . . [Namely,] that were the people in the territories to choose between the negotiating delegation which acts unconsciously as an alternative leadership [on the one hand], and the PLO, they would choose without vacillation the organization [the PLO], no matter how great and many their reservations and criticisms of it, which do not require elaboration."[73] In an ironic tone, Jamil al-Tarifi, the former deputy mayor of Ramallah and a participant in the talks, wondered how his appointed colleagues could act so unconstitutionally and refuse to obey the orders of the executive branch under the banner of institutionalizing the PLO.[74]

Ultimately, the PLO won the day. Sitting around a breakfast table in a Washington hotel a day before the opening of the eleventh round of talks, ʿAshrawi and her colleagues glumly conceded to an Israeli journalist of *Haʾaretz* that they had not read the agreement of principles that had been reached through the secret Oslo peace track. The journalist politely handed them an English version of the text that had appeared in another Israeli daily the previous day.[75]

ʿArafat, with Rabin's help, possessed the final trump card. He was to be neither Weizmann nor Hajj Amin even if it meant risking forfeiting east Jerusalem as the Palestinian capital. His willingness to accept an interim period of Palestinian rule that included neither Jerusalem nor cessation of settlements convinced Rabin to abandon the Zionist strategy for territorial Palestinians and to adopt the FLN model instead. The change was reflected in a letter in which Israel recognized the PLO as the representative of the Palestinian people signed four days before the declaration of principles on the White House on September 13, 1993. For Arafat it was also a learning experience on subject matter with which he was long familiar. The "delegation problem" had proved how correct his fears were and how right he was to secretly cultivate the Oslo process. Diplomacy had to remain the monopoly of the diaspora if Arafat was to secure his elusive kingdom in the promised land. Better less of it than sharing it or not having it at all.

7

Countdown to Statehood

In December 1947, the British government first announced its intention to withdraw all its troops from Palestine and terminate the Mandate on May 15, 1948 (later changed to May 14).[1] The leaders of the Jewish Yishuv knew they had five months to create effective state institutions that would fill the vacuum the British left behind. The countdown to Israeli statehood had begun. On September 13, 1993, when Arafat and Rabin exchanged an historic handshake on the White House lawn confirming the declaration of principles (DOP) between Israel and the PLO, the Palestinians were placed in a similar position. According to the agreement that was to come into effect on October 13, Israel would begin to withdraw its troops within two months from Gaza and the city of Jericho and complete its withdrawal three months later. Thus, Palestinians also had five months to prepare for self-rule, the details of which were to be ironed out by an interim agreement. In actual fact, the Palestinians had much longer. The Cairo Agreement, which translated the DOP into reality by creating the Palestinian Authority (PA) in Gaza and Jericho, was only signed on May 4, 1994, and the elections, originally scheduled for early 1994, took place two years later. But these delays could not have been known when the countdown to Palestinian self-rule began.

The following chapter analyzes the behavior of the PLO in the critical months before the creation of the PA, its impact on the PA's subsequent consolidation under Yasser Arafat when the outside finally territorialized under international agreement, and the likely impact of the elections of the future Palestinian state in relation to the themes developed throughout this book.

From DOP to the Cairo Agreement: Deinstitutionalization instead of State Building

For the political analyst, the Zionist state building that took place immediately before Israel's declaration of independence provides a unique comparison with which to examine Palestinian state-building efforts between the signing of the DOP and the emergence of the Palestinian Authority in May 1994. Often the transition from national liberation movement to state, described in Arabic rhyme as the problem of transforming "*al-thawra*," the revolution, into "*al-dawla*," the state, calls for the depoliticization of society by the state elite. Former revolutionary organs and activists are absorbed into the state bureaucracy and security services.[2] This is what occurred in both the Zionist and Palestinian experiences. The difference, however, is the extent to which the pre-independence political organs and elites of each were absorbed into the new political center. In the Zionist experience, the new institutions both retained many former structures and absorbed their elites; old political parties and leaders continued to share in the decision-making process with David Ben-Gurion. In the Palestinian movement, by contrast, depoliticization hollowed out political structures both within the PLO and in the occupied territories, thus creating a political vacuum that facilitated autocratic patrimonial rule.[3]

The weakening of the PLO was probably more dramatic and eventful than the patterns of deinstitutionalization in the West Bank and Gaza. The PLO rarely followed clearly defined procedures for decision making, and it was hardly likely to alter its course in the face of massive elite opposition to the DOP. This elite included formerly close allies of Arafat's such as Faruq Qaddumi, Muhammad Darwish, and Khalid al-Hasan.[4] According to Bayan al-Hut, a noted historian of the Palestinian movement, Article 7 of the 1964 Fundamental Law (Al-Nizam al-Asasi) gave the PNC sole authorization to ratify international agreements.[5] Furthermore, since the agreement in her opinion contradicted the national covenant, to ratify it, it would be necessary to revise the covenant as a whole, a procedure requiring a two-thirds majority of the PNC. Arafat could hardly muster such support. Instead, he decided that the Central Committee, established at the 7th PNC in Cairo (June 1970) as an intermediary body between the 15-member Executive Committee and the 450-member PNC, would be authorized to accept or reject the agreement.[6] Yet even then, the ratification process was clouded in ambiguity. To begin with, none of the sources agreed upon either the number or composition of the committee (one source speaks of 100[7] members, another 107[8]). Many more attended than voted. Ghassan Khatib, a leading member of the PPP who supported the agreement, sharply criticized the selection process, claiming that all those chosen to attend belonged to Fath. He also asserted that the selections were made on the spur of the moment, as were the appointments of committee members in the Taba negotiation process.[9] Hanan ʿAshrawi voiced the same criticisms.[10]

Even more controversial was the voting itself. According to official PLO statements, a total of 82 delegates voted, 63 of which supported the agreement, 8 rejected it, and 11 abstained.[11] On the other hand, the DFLP, insisting that the Central Committee numbered 107 members, claimed that 33 members were either prevented from attending or chose of their own volition to boycott the meeting, 10 attended and abstained from voting, 8 rejected the agreement, an additional 3 who attended left before the voting, and one Fath member who opposed the agreement was reported to have been forced by Arafat to accept observer status so as not to vote.[12] All of these persons were mentioned by name, reinforcing the credibility of the DFLP's reservations. All told, the DFLP claimed 55 of 107 members did not vote for the agreement as opposed to 52 who did and challenged Arafat to disprove their calculations. He never did. The PLO failed to provide a detailed list of those voting for the accords as the DFLP provided those who did not.

In general, the opposition bitterly contested the legitimacy of the voting process. Newspapers reported that Arafat had prevented Khalid al-Hasan, a founding member of Fath who opposed the accord, from attending, though he was a Central Committee member from its inception.[13] The DFLP questioned how Hakam Balʿawi, a close ally of Arafat, could legally replace al-Hasan, or how al-Tayyib ʿAbd al-Rahim could replace Fath activist and deportee Subhi Abu Kirsh, who was absent for health reasons and who, like al-Hasan, opposed the agreement.

Opposition to the DOP led Arafat to employ well-tested neopatrimonial practices that hurt even his own prominent lieutenants in the PLO. Bassam Abu Sharif, a prominent spokesman before the second negotiation process, disappeared from sight.[14] Hani al-Hasan, after having been designated as an official member of the Palestinian Economic Council for Development and Reconstruction (PECDAR), had been removed from PLO politics for his opposition to the agreement of principles.[15] Faruq Qaddumi, officially head of the PLO political office, was always unofficially referred to as the foreign minister. Yet in the agreement stage it was Mahmud ʿAbbas who deserved the title. Then he, too, suddenly seemed to disappear from center stage, with reports of his political seclusion.[16] The rotation of both friends and opponents can be juxtaposed to the constancy of Arafat's leadership. In addition, while never formally dismissed from any position, Khalid al-Hasan's house was raided and his bodyguards imprisoned for ostensibly making an assassination attempt on Arafat's life.

Personalization of rule increased just when the need for institutionalizing state building was most acute. Within the PLO, two historical phenomena contributed to the personalization of rule: the assassination of individuals who had checked Arafat's power within the PLO, and the fall of the Soviet Union. The assassination of Khalil al-Wazir (Abu Jihad) in April 1988, and the murder two years later of Salah Khalaf (Abu ʿIyad), placed Arafat in a far more authoritarian position than when he had shared the limelight with these two former colleagues. Then, he never designated, officially at least, a clear successor to Abu Jihad as commander of operations of the western front. One would also assume that the assassinations made Arafat feel far more vulnerable.

Institutional pressures constraining Arafat's control weakened following the inception of the intifada. The fall of the Soviet Union and the blow to

Communism as an ideology considerably weakened the two leftist factions, the PFLP and the DFLP, who as opposed to the Syrian-backed groups, had been the PLO's loyal opposition. The Palestinian Communist Party shared their fate, as their restraining influence on Arafat, never considerable to begin with, simultaneously declined.[17]

De-Institutionalization in the West Bank and Gaza

In the West Bank and Gaza, the crisis was originally financial. The national institutions supported by the PLO in the territories had been facing severe financial problems long before the signing of the DOP in 1993. The PLO, presumably in deep financial straits itself, closed a number of important political institutions that summer, sharply curtailing the mainstream press traditionally associated with Fath. The most prominent casualty was *Al-Fajr*, the Jerusalem newspaper that first appeared in 1972 and later became the mouthpiece of Fath and its Shabiba movement. Though it was the voice of the outside, it had consistently promoted territorial state-building efforts and for this reason had been highly critical of mobilization patterns during the intifada and the lack of institutionalization within the PLO (see chapter 5). A similar fate befell the two weeklies *Al-Bayadir al-Siyasi* and *Al-Fajr al-Jadid*.

The leftist press faced the same crisis. The monthly journal *Al-Katib*, published in Ramallah, and the Communist *Al-Tali*ᶜ*a* ceased to appear in orderly fashion after fourteen years of publication. Both organs had been excessively critical of PLO bureaucratization. *Al-Katib* had published the interviews with Faysal Husayni and ᶜAli al-Jarbawi so critical of Arafat that were discussed in the previous chapter. Sari Nusseibeh's Jerusalem Center for Strategic Studies, MAQDES, and its journal, *Al-Nashra al-Istratijiyya,* were other casualties of the financial crisis. The journal had attempted to be a vehicle for discussing state-building strategies and promoting state-building institutions, and it strongly advocated democratic governmental procedures.[18] It focused exclusively on institutions, not on personalities (not one was mentioned by name in the first eighteen issues). Even though it paid special tribute to brother Abu ᶜAmmar (Arafat) in one of its later issues to compensate for failure to give him his due, funds nevertheless dried up, forcing the ending of the journal.[19]

Palestinian educational institutions were also facing hard times. The decline of the Islamic al-Aqsa educational system (Madaris Riad al-Aqsa al-Islamiyya) in Jerusalem was particularly significant, for its decline proved a boon to the Israeli-run school system, thus contributing to regular Israeli hegemony in the eastern part of the city. While enrollment had dwarfed the Israeli-run municipal system in 1990 (14,000 to 8,000 students), the situation in 1992 had reversed itself: enrollment in the al-Aqsa schools had declined to 8,000 while enrollment in the schools run by the (Israeli) Jerusalem municipality had increased from 8,000 to 12,000.[20] Teachers in the al-Aqsa school system went on strike on the first day of the 1993 school year in protest against four-month arrears in the payment of salaries. Palestinians feared that the decline would bolster Israeli efforts at Judaicizing the city during the five-year interim period. Additional faculty strikes were recorded in a number of junior colleges and at Hebron University. Day after day, the newspapers reported Palestinian civil society's harmful dependence on PLO sources.[21]

Did Arafat deliberately seek the de-institutionalization of the occupied territories? The answer depends on the extent of the PLO's financial woes, which is difficult to ascertain. PLO finances have always been shrouded in mystery. It is therefore difficult to come up with a conclusive answer as to whether the plight of national institutions was deliberate or not. We know, however, that many questioned the severity of the crisis. Some wondered how Fath spent so much on festivities in the wake of the Rabin-Arafat accord at a time when universities and schools were closing and subsidies to prisoners and their families were being seriously reduced.[22] Asad al-Asᶜad, former editor of *Al-Katib*, wondered why the PPP and the Fida had so much money to spend on real estate purchases during such financial crisis.[23] Fida, the Palestinian Democratic Federation Party (Hizb al-Ittihad al-Dimuqrati al-Filastini), founded by Muhammad ᶜAbd Rabbu and headed locally by former assistant mayor of Ramallah and deportee ᶜAzmi Shuᶜaybi, had broken off from the DFLP. The two parties had sided with Fath over the peace accords and were financially beholden to the PLO.[24] George Habash, in an interview in late October 1993, was sure that the financial crisis was contrived due to political motives: "Arafat has enough money in his secret accounts. Arafat deliberately withheld the money to wear down the people in the occupied territories. Now he wants to buy the people's sympathies with money."[25] *Al-Hurriyya*, the official publication of the DFLP, claimed that Arafat had transferred $800 million to Egyptian banks in preparation for self-rule.[26] Yigal Karmon, former security adviser to Rabin and Shamir, felt that the PLO possessed considerable sums even after the Gulf crisis.[27] One indication that the PLO's financial woes were less than they appeared was the PA's financing, once off the ground, of *Al-Hayat al-Jadida*, a semi-official paper published in Gaza, and the restarting of *Al-ᶜAwda*, a staunchly pro-Arafat weekly that had been closed down by the Israeli authorities.

Institutionalization did not unfold after the countdown to self-rule began either. Essential to state building is the establishment of a central organization that resolves conflicts, allocates resources, sets up manpower commissions, prioritizes the functions necessary for an orderly transfer of power, and adumbrates, where necessary, the future legal system. In the countdown to the Zionist state, for instance, power resided in two institutions: the Jewish Agency and the Vaad Leumi. A division of labor, albeit not devoid of friction, marked the two institutions, and both drew their legitimacy from the Zionist Executive of the World Zionist Organization. The partition decision set off an amalgamation process that produced on April 1, 1948, the National Administration consisting of thirteen elected members and the thirty-seven-member National Council, "which were destined after the declaration of independence to be the Provisional Government and the Provisional Council of the State."[28] Both organs, which naturally included members from the Vaad Leumi and the Jewish Agency, took over almost all the functions the latter institutions performed and which were often bitterly contested between them.

Among the Palestinians, political developments took the opposite course. Instead of integrating central structures, political partisanship, geographical differentiation, and polarization grew. Most striking was the absence of a central authority. Fath, rather than the PLO, became the highest organ to address the public in "official" communiqués.[29]

Moreover, the same organization appeared in the West Bank and Gaza in different forms. Local newspapers reported the creation and composition of an executive committee and council in Gaza drawn from existing political steering committees to supervise the various committees. Yet there was no such reference to these organs or to political steering committees in the West Bank. Fath's only reference to territory-wide political institutions concerned the identification of officially authorized bodies of Fath.[30] Even in Gaza, the overall political structure was unclear. In early November, Fath reported that it had set up a higher command under Salim al-Zari^{c}i, who had been the longest incarcerated Palestinian prisoner in Israeli prisons.[31] (He was obviously a figurehead, having held no important positions in Fath while in prison.) This higher command was to issue communiqués, supervise the organizational work of the four wings of Fath activity, the political steering committees, the women's committees, the Fath Hawks (the military wing), and the Shabiba (youth) movement, and act as the liaison to the "outside" in Tunis. Dhiab al-Lawh, the head of the council who announced the establishment of the higher command, made no mention of the relationship between this body to Fath bodies in the West Bank. Presumably, the two were linked exclusively to the outside rather than to each other. In addition, Fath was unwilling to follow the PPP and Fida's example and transform itself into a political party.[32]

The National Authority That Never Was

To meet the challenge of state building, Arafat responded with words rather than deeds. Throughout the period under discussion, reports of the impending establishment of a national authority abounded. In late September 1993, Sari Nusseibeh was sure that the Palestinian national authority would be established in the next few weeks.[33] So was he sure that the technical teams he headed, numbering 500 experts who drew up plans for the establishment of self-rule, would be regrouped into government ministries so that their talents could be fully utilized immediately after the establishment of the PA. Muhammad Sabih, the secretary of the PNC, announced that the PLO was committed to publishing a complete list for the national authority[34] that Arafat was to head and that was to be accountable both to the Executive Committee and the Central Council of the PLO, although both bodies had basically ceased to function. According to Sabih, the national authority was to comprise from 20 to 40 appointees divided equally between territorial and diaspora Palestinians. One month later, the Jordanian newspaper *Sawt al-Sha*ʿ*b* reported that the number had been revised downward to twenty.[35]

Since the beginning of the intifada, Nusseibeh had advocated a strategy of preempting negotiations by creating a "shadow state" and thereby demanding more from Israel at negotiations on the grounds that autonomy already existed in practice. Immediately after the DOP, he repeated his call: "The agreement is the first step and way station so that we can profit from developing the prerogatives (salahiyyat) of Palestinian authority on the path toward complete independence."[36]

Nevertheless, Nusseibeh's appeals were in vain. Only the formation of the Palestinian police force went beyond the drawing board stage in the critical months after the signing of the 1993 accords. Yet even in this domain, the results were surprisingly meager. In the last week of September, fourteen recruitment centers were inaugurated amid great fanfare.[37] Eleven-thousand recruits had filled out the necessary forms by September 26. [38] In the West Bank, however, the process had been quite problematic. Fida opened its own office of recruitment in Ramallah in an attempt to ensure a more politically diverse police force.[39]

Questions regarding the political affiliations of candidates appeared on the application forms, but they were not uniform. Conscription terminated four days prematurely. According to Ghassan Khatib, the premature termination was due to the "the way conscription was undertaken which raised fears among citizens that what was being created was a militia connected to factions rather than a responsible apparatus whose task was to safeguard the safety of the citizens."[40] He deplored both the fact that Palestinian organizations had set up their own recruitment centers and the absence of regulations and a uniform code that defined the framework for conscription.

Prominent personalities both inside and outside harshly criticized Arafat's personal rule and careless if not destructive disregard for effective state building. The communiqué signed in November 1993 by leaders such as Haydar ʿAbd al-Shafi in Gaza, Sulayman al-Najjab (the deported Palestinian Communist leader), and ʿAbdallah Hurani, the latter two members of the PLO Executive Committee in diaspora) represents the most comprehensive statement on the means and objectives of state formation during this period as well as one of the finest examples of opposition to Arafat's neopatrimonialism. It began by distinguishing between the politics of national liberation and the imperatives of creating the independent state. According to the signatories, the political leadership was neither doing a good job at the negotiating table nor taking the right steps in creating the national authority. The communiqué censured the PLO for failing to come to terms with the opposition or explain the agreement to the people, refusing to hire experts to conduct negotiations, and somewhat contradictorily, negotiating in a bureaucratic manner rather than continuing to view negotiations as a means of struggle in the attainment of the basic goals of the PLO. The communiqué called for the establishment of professional committees concerned with aspects of self-government and relations with foreign actors and a department to locate and place highly qualified professionals in appropriate government posts. It also sought the eradication of allocation by faction and favoritism, the planning of a comprehensive program on the basis of the DOP, and the establishment of a narrow leadership body that would direct the negotiations and coordinate between the various components. The completion of the legal council's work in drawing up a constitutional document was also deemed a high priority. Finally, the signatories called for the establishment of a council with planning, coordinating, and advisory capacities that would operate side by side with the PLO executive. Membership would be limited to professionals only.

Fearful that their communiqué would collect dust in Arafat's office, the authors asserted in their closing remarks that "we do not agree that our fateful decisions will fall victim to the negative situation in which we live and have, therefore, established from among us a body that will follow up in a consistent manner the realization of these demands."[41]

Despite the assertiveness of this group, it had failed to address crucial issues: the communiqué did not adequately address the lack of decision making through formal channels, the need to formally designate the official bodies that would nominate the people who would staff these organs, and the establishment of institutions and procedures that could contain Arafat's freedom to maneuver and make him and other officials accountable. The use of the passive form in presenting their demands ("an organ should emerge") was an open evasion of responsibility. Six weeks after the communiqué was issued, ʿAbd al-Shafi acknowledged the failure of the mission to reform politics within the PLO after meeting with Arafat and other members of the Executive Committee in Tunis.[42]

Territorializing Neopatrimonial Rule: The Emergence of the PA

Only when the two elements central to neopatrimonial rule, Arafat himself and his security forces (the *mukhabarat*) arrived physically in the territories did the PA begin to take shape. This it did on a martial note common to "revolutionary" governments. Arafat was, of course, unencumbered by the promulgation of a constitution, a bill of rights, the swearing in of a government, and the modalities of elections. Instead, in the second week of May 1994, convoy after convoy of 1,500 "policemen" dressed in the military uniform of the Palestine Liberation Army crossed over bridges linking Jordan with the West Bank and the Rafah border crossing that links Gaza to Egypt. Atop the front windshields of the lorries loomed large portraits of Yasser Arafat in military uniform. While the long familiar photograph showed him from the chest up, it took little imagination to imagine his holster and gun as well. Local inhabitants had seen these signs of personal loyalty even before the establishment of the PA. Only half a year before, the second contingent of Palestinian policemen trained in Jordan were filmed by Israeli television on the steps of the entrance to Orient House, the unofficial seat of the Palestinian delegation in East Jerusalem, thrice snapping the salute, "Long live Abu ʿAmmar." [43]

By the end of May, the number of diaspora soldiers turned policemen was up to 6,000. By April 1995, there were 17,000, including local inhabitants, recruited into the police and the various arms of the security network.[44] Even the civilians who arrived from the diaspora did little to dispel the concentration of politico-military power that descended on Gaza soon after Israeli evacuation. Most of those who arrived in early and mid-May were men handpicked to hold top positions in the emerging internal security network, which eventually encompassed six agencies in an area of control one-third the area of Long Island.[45] Undeniably, the foundation of Palestinian government resembled a military takeover.[46]

The first sign of civilian rule occurred on July 1, at the initial meeting of the PA Executive. Nevertheless, there too Arafat took his seat as chairman while still in uniform. It was his first day in Gaza. Since then, he was never seen publicly in Gaza out of uniform, and only rarely, such as when abroad, was he photographed without his gun and holster.

From that time on, an almost feverish spate of state building took place. Within one year, the PA was a state to its citizens in all but name. By the summer of 1995, the PA consisted of a cabinet (chaired by President Arafat), the managing director of the Office of the Presidency (Maktabat al-Riyasa), and the ministers (wuzara). These ministers, in turn, presided over ministries (*wizarat*) typical of any state, Finance, Economics, Planning, Information, and, more recently, Interior. Even without an official foreign ministry (it was instead called the Ministry of Planning and International Cooperation), the PA managed to conduct more foreign policy and to be visited by more world leaders and officials than many states. Completing the organizational portrayal of a state-in-the-making were an impressive array, on paper at least, of functionally specific state authorities such as the Palestinian Monetary Agency, a bureau of statistics, an environmental control agency, and a civil service commission.

The PA not only attempts to look like a state, but also to behave as a highly centralized one. Taking its cue from Israeli government practice of holding weekly cabinet meetings, the PA cabinet consistently holds weekly meetings every Saturday, and its decisions and agenda are then relayed to the local Palestinian press by the government spokesman. A continuous barrage of official announcements reflecting typical government business connects the citizen to the state. These announcements include: tax matters, competition for civil service positions, tender bids for projects by the different ministries, exhortations to citizens to pay electricity and telephone bills owed to Israeli public companies, warnings against building on "state" lands, and information regarding official policy positions. The "state" also reflects its "revolutionary" past. The Mufawidiyyat al-Tawjih al-Watani, (the Commissariat of National Direction) an organ of the Presidential Office, is responsible for political education both in the security branches and government offices of the PA.[47] Finally, as stipulated in the Cairo Agreement, the PA secured territorial inviolability from Israel for areas in Gaza where there are no settlements or roads. The Israeli government also refrained almost completely from exercising the right of hot pursuit in Gaza accorded to it in the Cairo Agreement, despite considerable pressure from Israeli parties on the right. In short, the PA, in transition, is probably more of a state than many "juridical" states in Africa.[48]

The PA also became the dominant force in the territories economically. In 1995 it had a budget of $440 million, approximately one-third of the GNP of the area it controlled at the time. It was the largest employer in Gaza and the source of most new jobs as the state bureaucracy and security apparatus rapidly expanded. The international aid regime originally set up to aid the Palestinians had conceived of a much smaller Authority. The Emergency Assistance Plan (EAP) drafted by the World Bank during the latter six months of 1993 in cooperation with Palestinians from the PLO and the occupied territories earmarked $100 million of a $1.3 billion total, less than 10 percent of the total aid package, for the initial costs of the PA.[49] The reality was strikingly different. In the latter half of 1994 alone, disbursements for PA budget support equaled $154 million, accounting for 39.7 percent of total expenditure. Government expenditures of $123 million in the first five months of 1995 accounted for 80 percent of this total. The overwhelming share of aid paid the salaries of the growing bureaucracy and security complex.[50]

Judging from this trend it seems that the EAP will primarily become a framework for setting up the state, rather than for promoting economic development. The number of salaried civil employees grew in the course of ten months from 20,000 to 27,000 and security personnel from 6,000 to 17,000. Thirty million dollars were expended monthly on these salaries alone.[51] A special multilateral fund, the Holst Fund, named after the Norwegian minister of foreign affairs who hosted the secret negotiations, was set up to meet these expenses.

Yet neither formal organizational charts of the PA nor numerical indicators of its imposing presence in society could hide the PA's neopatrimonial nature. Like many autocrats in the Arab world and elsewhere, Arafat created multiple agencies to perform similar tasks and did not delegate to institutions specific powers. He also developed strike forces linked directly to him rather than to the organization, a securitate model highly developed in autocracies. The special forces were far better equipped and more mobile than conventional forces, so that what they lacked in numbers, they made up in quality.[52]

Depoliticizing Society: The Weakening of Fath "Inside"

The major casualty of Arafat's takeover was the Fath "inside." While Arafat sought to weaken rather than destroy Fath's popular base, he still needed the organization's weight to counteract the Islamic opposition. Tensions between the territorial elements of Fath and Arafat had already surfaced before the emergence of the PA when Arafat and his adviser on West Bank affairs, former deportee Jibril Rajub, announced on January 1, 1994, the establishment of Force 17, whose aim was to establish a force loyal to Arafat that would "assure the security and stability of our people." Muhammad Nasr, an engineer employed in the Civil Administration, the civilian wing of the military administration, and formerly involved in the Israeli-sponsored and funded Village Leagues, was to head it.[53] Three Fath activists, the lawyer Dhiab Sharbati, Ihsan al-Nazzar, and Jibril al-Bakri, resigned in protest against this move specifically and, in general, because of the absence of institutional and democratic procedures within Fath. Before this, four activists in Gaza had resigned a month earlier to protest the lack of democracy and the nomination of Dr. Zakaria al-Agha as head of Fath.[54] These issues were closely linked to the problems of territorialization and the desire of the "inside" to assure their stake in the future entity. As al-Nazzar explained it,

> The feeling grew among us that there are no democratic procedures in Fath. The leadership abroad does not update the leaders in the organization "inside" concerning foreign policy developments, and does not coordinate organizational moves with them. This situation makes it difficult in our opinion to bring about a proper decision making process.

Asked whether the establishment of the Force 17 in the area led him to resign, he responded:

> It was one of the reasons. The leadership appointed men who were not affiliated with one of the Fath frameworks and do not have past experience in the struggle. There are opportunists in the Fath organization and among the people. In the past they operated against the people, for they defined themselves as the security apparatus, and as such they will be able in the future to enter homes, carry out searches, and do as they please.
>
> Arafat is the leader of all of us, and he does not require protection from the Palestinian masses with the help of such a body. For if there is a need to protect him, then we, the soldiers of Arafat, are those appropriate to do so. If one seeks to establish Force 17, then one has to place honorable men at its head.[55]

By the time the PA emerged, the challenges to the dominance of the outside developed far beyond the issue of recruitment into the security branches. The "middle command," the activists in the Shabiba and Fath in the Ramallah area under Marwan al-Barghuthi, the secretary general of the Higher Movement Committee for the West Bank (al-Lajna al-Harakiyya al-ᶜUlya lil-Diffa al-Gharbiyya), initiated a drive toward internal Fath elections on the district level, which ultimately took place only in Ramallah in October 1994. A member of the "middle command" deported in 1987, Al-Barghuthi was one of the few exiles from the "inside" to be accorded membership to the Revolutionary Council in the 5th Fath Assembly in August 1989. Yet he did not, at least during the first year of the PA, play the role of one beholden to his patron. Highly critical of the outside leadership, particularly Arafat, for their monopolization of power, Barghuthi claimed that "there is no doubt that the Madrid Conference and the composition of the delegation from the inside gave a big and important push to the role of the inside, but now part of the leadership returned. In other words, the leadership has returned to the homeland, because the leadership essentially is Yasser Arafat. Wherever Yasser Arafat is to be found, the Palestinian leadership is to be found, because it is clear historically and in the last few years that the power of Yasser Arafat makes him the sole leader and the sole decision maker regarding the Palestinian people."[56]

The omnipotence of one leader and the absence of any role for the most important collective bodies in the PLO was exacerbated by the way PA officials were chosen, which, Barghuthi claimed, is based on the desire to coopt and strengthen the role of families and extended clans.[57] Both Sufian Abu Zaida, a fellow Fath activist from Gaza, and Nabil ᶜAmru, a member of the Revolutionary Council from the "outside" and editor of the *Al-Hayat al-Jadida* daily, generally concurred with Barghuthi. Even though ᶜAmru was an editor of the semi-official newspaper of the PA, he nevertheless censured the "Fath base" for "making a big mistake when it did not continue, despite the leadership [i.e., Arafat], the process of holding elections that began in Ramallah."[58]

The possibility of democratization in Fath became even more remote following the above interviews, conducted in February 1995. First, key Fath personalities on the "inside" who had championed the cause of elections were being effectively coopted by the PA. An excellent example is Nayif Suwaytat, a founder of the Shabiba movement in the north, president of the student council in Bir-Zeit University in 1984, who was appointed as general political adviser to the governor of Jenin.[59] Second, in November 1995, a ruling council was formed for the election campaign (al-Majlis al-Qiyadi li-ʿAmaliyyat al-Intikhabat) that was composed of members appointed by the Fath Central Committee rather than elected by the rank and file. The decision reveals how closely linked are the issues of democratization, effective politicization, and the inside activists' loss of power. The Fath Central Committee that made the decision was composed solely of PLO leaders from the "outside," who allotted four chairmanships of the six committees in the new council to outsiders, only two to insiders, Faysal Husayni and Zakariya al-Agha, and none to former inside organization members who at the time headed the higher movement committee in the West Bank.[60] Needless to say, the two most important committee chairs, the political and the financial, went to Mahmud ʿAbbas (Abu Mazin) and Ahmad Qariʿ (Abu ʿAlaʾ), both longstanding members of Fath in the diaspora. The political committee was responsible for strategy and choosing the nominees, the latter in financing their campaign. The "inside" was left then with mobilizing cadres on the basis of the decisions made by the returnees. Such an allocation of roles perpetuated the traditional division of labor between the PLO and Fath on the outside and the territorial organizational command that prevailed since 1967 right through the intifada.[61]

What happened in Fath was reflected in the PA itself. The "outside" received the key posts in the Palestinian Authority, especially in the higher levels of bureaucracy, the security forces, and district governorships. On the ministerial level, officials from the outside headed the three major ministries in the PA: Nabil Shaʿth was appointed minister of planning and cooperation; Ahmad Qariʿ, minister of economy, trade, and industry; and Muhammad Zahdi Nashashibi, minister of finance. Another veteran PLO official, Al-Tayyib ʿAbd al-Rahim, became the secretary of the presidential office. Those from the inside, who were appointed head of the more minor ministries, Saʾib Ariqat, Jamil al-Tarifi, and Furayh Abu Middayn, were never members of the middle command. Those relatively highly placed local politicians such as Faysal Husayni, Saʾib ʿAriqat (minister of local government affairs), and Jamil Tarifi (head of the liaison committee with Israel) also did not emerge from the "inside" organizational command of Fath.

Even in Jenin where the PA tried to be more even-handed and appointed major figures from the territorial Fath organization, it was Hikmat Zaid al-Kaylani, a former exile, who received the key position of governor. It is important to realize that the categorization of officials and activists within Fath between inside and outside is organizational rather than locational. Cadres belonging to the "inside" are those who possessed a power base in the front organizations of Fath they helped set up in the occupied territories in the late 1970s and early 1980s even if they were exiled afterwards.[62] Obverse, a person like Jibril Rajub, head of the Preventive Security Apparatus (Jihaz al-Amn al-Wiqaʾi), who does not have such a background can be regarded as an outsider, even though he was incarcerated inside. Similarly, those locationally from the outside could never be insiders.

The Traditionalization of Politics

Arafat was hardly alone in his quest to depoliticize society. After seven years of intifada, many intellectuals urged that national institutions depoliticize and address the specific public concerns for which they were formally established and which they often neglected for the sake of political mobilization.[63] The difference between their perspective and Arafat's lies in the context. Whereas these elites saw depoliticization within the context of establishing a strong civil society and democracy and wanted to separate institutions with public agendas from simple political parties in order that the former would protect, not dominate, the latter, Arafat saw it as a prelude to traditionalizing politics.[64]

To be sure, much of the groundwork had been laid beforehand. The high level of internal violence and the absence of conflict-resolution mechanisms had paradoxically strengthened the identity of family and kin at the expense of other forms of union and identity.[65] Primordial ties frequently become more important with the breakdown of institutional authority.

It is hardly surprising then that the political announcements that appeared in the Jerusalem Arab press after the meeting at the White House on September 13 were remarkably similar to those gracing the pages of Jordanian newspapers in honor of special occasions associated with King Hussein and his family. Out of 87 such announcements, only 11 referred to collective and institutional concepts such as the Palestinian people and the PLO in their main headings; 65 congratulated President Arafat, employing his official title; and 11 congratulated Abu ʿAmmar, "the commander and symbol" (al-qaʾid wal-ramz), without any reference to his formal title. In 40 announcements, the traditional word "homage" (mubayaʿa) appeared in the major headline.[66] The announcements were made both by kinship and corporate groups. These findings indicate just how prevalent feelings of personal fealty and traditional stratification of society continued to be and, as a result, to what extent Arafat could effectively employ strategies based on kin-based patronage.[67]

One announcement particularly demonstrated the continued strength of ascriptive rather than ideological group affiliation. A sweeping victory of the

Fath-affiliated list over the fundamentalist opponents in the February 1994 elections for the administrative council of the Arab Medical Society (al-Jamᶜiyya al-Tibbiyya al-ᶜArabiyya) prodded the Shaᶜth family of Khan Yunis to congratulate the victors in a paid announcement in *Al-Quds*:

> The members [literally "sons"] of the Shaᶜth family in the Palestinian National Liberation Movement/Fath and the Palestinian People's Party headed by Jamal Ahmad Shaᶜth, Jamal Ahmidan Shaᶜth, and Muhammad ᶜAbd al-Majid Shaᶜth extend their warmest congratulations to the National Independence Bloc upon their sweeping victory in the Medical Society elections. At the same time they congratulate the son of Fath and the son of the family, brother Ziad Shaᶜth, and all the members of the administrative council [of the society], wishing all of them success in the service of the homeland (al-watan). [On the left side of the announcement appears a photograph of Arafat.][68]

Ascriptive ties blend naturally into organizational forms in this announcement. Initially the family is the organizing principle behind the announcement as members of two parties from the same family gather together to make the announcement in the family's name. This is later tempered by the second congratulations to a family member whose political affiliation precedes his filial relationship. The difference is marginalized, however, by the fact that in Fath the individual member is identified by the appellation "*al-akh*," brother, thereby conceiving national and organizational affiliation in terms of blood ties. The factions of the left, in contrast, always used the more impersonal term "*rafiq*" (comrade). Between the two congratulations are three names of brothers distinguished from the rest of the family. Status (in this case based on gender) within the family is important in kinship-based announcements. Finally, there is the linkage between family and the personalism of Arafat by way of the photograph. This is by far the most prominent and pertinent fact in an otherwise complex announcement from a family composed of party activists who had contested an election of a prominent local organization. Arafat, in short, looms above them all.

No wonder that while David Ben-Gurion responded to internal political divisions with an ideology of elitism, Arafat bolstered a social structure that facilitated the diffusion of power. The establishment of the "the Office of the President for Tribal Affairs" (Maktab al-Raᵓis li-Idarat Shuᵓun al-ᶜAshaᵓir) to adjudicate problems between families in October 1995 is probably the best example of deliberate traditionalization. In early November 1995, for example, some members of the Daᵓud family who were refugees from Majdal/Asqalan thanked the PA for refraining from recognizing the present family council whose legitimacy they contested.[69] A month later, the Ministry of Interior licensed the newly founded Association of the Confederation of the

Sons of the Tribes of Beersheba (Jamᶜiyyat Rabitat Abnaᵓ Qabaᵓil Bir al-Sabᶜa). In response, the members of the association, which included Furaykh Abu Middayn, the minister of justice, thanked "President Yasser Arafat for placing [in us] precious trust, enabling the Association to take a role in the service of the Palestinian people so that it may be forever a constructive organ in building our Palestinian state."[70] The announcement reflects the various strands of neopatrimony: the modernization in the organization of tribes based on geographical origin; the modern division of labor apparent in the list of the members of the Executive Committee, their positions, and telephone numbers; and the fact that the information is couched in terms of Palestinian state building. It should be noted, however, that in this particular case the official title and Arafat's full name are given rather than the "paternal" code name and his designation as "leader."

A Shariᶜa ruling by an arbitration committee headed by the Mufti of Gaza "under the sponsorship of the honorable President, the leader and symbol 'Abu ᶜAmmar,' may God keep him," indicated tolerance of a traditional legal system that competes on the turf of the state directed legal system.[71] The gravity of this example is evinced by the fact that it involved the homicide of a member of the ᶜAbid family in October 1995, jurisdiction over which is normally part of the monopoly over violence and should be left to the civil courts who formally posses it.

While the subject matter of the ruling indicates just how little the PA was striving to assert the supremacy of the civil system, the flowery reference to Abu ᶜAmmar highlights the close connection between legal pluralism and neopatrimonialism. Personal fealty is often achieved by the absence of formal jurisdictional division of labor between the organs of the state. It is, in fact, the very competition between individuals and organizations generated by institutional pluralism that serves as a means of assuring loyalty. Arafat, it appears, preferred personal loyalty at the expense of state building. It is no mere coincidence that the newly appointed attorney general in the Palestinian Authority, Khalid al-Qidra, five months before the ruling of the Mufti, ruled out the possibility that such a ruling could ever take place.[72]

The participation of PA officials in customary law is another indication of the traditionalization of society. On September 30, 1995, a ceremony of reconciliation (*sulh*) proscribed by customary law took place between two families in the headquarters of Force 17 "with the blessing of the [Palestinian] Authority and Force 17," and in the presence of leading security personnel and dignitaries.[73] On November 1, the lawyer Ibrahim Qandalaft, the PA official in charge of Christian religious affairs represented the PA in the procession (*jaha*) of notables in a *sulh* between the Taha Abu Sanina family and the Christian Habash family, concerning a fight that broke out two months previously in the old city of Jerusalem.[74] In October, the *sulh* in the village of Irtas resolved a fight that broke out on August 4, 1995 between two families. The procession included Da'ud al-Zir, a former PLO official, Abu Khalid al-Lahham (a PLO adviser) "representing Mr. President Yasser Arafat"), and the representatives of both Fath and the Preventive Security Apparatus (Jihaz al-Amn al-Wiqa'i) in Bethlehem.[75]

The PA and the Rule of Law

In the conclusion to his book *Neopatriarchy*, Hisham Sharabi claims that the rule of law is the only way out of the neopatrimonial predicament most Arab societies face.[76] Many fellow Palestinians, agreeing with Sharabi's analysis, looked for ways to establish a framework for the rule of law before the creation of the PA. One of the most serious attempts was the drafting of an interim constitutional order (al-nizam al-dusturi) after the 20th PNC in September 1991. The project, basing its mandate on decisions made in the PNC in November 1988, was headed by Anis al-Qasim, an international affairs lawyer who had helped draft the PLO basic law in 1965 and was later the chairman of the legal committee of the PNC.[77] The committee, with Arafat's permission, circulated the first draft in December 1993 among the various factions, independents in the PNC, and at a conference of Jordanian lawyers in Amman, where it was discussed at length. It was subsequently revised by the PLO in January 1994.[78] A third draft was published on May 1, 1994.[79] According to al-Qasim, the central committee of the PLO was supposed to activate constitutional order simultaneously with the appointment of the Palestinian Authority.[80]

Few constitutional documents have been drafted so heavily in favor of the president, a title Arafat had held since the 1988 declaration of Palestinian independence. This favoritism is illustrated best by the scant attention given to the legislative assembly, dealt with in three articles as opposed to the nine articles defining the role of the president. True, the interim constitutional order was only to be in effect until elections to the legislative council occurred. The assembly was then free to define the constitutional relationship between the executive and legislative branches (Article 48). Yet given the subordinate status of the legislative assembly compared to PLO institutions, it was obvious that once empowered, the executive would be hardly likely to cede power. In addition, it was clear that Arafat stood at the apex of both: Article 49 reads that "The chairman of the Executive Committee shall be the President and head of the National Authority,"[81] while Article 60 made him the prime minister of the legislative council.[82]

Despite these assurances of executive power, the Palestinian interim constitutional order never saw the light of day. One excuse for its neglect was Israeli opposition. Prime Minister Rabin's disparaging remarks at the end of May that "it is all meaningless patter" was followed by a clear warning that its publication would be an intolerable infringement of the DOP and Cairo agreements.[83] In retrospect, this excuse hardly sounds convincing. The PA's decision to abrogate the validity of past military orders on the same day that Arafat had announced his intentions to implement the constitutional order[84] had also aroused the anger of Israel, but was stated as law in Al-Waqaʿi al-Filastiniyya, the official law registrar first issued in November 1994. This matter might have also been overlooked in the same manner.

One man who hardly doubted the feasibility of its implementation was Anis al-Qasim. On December 7, 1994, almost five months after the PA's establishment, Al-Qasim was still hoping in vain that the central council would convene and ratify the document in order to solve problems related to civil rights and legislation.[85] The issue resurfaced after the elections, in February 1996, as if the matter had never been on the agenda previously, when "President Arafat decided to form a committee to draft the basic law for government." One of its members was, not surprisingly, Anis al-Qasim.[86]

Al-Qasim must have regretted the absence of judicial oversight of the little legislation the PA did enact or propose in the first two years of its existence. All this legislation was imbued with the strong autocratic stamp typical of Arab regimes. One of the most controversial was the law regarding voluntary societies that was heatedly contested between the PA and the Palestinian nongovernmental organizations (PNGOs). Three central issues were at stake: funding, licensing, and participation in policy formulation. Of the three, the funding issue was probably the most crucial. The emerging PA had decided that the only conditions under which PNGOs could receive financial support either from government or from international donors (the European Community, the UN agencies, and international nongovernmental organizations [INGOs]) were that the state approved such aid and that the aid was coordinated with the relevant state agencies. Ironically, but naturally, the deputy minister for international cooperation, who explained this position to the PNGOs, had held a totally different view before the emergence of the PA.[87] As founder and former chairman of the largest nongovernmental provider of public health services in the West Bank, he had written a detailed article in *Al-Quds* defending a decentralized public health service and opposing the role of the state as the major health service provider.[88] As a senior government official, however, he faithfully set about marginalizing the role of civil society.

Licensing had also become an important issue. On September 24, 1994, the PA called on all private voluntary organizations to register with the authorities by November 2 or else be considered "nonoperational." With considerable foresight, the PNGOs had anticipated state encroachment, and one month after the signing of the Declaration of Principles (DOP), twenty of them formed the Network of PNGOs, stressing their right to international funding, immunity from any form of licensing, and opposition to registration until a law was promulgated that defined the relationship between PNGOs and the PA. Members of the network feared that the outside PLO, influenced by Arab politics around it, would impose its political culture on the more democratic inside in the West Bank and Gaza.[89] They little realized, however, that the outside would find support for the centralization of public services, at the PNGOs' expense, from former colleagues in Palestinian civil society now well placed in the PA bureaucracy.

To gain legitimacy in contesting the state, the network commissioned a local lawyer to make a comparative study of legislation regulating NGO work in six states: Denmark, Egypt, India, Israel, Jordan, and the United States. The study, completed in May 1995,[90] revealed that only Jordan required licensing, that Egypt required many more procedures of registration than the other states, and that both of these Arab states accorded officials considerable latitude to interfere in the workings of the NGOs. None of the six states specifically addressed the issue of international aid.

The upshot of the paper was clear. First, it established a clear correlation between the democratic nature of a state and noninterference in the affairs of NGOs beyond ensuring these organizations' financial accountability to their respective members and donors. The PA would therefore have to decide whether to adopt the democratic mode and join the ranks of the United States and Denmark, or to adopt the autocratic mode that characterizes such states as Egypt, Brazil, and to a lesser extent India. Second, the paper suggested that by placing limitations on international funding to PNGOs, the PA would place itself in the unenviable position of being in a class of its own in its heavy-handed treatment of NGOs. The PNGO Network's challenge to the PA reflected one of the PA's most basic failings , the almost total absence of any lawmaking, even in the form of ordinances. By 1996, only twelve laws had been put into effect. Compare this to the Israeli experience, where nearly 100 laws (formally called ordinances) were issued between its declaration of independence on May 14, 1948, and the convening of the first Knesset nine months later.

In the year after its establishment, the PA succeeded in attracting to its ranks only 62 out of a total of 1,200 voluntary organizations operating in the occupied territories. Though some of these organizations ranked among the biggest in the occupied territories, they represented but a small fraction of total voluntary activity[91] and were not evenly spread throughout the area. Only 16 of the 62 organizations were based in Gaza, though Gaza represents over 40 percent of the total Palestinian population. The general profile of these organizations was highly urban and elitist.

The PNGOs, moreover, operated in a political environment where opposition political parties sympathetic to their cause were weak. Polls conducted in the occupied territories since the establishment of the PA indicated the extreme weakness of non-Islamic opposition groups.[92] International aid was thus crucial in enabling the network to challenge the state.[93]

That such aid was not forthcoming in sufficient quantity was attested to by a proposed law governing voluntary organizations unveiled by the Ministry of Social Affairs in August 1995. This law, which was drafted without consultation with the PNGOs, required the PNGOs to register and receive permits, empowered either the minister of social affairs or the minister of the interior, or both, to suspend organizational activity without recourse to judicial review, and placed restrictions on foreign funding.[94] The PNGOs highlighted the proposed involvement of the ministry of the interior which in most Arab states is closely linked to public security matters.[95]

The Election Laws, Process, and Results

Neopatrimonialism, as a hybrid product of modernity and tradition, is linked to the preference of a particular electoral system over others. One of the most problematic and intricate aspects of the interim peace process between Israel and the Palestinians was related to the holding of elections and the creation of an elected government. For both sides the issue of elections, even regarding aspects that could be considered procedural, was subsumed under the more immediate issue of sovereignty. And the issue of sovereignty was closely related both to the size of the proposed legislative council and to the powers it would wield. Israel wished to limit the number and powers of the council to a level appropriate to the council of an autonomy.[96] In contrast, the Palestinians proposed a 100-member council with extensive legislative powers that would bring the Palestinians closer to de facto statehood. The PLO insisted that the elections for the PA take place in East Jerusalem and that its Arab inhabitants should have the right both to elect and to be elected.[97] Israel was prepared to allow them to vote only outside of Jerusalem (formally annexed to Israel) and would not allow East Jerusalemites to present themselves as candidates to the council. Finally, the elections were held up because Israel insisted that the candidates and parties running for election support the peace process and renounce violence. Palestinian acceptance of these conditions would probably have led to the exclusion of the Hamas and al-Jihad al-Islamic groups, which, according to opinion polls of the time, had the support of approximately one-sixth of the population.[98] The Oslo B agreement, concluded on September 28, 1995, finally resolved the issue of elections in Jerusalem and set the size of the Palestinian Assembly at 83 members, later revised to 89.[99]

Less well known was the controversy generated over the election law that adopted the multiseat, multidistrict system. Voters chose from among individual candidates (though they might belong to a party), and the number of voting choices equaled the number of seats allotted to that district.[100] Such a system tends to maximize the power of the largest political formation, strengthen independents affiliated to that formation, and, in general, weaken party organization. This last effect is particularly strong in Arab societies, including the Palestinian, where clans remain important and can be coopted by the government. It is not surprising then that the Independent Palestinian Group for Elections, composed of leading figures in Palestinian civil society, proposed instead a single-district proportional representation system.[101] It was the first model, however, that was inscribed in law in December 1995 and formed the basis for the elections.[102]

The proposed law regulating political parties likewise generated criticism for the limitations it placed on political freedom and for its resemblance to laws governing political parties in neighboring Arab, particularly one-party, states.[103] Article 3 limited participation only to political parties that "are formed according to the provisions of this law in realizing political and social progress on the basis of national unity"[104]—criteria so broad and ambiguous as to make it a tool for possible government intervention. Clauses 4 and 5 of Article 4 added the provisos that a party was only lawful if it ascribed to political pluralism and was distinguishable by its programs from other parties. These clauses, together with the prohibition on affiliation or even cooperation with "groups, organizations, or forces inimical to the Palestinian people," could easily be used against the Islamic parties. The Islamic opposition parties' refusal to participate in the January 20, 1996 elections did not test the PA's potential uses of this law, however. Many of these deficiencies were too easily overlooked in the festive atmosphere that prevailed before and after the first Palestinian elections.

Both Arafat and the Israeli government had much to be pleased about. The massive turnout, particularly in Gaza (90 percent), where Arafat's PA had governed longest, was a sharp slap in the face to both the Islamic and left-wing opposition.[105] The Hamas, while refraining from calling for a boycott, had prevailed upon three members who had decided to contest the elections as a bloc unaffiliated to the Hamas, to rescind their decision seventeen days before the elections.[106] The PFLP and DFLP were less successful in controlling their members. Prominent activists such as Ghazi Abu Jiab, Riad al-Maliki and Raʾfat al-Najjar of the PFLP, and Bilal Shakhshir of the DFLP, refused to follow the decisions of the factions in Syria, and contested the elections as independents.[107] Israel was pleased because it had created a vehicle, the legislative assembly, that could potentially change the PLO Covenant and construct modalities that could institutionalize leadership change after Arafat.

The first Palestinian "national" elections hardly ushered in an age of democracy. But all said and done, it did finally territorialize a national movement and give that movement both shape and legitimacy to transform itself into a state and to live up to its international commitments.

Conclusion

To a student of transitions from national movement to territorial state and modern state formation, neopatrimonialism is not all bad. Assuring personal safety and property of the population certainly ranks high in the satisfaction of wants. The West Bank and Gaza population could hardly forget the situation prevailing immediately after the DOP was signed in which thieves systematically stole telephone cables in Gaza in order to sell their copper content, that factories were being burnt to the ground because of the owners' assumed political affiliations,[108] and that at least three prominent Fath activists were killed in a spate of political murders. They hardly had to read Graham Usher writing in *Middle East International*, a weekly sympathetic to the Palestinian cause, who described Gaza as of February 1994 as being in a state of chaos, and Fath, the major political force in the area, in a state of disintegration.[109] These events underscored the need for strong central authority. Arafat's military conquest succeeded considerably in reducing lawlessness.

Most people in precarious, unsettled conditions are risk-averse; they want first and foremost to ensure that conditions do not deteriorate further before they seek to improve them. Arafat might have succeeded where local society and the Israeli authorities failed, at least according to research data collected by the Nablus-based Center for Palestine Research and Studies.[110] The preference for Arafat as head of the Palestinian Authority had been increasing steadily from the time that the PA began administering Gaza and Jericho. There was no better proof of his success, particularly in Gaza, than the overwhelming turnout in the January 20 elections in support of Arafat.

The problem, however, lies in the trade-off between present stability and the future costs of an institutionalized neopatrimonialism. As the experience in many Third World states demonstrates, such regimes are usually characterized by a long-term decline in the capacity to govern, due in part to the increasingly stringent control and cooptation of civil society. A vicious cycle of conflict between state and society ensues that is extremely difficult to break.

Nor can one disregard the dependent relationship of the PLO and the Palestinians on Israel and the United States, which reflects the dynamics of peripheral and hybrid state formation in an international system characterized by core, semiperipheral, and peripheral states. Arafat may be the patriarch of the PA, but he is a child to the forces that surround him; and the PA if it achieves statehood will, like other neopatrimonial regimes, join the ranks of the peripheral states. To the few Palestinians who fought on the ground for something different, this might be a tragedy, but it will be a blight shared by many states-in-the-making. Palestinian state building is likely to be one more example that there are no shortcuts either to democracy or to sustainable development.

Conclusion

Palestinian State Building and the Postcolonial State

This book has focused mainly on the relationship between territorialization and modern state formation. What we saw is that national movements, like that of the Palestinians, must challenge territorial states in a politically crowded world. Likely to have to operate from the outside the territory they seek to liberate, nationalists will find it difficult to penetrate into a contested area. But given the territorial focus of the state system, they must territorialize also. As a result, the tensions between a nation's inside and outside wings will increase as diaspora leaders seek to territorialize while assuring their hegemony over the activists in the homeland. This imperative, in turn, gives birth to a dilemma. On the one hand, it is necessary to mobilize resistance on the inside; on the other hand, state formation in the homeland must be avoided at least until the diaspora leaders come home. Consequently, neopatrimonial techniques of mobilization through diffusion come into play. Power is personalized and functional agencies are bureaucratized at the center, while the outside works to diffuse, segment, and multiply those agencies on the inside in order to play off one organization against the other. The gulf between inside and outside exacerbates strains within national movements that operate anyway in an atmosphere of crisis, pushing them toward either autocratic personal rule or organizational fragmentation.

Violence and Institution Building

From the foregoing, we may ask how the Palestinian experience, both similar and different from the Zionist case, may shed light on other cases of state building in the postcolonial era. To this end, our analysis can relate especially to two factors that play crucial roles in determining the success, or failure, of new state-building endeavors: (1) the role of violence in establishing prestate institutions, and (2) the importance of pre-independence institution building in the establishment of the state.

Let us begin with violence. In his analysis of Western European state building, Charles Tilly concluded that war makes states.[1] It was in the process of making war that principalities developed fiscal systems to finance war and bureaucracies to assure more universal conscription. War thus became a catalyst for state building. Several scholars have used this argument to comment on the formation of postcolonial states. Sheldon Gellar argues that in peaceful transitions in Africa, the state regressed into neopatrimonial forms of rule more debilitating than the bureaucratized colonial regime they inherited. In more conflictual situations, as for example was the case in Guinea-Bissau, conflict bred indigenous institution building, which facilitated greater social transformation and nation building, as well as a higher degree of institutionalization of party rule.[2] According to this thesis, conflict should facilitate post-independence state consolidation. Patrick Chabal, John Saul, and, most eloquently, Basil Davidson, concur with Gellar that, with violence, the legacy of colonial rule is considerably weakened,[3] and the chances for successful state consolidation are enhanced.

The Communist Chinese experience provides a striking example of how conflict can positively influence modern state building. Thus, it was while waging *war* that the Chinese established a revolutionary *state*. But the Chinese experience also demonstrates that the linkage between these two can be illusory. First, the Chinese conflict was a civil war waged against a foe of equal strength, not a hegemonic one. Second, and more importantly, one of Mao Tse-tung's major strategic goals was the establishment and expansion of a liberated area, in which institution building could freely take place.[4] Rather than regarding violence as the midwife of state building, then, Mao believed that it was only far away from the conflict zone that state building could take place. After all, to build institutions in virgin territory is a far easier task to accomplish than to build them in the face of a competing infrastructure.

Accordingly, one may conclude from the Chinese case that it is the creation of liberated areas while in conflict, not the conflict itself, that contributes to institutionalization. This is the gist of Ronald Weitzer's critique on Tilly-like reasoning in an article on Zimbabwe. Weitzer contests the idea that mobilization in protracted conflict creates institutions that can lead to effective state building.[5] He argues that there is no demonstrable evidence from modern patterns of state consolidation in Africa, even where born violently, that these states produced better governments than the colonial states they replaced. However much they waged struggle against the former colonial power, states that inherited colonial forms of government and administration, particularly in multi-ethnic societies, quickly degenerated into neopatrimonialism. Only in the case of Mozambique, where guerrillas established effective liberation zones, does Weitzer note that there was indeed greater institutionalization, less of a colonial legacy, and more healthy state consolidation.[6] In the occupied territories, so unequally arrayed are the state and the opposing national movement that it would be difficult to conceive of such liberated areas.

The pursuit of violence alone compromises institution building in at least three ways. One, manpower and resources are diverted from institution building to the mobilization of violence. Second, the propensity to violence, even when it is contained as was the case during the intifada, tends to generate internal violence, compromising institution building even further.[7] Finally, violence invites state repression, not only against those personally engaged in violent acts, but also against the institutions the national movement creates. Conversely, apart from what may be a necessary measure of violence, the more a movement avoids conflict, the greater the level of institutionalization, yielding greater dividends in the period of state consolidation. In a liberation struggle against the nation-state, therefore, it is not war that makes the state, but achieving the right mix between the exercise of violence and the enterprise of institution building.

Can national movements themselves decide what kind of compromise to strike between the two, or will it be determined by the nature of the conflict and the policies of the opposing power? Migdal demonstrates, through six case studies, the ways in which foreign rulers may help to determine the extent to which national movements will take the institution-building route.[8] He argues that the greater the willingness of the foreign ruler to allow voluntary center building by forces working toward independence, the more likely the emergence of a strong and stable state. Thus, a violent colonial regime begets violence, while a more benign regime will beget an institution-building reaction. Migdal also emphasizes the importance whether or not the indigenous population is undergoing modernization. Both of these factors, at least in the short term, are not easily controlled by any national movement. For Migdal, the state of Israel is an example of the strong state, while he regards Sierra Leone as a weak state. In the Jewish Yishuv, the British fostered state building by encouraging the creation of a Jewish Agency, while the immigrant population was characterized by a relatively high level of modernization. In Sierra Leone, in contrast, the British strengthened the hand of ethnic "strong men," maintaining the disunity of a traditionally fragmented society.[9]

The role of foreign rulers may be further highlighted by comparing between Indian and Algerian state formation, where regime policies determined the level of violence. In the first part of the century, British policy toward India fostered a reasonable amount of institution and center building. Indians were allowed electoral participation, first at the local level, and then regionally, without undue interference. Where the British deviated from center-building facilitation, as in the case of India's Muslims, the outcome was bloody. In Algeria, the French were very unsympathetic to institution building because of settler opposition. The FLN's reaction was correspondingly more violent than in the Indian case.

Foreign rulers also affected the evolution of Palestinian nationalism. While it may be argued that the outside, because it was prevented from territorializing, never seriously attempted to strike the right balance between violence and institution building, one cannot assume that if it had allowed the "inside" to pursue institution building they would have succeeded. Israel, after all, was as hostile to their efforts as it was to PLO territorialization. If Israel was not as ruthless as the French were in Algeria, and therefore enabled some Palestinian institution-building, this was in part because, as a small state, it was more sensitive to international pressure than France.

Prior Institutionalization and State Formation

If violence is not conducive to institution building before independence, how important is the establishment of prestate institutions for the eventual consolidation of a new state? The Israeli experience is an excellent example of how pre-independence state-building patterns can predict the character of the state after independence. Only in 1977, nearly thirty years after the establishment of the state, did the right-wing Likud party take the reins of power from the hegemonic state-building political elite. In the emerging Palestinian entity, the legacy of Arafat's neopatrimonialism will probably be even more considerable. As in the Israeli case, Palestinian patterns of state building are likely, after the assumption of self-government, to predict the type of state consolidation for a considerable period of time.

Joel Migdal, the only researcher I know who addresses the relationship between state formation and state consolidation in these terms, assigns pre-independence institutions considerable weight.[10] He has shown that where the British intervened in the Zionist state-building experience and sanctioned pluralism within the Mandate framework, through, for example, religious law and the authority of various religious courts, rule-making indeed became a problem later on for an otherwise strong Jewish state. By contrast, the state emerged strong in those fields where the British did not interfere or, in fact, abetted local Zionist initiatives. On this score, what emerged from "benign neglect" was the protracted maturation of a collective decision-making process and the development of rules of the game.[11]

Ruth Collier confirms this view in her work on African state building.[12] Collier studies the relationship between (1) the institutionalization of modern forms of participation in the pre-independence era, and (2) regime types following independence in tropical Africa. She looks at three variables:

1. The rate, or extent, of participation in electoral politics in the pre-independence era and the party configuration that it yielded

2. Sequence, or the level of socioeconomic modernization of the population, as measured by indices such as economic welfare and level of education in the immediate pre-independence era
3. Colonial regime type, that is, French direct rule, British indirect rule, and other distinctions.

Although Migdal's variables and those suggested by Collier differ, some correspondence does exist. What Collier operationalizes as rate corresponds roughly to what Migdal terms prior institutionalization; "sequence" can be likened to Migdal's concept of "embeddedness," and regime type relates to the form of state consolidation. Thus while eventually most tropical African regimes succumbed to unstable military rule, Collier shows that where parties had achieved a higher level of institutionalization and where elections were more frequently held in the pre-independence stage, the slide to authoritarianism was slower.[13]

Namibia, which achieved statehood in 1990, and seems to have made a promising start, further confirms the importance of prior institutionalization inside the contested territory. The leading guerrilla group in the struggle against South Africa, the South West African People's Organization (SWAPO), had been forced to operate from outside the territories it claimed. Though the conflict was violent and protracted (SWAPO initiated guerrilla warfare in 1959 and continued for thirty years), a constituent assembly formed within the contested territory in 1975 and inaugurated considerable reform, even though it was boycotted by SWAPO.

Of critical importance in Namibia was the early emergence of institutionalized parties such as the Democratic Turnhalle Alliance (DTA), a coalition of minority ethnic groups and predominantly settler parties that became a loyal but active opposition when independence came and a SWAPO-led government emerged following free elections in 1990.[14] Both the reforms inaugurated under DTA and the integrity of the party impressed SWAPO leaders who returned to Namibia after long years of exile.[15] It is important to note, too, that some SWAPO political activity was tolerated by the settler regime.[16] Perhaps the DTA's cohesion and performance persuaded SWAPO to transform itself into a political party three years before independence.[17] At any rate, it was one of the few hegemonic national movements that agreed to become a party and contest multiparty elections rather than insist on acting as a surrogate state. In cases where this did not occur, the national movement became almost inevitably a one-party authoritarian state.[18]

The Namibian experience confirms what is known from Zionist state building about the importance of the emergence of effective territorially based political parties in the pre-independence era. As we have seen, however, the conditions facing the Palestinian national movement are hardly conducive to an emulation of Namibia's promising start. For example, local Palestinians never had the opportunity to organize territorial political parties. Israel stopped any kind of political reform when it decided that the 1976 West Bank municipal elections were the last under Israeli rule. Israel never seriously contemplated allowing the formation of legal political parties. But even when the Palestinians achieved autonomy through the PA and were in a position to institutionalize territorial political parties, the most important movements failed to do so. Thus neither Fath nor the organized Palestinian political opposition (consisting of the Hamas, the Islamic Resistance Movement, the PFLP, and the bulk of the DFLP) transformed themselves into political parties or indicated their willingness to contest other forces in the political arena.[19]

Finally, and again in comparison with the Namibian case, the PLO confronts severe difficulties emanating from its negotiating agenda. Fath must maintain its hold on the local population during protracted negotiations over a final agreement while presiding over an autonomy rather than a sovereign state. This in itself is a reflection of the power of a nation-state such as Israel, as compared to the sort of minority settler regime that controlled Namibia.

There are, however, three reasons for optimism with respect to the Palestinians. First, the era is marked by a wave of liberalization, the termination of superpower rivalry, and continuing prospects of regional peace in the Middle East, notwithstanding the present right-wing Israeli government under Binyamin Netanyahu. The recently signed agreement on redeployment in Hebron is one such indication. Second, the nonpenetrative nature of the Israeli regime allowed for the emergence of a vibrant, if fragmented, Palestinian civil society (as opposed to state-building institutions such as strong political parties). The third reason for optimism of hope lies in the relationship between local civil society and worldwide change in the role of the state. Palestinian state building is taking place in an era when society is disengaging from the state and the state is retreating from society. These two phenomena could have ominous consequences, were it not for the fact that both theorists and practitioners and local and international civil societies (who possess the clout to pressure Third World countries) share a "third wave" perspective of the state. The first wave of theorists glorified the state as the key engine of social and economic modernization, while the second wave of civil society theorists minimized its importance. Scholars of the third wave seek to strike a balance between the state's watchdog functions and the need to supply basic public goods, such as education, with the need to maintain the autonomy of civil society.[20] Thus, both the penetrative and neopatrimonial state regimes are placed on the defensive; the former because it stifles civil society, and the latter because it does not provide public goods efficiently.

Perhaps these forces will prevail over the internal structural constraints that thwarted institutionalization and will alleviate the painful dilemma in which the inside, more qualified to engage in state consolidation, is defeated by the outside, which hastens the process of statehood but fails to consolidate the state. It would be tragic if the Palestinians, who suffered so much at the hands of others, should create an entity where suffering will be self-inflicted.

ZIONIST AND PALESTINIAN STATE FORMATION AND THEORY

Social scientists sometimes try not only to draw on theory to understand a particular case but to use the analysis of the special case to revise theory. To this end, what might the comparison of Palestinian state building with its Zionist predecessor imply regarding scholarly models of state formation in the postcolonial age?

These findings, I believe, suggest that the absolutist model of state formation developed by Charles Tilly should be applied only cautiously, if at all, to Third World settings. To recall, for Tilly, state formation is the consequence of conflict to the point where the state becomes almost synonymous with institutionalized violence. The more the prince and then the state monopolizes violence internally and exercises it externally, the more stately the state. Tilly points out that his formula for successful state making emphasizing extraction, control, and coalition building, "deals primarily with penetration, secondarily with legitimacy, less with integration and identity, and hardly at all with participation and distribution."[21] According to Thomas Callaghy, all of this shows up in the Third World in a three-way conflict between leaders of national movements of newly founded states and (1) the state and society that it wishes to dominate, (2) contestation with external groups, organizations, and states, and (3) the struggle within the state between the ruler and his staff.[22]

Similarly, in their analysis of the "juridical state," Jackson and Rosberg claim that Third World states are weak because they are prevented by the international community from waging war.[23] Consider, for example, what happens to various Third World rulers who sought to expand their territories in an hegemonic state system. Nasser, Saddam Hussein, and Muhammad ʿAli, the Albanian despot who ruled Egypt in the first part of the nineteenth century, did not recognize to what extent the division of power between states ensured the juridical persistence of even weaker states. These leaders paid dearly for their oversight, and the cost of not heeding the lesson increased over time. Thus, after severely defeating the Ottoman forces, ʿAli was thwarted by anxious Western powers in his imperial designs (it would be called "state formation" in previous centuries) aimed at wresting territory from the Ottoman Empire. Then, Nasser, the charismatic Egyptian president, was stalemated by conservative regimes who, aided by the West, challenged his support of the republican regime in Yemen during the civil war there in the 1960s. And Saddam Hussein, for his invasion of Kuwait, may yet pay with partition of the Iraqi state into its Sunni, Shiite, and Kurd components. In the Palestinian case, Arafat's pro-Iraqi policy in the Gulf crisis and his unwillingness to recognize the dynamics of an hegemonic world dealt the Palestinians a blow from which they have yet to recover.

Yet even if rulers could continue to make war, it is not the absence of external conflict that has led to the atrophy of many African states. Revisionists argued two decades ago that authoritarianism actually increased the rapaciousness of elites promoting secession rather than decreasing it.[24] Azarya and Chazan, for example, point to the paradox that the stronger the state, the more limited its hold on civil society. They suggest a more Tocquevillian understanding of the strong state that conservatives recognized long ago.[25] Wunsch and Olowu's *The Failure of the Centralized State*, written from an economic development perspective, and Migdal's more theoretical *Strong Societies and Weak States*, agree that the strong state was never what it was presumed to be. The state without the participation of civil institutions, such scholars indicate, is structurally deficient. Rather than dominating society the leader and his organization must work with it.

Callaghy's third assertion, that leaders of nascent states should seek, perhaps forcefully, to dominate their staff may also deserve revision. The importance of forging autonomy, not dominating a budding bureaucracy, is strongly argued in the literature on economic development, indeed by Callaghy's own work on economic structural adjustment. Peter Evans has stressed the importance of an autonomous and professional bureaucracy for its ability to foster economic growth among "Asian tigers" and Japan as part of a third wave of thinking on successful state consolidation.[26] Why, then, fight the bureaucrats when they can so promote the development of the state and curb the destructive predatory rent-seeking that plagues Third World states? This point perhaps is particularly relevant to territorial Palestinians who cultivated a public policy and administrative elite that is now systematically being marginalized and overpowered by autocratic neopatrimonialism.

In sum, institutionalization and institution building in a pluralist structure should unfold in an evolutionary manner. This is a more suitable road to the truly strong state than is the absolutist route. If restraint from violence rather than violence itself will lead to the good state, then the very goodness of that state can justify the additional time it takes to build.

NOTES

Preface

1. Mark A. Heller and Sari Nusseibeh, *No Trumpets, No Drums* (New York: Hill and Wang, 1991).

1. Territorialization and State Formation

1. The distinctions between nation building and national identity, and state building and state formation date back to the works of Peter Nettl, Haans Dalder, Robert Dahl., Val Lorwin, and Stein Rokkan, all of whom distinguished between the "stateness," and "nation-ness" of pluralist states in Western Europe. For a discussion of this distinction, see Stein Rokkan, "Center Formation, Nation-Building and Cultural Diversity: Report on a UNESCO Programme," in S. N. Eisenstadt and Stein Rokkan, eds., *Building States and Nations*, vol. 1 (Beverly Hills, Calif.: Sage, 1973), 18.

2. On the importance of the diaspora experience in the cultivation of *la negritude* and more radical Africanist ideologies, see Michael C. Lambert, "From Citizenship to Negritude, 'Making a Difference' in Elite Ideologies of Colonized Francophone in West Africa," *Comparative Studies in Society and History*, 35.2 (April 1993): 247–51; for the contribution of Lebanese emigres to the development of a secular Lebanese nationalism, see Meir Zamir, *The Formation of Modern Lebanon* (London: Croom Helm, 1985), 23. An even stronger case can be made for the Algerian experience. The first Algerian nationalist party, L'Étoile Nord-Africaine, was founded in Paris in 1926, ten years before the establishment of the branch in Algeria, which one year later was renamed Parti du Peuple Algerien. Charles-Robert Ageron, *Modern Algeria: A History from 1830 to the Present* (Trenton, N.J.: Africa World Press, 1993), 93–94. Emigrés comprised twelve out of the twenty-three delegates of the first Syrian-Arab Congress, held in Paris in 1913. Eliezer Tauber, *The Emergence of the Arab National Movements* (London: Frank Cass, 1993), 185–86.

3. For a cogent argument that the world is heading toward a postterritorial era, see John Gerard Ruggie, "Territoriality and Beyond: Problematizing Modernity in International Relations," *International Organization* 47.1 (Winter 1993): 139–47. Recall, however, that John Herz predicted the demise of the territorial state in 1957, only to apologize for his rashness ten years later. At that time, the nuclear stalemate was supposed to have rendered territoriality obsolete. See John L. Herz, "Rise and Demise

of the Territorial State," *World Politics* 9.4 (July 1957): pp. 473–93. Today the phenomenon is linked to international economic integration and information systems. The problem with Ruggie's argument is that the impact of these forces are not evenly distributed across the globe, and perhaps in the case of Eastern Europe their effects are almost deliberately withheld, so that one may assume that where they are weak, the territorial state as an institutional feature will remain and so will the conflicts between national movements and jealous ethnically based nation states.

4. Laurie A. Brand's *Palestinians in the Arab World: Institution Building and the Search for State* (New York: Columbia University Press, 1988) is an excellent demonstration of state building failure in diaspora, although this is not a point explicitly made by the author.

5. For a discussion both of the sanctuary state as a general concept and in its specific Palestinian context, see Rex Brynen, *Sanctuary and Survival: The PLO in Lebanon* (Boulder, Colo.: Westview, 1990).

6. The territorial imperative is the outcome of a world divided into sovereign nation states. "With the disappearance of 'nonstate, semistate, or pseudostate areas of the world,' every state is embedded in a system of coordinate territorial states. . . . Jointly, these territorial jurisdictions exhaust the inhabitable surface of the earth." Rogers Brubaker, *Citizenship and Nationhood in France and Germany* (Cambridge, Mass.: Harvard University Press, 1992), 26. Therefore, diaspora movements can only achieve recognition if they prevail in a given territory, because territory becomes "the ultimate object of political life." James Mayall, *Nationalism and International Society*, Cambridge Studies in International Relations 10 (Cambridge: Cambridge University Press 1993), 19; see also Anthony Giddens. *The Nation State and Violence* (Berkeley: University of California Press, 1987), 172; Peter Sahlins, *Boundaries: The Making of France and Spain in the Pyrenees* (Berkeley: University of California Press, 1989), 61–63, and on territorialization of rule, 78–89, 93–97, 168–70, and 190–92.

7. "The idea which I have developed in this pamphlet is an ancient one: It is the restoration of the Jewish State." So began the pamphlet Herzl addressed to the Rothschilds which he wrote feverishly in five days in February 1896. See Arthur Hertzberg, *The Zionist Idea* (New York: Atheneum, 1977), 202, 204.

8. Michael Doyle, *Empires* (Ithaca, N.Y.: Cornell University Press, 1986), 370.

9. Willie Breytenbach, chapter 3, in Johannes Albertus Venter, *Challenge: South Africa within the African Revolutionary Context* (Gilbratar, Ashkanti Publishers, 1989), 63–88.

10. Ian S. Lustick, *Unsettled States: Disputed Lands* (Ithaca, N.Y.: Cornell University Press, 1993), 111, 134.

11. These observations are distilled from summaries on nationalist struggles in Africa that appear in Ali A. Mazrui and Michael Tidy, *Nationalism and New States in Africa* (London: Heinemann, 1984), 134–59, and relevant chapters from Prosser Gifford and William Roger Lewis, eds., *Decolonization and African Independence: The Transfers of Power, 1960–1980* (New Haven, Conn.: Yale University Press, 1988).

12. Based on a series of random representative samples conducted during 1991, 69 percent of the Jews answered that Israel would be worse off if a Palestinian state were to be established, 13 percent felt that the situation would remain the same, and only 18 percent felt that Israel's situation would improve. See Majid al-Haj, Elihu Katz, and Shmuel Shye, "Arab and Jewish Attitudes: Toward a Palestinian State," *Journal of Conflict Studies*, 37.4 (December 1993): 619–32.

13. Indeed one of the findings in the study previously cited was that 51 percent of the Jews sampled felt that the Palestinian state would pursue actively irredentist policies and a further 28 percent felt that it would make territorial demands "to some extent." Ibid., 628.

14. Mayall, *Nationalism*, 39, 49; Dov Ronen, *The Quest for Self Determination* (New Haven, Conn.: Yale University Press, 1979), 15–23.

15. Mayall, *Nationalism*, 61.

16. Shmuel Sandler and Hillel Frisch, *Israel, the West Bank, and the Palestinians* (Lexington, Mass.: Lexington Books, 1984), 15–19.

17. Clement Henry Moore, *North Africa: Algeria, Morocco, and Tunisia* (Boston: Little, Brown, 1970), 86–87.

18. Elbaki Hermassi, *Leadership and National Development in North Africa: A Comparative Study* (Berkeley: University of California Press, 1972), 137.

19. William B. Quandt, *Revolution and Political Leadership: Algeria 1954–1968* (Cambridge, Mass.: MIT Press, 1969), 129.

20. Thus Abu Iyad of the Fath Central Committee drew inspiration from the Algerian experience because the FLN leadership, like the PLO, was "found outside the country." *Al-Taliʿa* (Cairo), June 1969, quoted in Mordechai Nisan, "The PLO and Vietnam: National Liberation Models for Palestinian Struggle," *Small Wars and Insurgencies* 4.2 (Autumn 1993): 186.

21. See Muhammad al-Yunis's article "Tariq al-Khilas," *Al-Fajr*, May 23, 1973. Yunis calls for the development of national institutions on national soil that he hoped could mature to statehood. On the relevance of the Zionist model to the forging of a truly national education system in the occupied territories, see Sami Husayn's article, "Al-Tarbiyya al-Mahaliyya Jahizatan ʿAn Taʿrif al-Watan," *Al-Fajr*, January 1, 1976.

22. Moshe Lissak and Don Horowitz, *The Origins of the Israeli Polity* (Chicago: Chicago University Press, 1978), 88–99.

23. This is distillation of five major works on Israeli state building by Moshe Lissak and Don Horowitz, *Origins of the Israeli Polity*; Gershon Shafir, *Land, Labor and the Origins of the Israeli-Palestinian Conflict, 1882–1914* (Cambridge: Cambridge University Press, 1989); Michael Shalev, *Labor and the Political Economy in Israel* (Oxford: Oxford University Press); Joel Migdal, *Strong Societies and Weak States* (Princeton, N.J.: Princeton University Press, 1988), chapter 4; and Yonathan Shapiro, *The Formative Years of the Israeli Labour Party* (Beverly Hills, Calif.: Sage, 1976).

24. Mitchell Cohen, *Zion and State: Nation, Class, and the Shaping of Modern Israel* (London: Basil Blackwell, 1987), 88–89.

25. Shafir, *Land, Labor*, 198.

26. Shapiro, *Formative Years*, 240.

27. Quoted in Shlomo Avineri, *The Makings of Modern Zionism: The Intellectual Origins of the Jewish State* (New York: Basic Books, 1981), 203.

28. Rawls writes:

> By an institution I shall understand a public system of rules which defines offices and positions with their rights and duties, powers, and the like. These rules specify certain forms of action as permissible, others as forbidden. . . . An institution may be thought of in two ways: first as an abstract system of rules; and second, as the actions specified by these rules. . . . A parliamentary institution exists at a certain time and place when certain people perform the appropriate actions, engage in these activities in the required way, with a reciprocal recognition of one another's understanding that their conduct accords with the rules they are to comply with. . . . A person taking part in an institution knows what the rulers demand of him and of the others. He also knows that the others know this and that they know that knows this, and so on.

John Rawls, *A Theory of Justice* (Cambridge, Mass.: Harvard University Press, 1971), 55–56, quoted in Robert H. Jackson and Carl G. Rosberg, *Personal Rule in Black Africa: Prince, Autocrat, Prophet, Tyrant* (Berkeley: University of California Press, 1982), 11. Institutionalization or state building is the process in which the above is translated into reality.

29. The distinction between these two levels, the macropolitical where the power of decision making is regulated, and between the microfunctional and bureaucratic, emanates from the theoretical weaknesses of Huntington's celebrated treatment of institutionalization in his analysis of political decay. Huntington applies concepts from the theoretical literature concerning voluntary organizations to the study of institutions of the state, claiming that the institutionalization of the latter is a function of their adaptability, complexity, autonomy, and coherence of its organizations and procedures. Samuel P. Huntington, *Political Order in Changing Societies* (New Haven, Conn.: Yale University Press, 1968), 12. States that score highly on these four dimensions, he claims, achieve a high level of stability and are highly valued, by which he means legitimated. This might be true of organizations whose scope and power are regulated in free social competition, and where members have effective exit options, it does not necessarily hold for state political structures that have to adjudicate between competing wants. Stability and value in politics are often obverse rather than complementary phenomena. It is the crisis of democracies and their temporary state of flux and instability that yields long-term durability; it is the fixity or short-term stability of totalitarian regimes that render them vulnerable to counterrevolution. Rules

must govern the allocation of power, while roles may be sufficient for bureaucratic organizations. An organization such as the state that structures the arena must be permeated by institutions in the form of rules as well as roles. The PLO, for example, rates relatively high on organization. The problem is institutionalizing the state. The Zionists, by contrast, possessed both. For an excellent article that relates to the theoretical shortcomings of Huntington but unfortunately never had the impact it deserved, see Gabriel Ben-Dor, "Institutionalization and Political Development: A Conceptual and Theoretical Analysis," *Comparative Studies in Society and History* 17 (1975): 309–25.

30. Shafir, *Land, Labor,* 46–55.

31. Cohen, *Zion and State*, 75.

32. Migdal, *Strong Societies*, 156–57.

33. Sandler and Frisch, *Israel, the West Bank*, 15–19.

34. Shmuel Sandler, "The Socio-Political Origins of the Israel-Diaspora Relationship: The Territorialization of the Zionist Movement, 1917–1935," *Israel and Diaspora Jewry: Ideological Political Perspectives* (Ramat-Gan: Bar-Ilan University Press, 1991), 151.

35. Charles Liebman, *Pressure without Sanctions* (Rutherford, N.J.: Fairleigh Dickinson University Press, 1966), 232–33.

36. Migdal, *Strong Societies*, 147.

37. S. N. Eisenstadt, *Traditional Patrimonialism and Modern Neopatrimonialism* (Beverly Hills, Calif.: Sage, 1973), 13–19. I use the term to define regimes with a stronger element of personalism than discussed by either Eisenstadt or John Waterbury in his *Commander of the Faithful* (London: Nicolson and Weidenfield, 1970), 150. Yet I am not willing to minimize the bureaucratic or social foundations of neopatrimonialism that would make me opt instead to use the terms *personal rule* and *personalism*, which appear in Robert Jackson and Carl G. Rosberg, *Personal Rule in Black Africa: Prince, Autocrat, Prophet, Tyrant* (Berkeley: University of California Press, 1978), 17–22. A competing term, *authoritarianism*, is inappropriate for a nonstate organization whose members and adherents have considerable latitude to exit or protest. ʿArafat maintains the most relative power, but he does not aim to totally monopolize it.

38. John Waterbury, *Commander of the Faithful*, 155–64.

39. ʿUmar ʿAsaf, "Hata Nasuna Munazamat al-Tahrir wa Naqif u al-Inhiyar," *Al-Quds*, August 8, 1993.

40. Sabri Jiryis, "Hawar Min Nawʿi Aakhar Hawla: "Al-Hawar" wa al-Wahda al-Wataniyya," *Shuʾun Filastiniyya* 170–71 (May–June 1987): 4.

41. Ibid., 30.

42. BBC Radio in Arabic, August 28, 1993.

43. Migdal, *Strong Societies*, 11–12.

44. The United States and Australia are both examples of colonizing societies where immigrants overwhelmed the indigenous population and where the development of "stateness" was diffuse and slow. South Africa and Israel, on the other hand, are examples of "big" states characterized by large bureaucracies and high levels of fiscal extraction from members of the community even in prestate days, because of the unfavorable ratio between colonizers and colonized. Shafir, *Land, Labor*, 14–15.

45. Emile Sahliyeh, *In Search of Leadership: West Bank Politics since 1967* (Washington, D.C.: Brookings Institution, 1988), 7.

2. The PLO, Territorialization, and Palestinian State Formation

1. Wahid ʿAbd al-Majid, "Al-Intifada al-Filastiniyya: Al-Siaq al-Taʾarihi—Al-Quwa al-Faʿila—Al-Massar wal-Mustaqbal," *Al-Mustaqbal al-ʿArabi*, 11 (May 1988): 8–9.

2. Baghdad Radio, December 15, 1959, quoted in Moshe Shemesh, *The Palestinian Entity 1959–1974: Arab Politics and the PLO* (London: Frank Cass, 1988), 12.

3. Shemesh, *Palestinian Entity*, 8.

4. Yehoshafat Harkabi, ed., *Arav ve-Israel* 3–4 (Tel-Aviv: Am Oved, 1975), 18.

5. Shemesh, *Palestinian Entity*, 6.

6. Harkabi, *Arav re-Israel*, 18.

7. Shemesh, *Palestinian Entity*, 81–82.

8. Ibid., 83.

9. Ibid., 42.

10. John W. Amos II, *Palestinian Resistance: Organization of a Nationalist Movement* (New York: Pergamon Press, 1980), 48–55.

11. The biographical information was collated from Dr. Salih ʿAbd al-Jawad Salih, "Dirasa fi Qiyadat Harakat Fath," *Qadaya*, 4 (August 1990): 39–40; Ziad Abu ʿAmru, *Usul al-Harakat al-Siyasiya Fi Qutaʿ Ghazza 1948–1967* (Accre, Israel: Dar al-Aswar, 1947), 85–97. Abu ʿAmru attempts to demonstrate the important role played by the Gaza group (the remaining four emerged abroad) in the development of Fath, but appears to demonstrate its marginality. The Gaza group consists of 7 of a total of 23 founding members, but only 2 of them, Salah Khalaf and Salim al-Zaʿnun, are included among the 23 leaders of Fath in ʿAbd al-Salih's list of Fath leaders during its formative years. The remaining five, Fathi al-Baʿlawi, ʿAwni al-Qishawi, Majid Sadiq al-Mazini, Muhammad Ghassan al-Faranji, and Asʿad al-Siftawi did not carry much weight within the organization (p. 96). The two prominent leaders, to recall, had left Gaza by the time Fath was founded. Only one of them, Asʿad al-Siftawi, continued

to be prominent under the Israeli occupation. He was murdered in September 1993. Abu ʿAmru's findings then only serve to strengthen the claim that the Fath leadership was overwhelmingly based in the diaspora.

12. Ibid., 39. ʿAbd al-Salih reflects on the class transformation that took place, juxtaposing the leadership during the Mandate and early period of the PLO to the leadership after the Fath takeover. The former he portrays as belonging to the social elite, the latter members of the lower professional middle class. His findings have ramifications on state formation in two ways. Historically we see the eclipse of the upper strata first in the diaspora, and then in the act of territorializing PLO and Fath hegemony.

13. Cited in Abu ʿAmru, 33. Shemesh, *Palestinian Entity*, 48, gives seven as a figure but does not provide a source.

14. Moshe Shemesh, "The West Bank: Rise and Decline of Traditional Leadership, June 1967 to October 1973," *Middle Eastern Studies* 20.3 (July 1984): 288–92. Initially, some of these structures were very weak. Yezid Sayigh quotes one Arab Nationalist Movement cadre telling George Habash, "we have no organization in the West Bank or Jordan, everyone is in prison, and those who have escaped have lost confidence and distrust their colleagues." See his "Turning Defeat into Opportunity: The Palestinian Guerrillas after the June 1967 War," *Middle East Journal* 46.2 (Spring 1992): 247, 254.

15. ʿAbd Al-Jawad Salih, 21–22; Harkabi, *Arav ve-Israel* (3–4), 25, 84, 124, 129, 171.

16. Ibid.

17. Shemesh, *Palestinian Entity*, 42; Harkabi, *Israel-Arav* (3–4), 84.

18. See Phillip Matar, *The Mufti of Jerusalem—Al-Hajj Amin Husayni and the Palestine National Movement* (New York: Columbia University Press, 1988), 111.

19. See Shemesh, "The West Bank," 293.

20. Ehud Yaari, *Strike Terror: The Story of Fatah* (New York: Sabra, 1970), 150, quoted in Helena Cobban, *The Palestinian Liberation Organization: People, Power, and Politics* (Cambridge: Cambridge University Press, 1984) 37.

21. Ibid.

22. *Middle East Record-1968* (Jerusalem: Shiloah Institute for Middle Eastern and African Studies, Israeli University Press, 1973), 352.

23. Cobban, *Palestinian Liberation Organization*, 52.

24. Munir Shafiq "Limadha Yarfud al-Filastiniyyun Mashruᶜ al-Dawla fi al-Diffa al-Gharbiyya wa-Qitaᶜ Ghazza," *Shuʾun Filastiniyya* 7 (March 1972): 65.

25. For the most comprehensive series of articles in the English language by advocates of the Palestinian entity idea, see ʿAziz Shahada's articles in the magazine *The New Middle East*: "The Voice of the Forgotten Palestinian" (December 1968),

"Why Fatah Does Not Speak for Democratic Palestine" (March 1969), and "Must History Repeat Itself?" (January 1971). Over a hundred articles appeared on the subject in *Al-Quds* between the years 1969 and 1972.

26. *Al-Quds*, August 10, 1970.

27. In the 11th PNC, the number of representatives was set at 180 to enable more independents to attend, in keeping with the recommendations of the Palestinian Popular Congress held in April 1972 and attended by over 400 representatives. Harkabi, *Arav ve-Israel* (3–4), 204, and the same number was designated for the 12th PNC in 1974 (ibid., 216).

28. Avraham Diskin, "Trends in Intensity Variation of Palestinian Military Activity, 1967–1978," *Canadian Journal of Political Science* 16.2 (June/July 1983): 344.

29. *Annual Report—1974 -The Israel Police Force*, (Tel Aviv, 1975), 50; *Annual Report—1976—The Israel Police Force*, 24.

30. In a study of files of court cases of 492 subjects randomly selected from the Ramallah and Nablus districts and Gaza tried and sentenced for guerrilla and political activity against the authorities during the years 1976–1983, only 4 percent came from abroad, indicating that at least from the mid-seventies on the overwhelming percentage of those involved in resistance to the authorities came from the occupied territories themselves. See Eliezer Ben-Rafael, *Israel-Palestine: A Guerrilla Conflict in International Politics* (Westport, Conn.: Greenwood, 1984), 110.

31. Ann Lesch, *Political Perceptions of the Palestinians on the West Bank and the Gaza Strip* (Washington, D.C.: Middle East Institute, 1980), 72; see also "ʿArafat: The Results of the Elections in the [West] Bank: A Victory for the People," *Al-Quds*, April 28, 1976.

32. *Davar*, March 13, 1980.

33. *Al-Fajr*, April 17 and June 15, 1976.

34. *Al-Fajr*, July 31, 1976.

35. On the cooperation of the Jericho municipality with VWCs, see *Al-Fajr*, June 20, 1976; in Ramallah and Al-Bireh, see *Al-Fajr*, June 15, 1976; on a visit of the Ramallah VWC to Hebron and its meeting with Fahd Kawasmi, the mayor, see *Al-Fajr*, June 17, 1976.

36. Sabri Jiryis, "Hawar Min Nawʿin Ahirin Hawla "al-Hawar" wa "al-Wahda al-Wataniyya," *Shuʾun Filastiniyya* 170–71 (May–June 1987): 14.

37. Jamil Hilal, "Lahzat Hasima fi-Taʾarikh al-Nidal al-Watani al-Filastini," *Al-Fikr al-Dimuqrati* 4 (Winter 1988): 4–13, esp. 4–7. Hilal is a member of long standing of the central committee of the DFLP and presently serves as spokesman of the PLO.

38. Rashid Khalidi, *Under Seige: PLO Decision Making during the 1982 War* (New York: Columbia University Press, 1986), 28–36, 136–43.

39. See Rashid Khalidi, "The Palestinians in Lebanon: Social Repercussions of Israel's Invasion," *Middle East Journal* 38.2 (Spring 1984): 255–66.

40. Baruch Kimmerling and Joel S. Migdal, *The Palestinians: The Making of a People* (New York: The Free Press, 1993), 223.

41. Khalidi, *Under Siege*, 59.

42. Adam Zagorin, "Auditing the PLO," in Norton and Greenberg, eds., *The International Relations of the Palestine Liberation Organization*, 197–98. Cited in Kimmerling and Migdal, *Palestinians*, 233.

43. Ibid.

44. Jiryis, *Shu'un Filastiniyya* 170–71 (May–June 1987): 14, 25.

45. Mustafa ʿAbd al-Aziz Marsi, *Al-ʿArab fi Muftaraq al Tariq: Bayna Darurat Tajdid al-Mahsruʿ al-Qawmi wa-Mahatir al-Mashruʿ al-Sharq al-Awsati* (Cairo: al-Shuruq, 1995), 9.

46. One of the most longstanding debates in the social sciences is the relationship between ideas (both as ideological and cultural constructs) and praxis, known in the political science nomenclature as the debate between idealism and structuralism. For a concise and cogent argument for a middle ground approach between structuralism and idealism adopted in this work, see Robert H. Jackson, *Quasi-States: Sovereignty, International Relations, and the Third World* (Cambridge: Cambridge University Press, 1990), 6–7.

47. My analysis again differs widely from conclusions drawn by Sadik J. Al-ʿAzm in his "Palestinian Zionism," *Die Welt des Islams* 28 (1988): 97. It is especially interesting that he likens Arafat to Weizmann when the comparison should be made to Ben-Gurion.

48. For an excellent example of the importance of return, not functional institution-building redemption, see, Ali Tibawi, "Visions of Return: The Palestinian Refugees in Arabic Poetry and Art," *Middle East Journal* 17.5 (1963): 507–26.

49. See, for example, the write-up on the Shabiba Youth Committee for Social Work in the Balata Refugee Camp in Nablus, *Al-Bayadir al-Siyassi*, September 17, 1983. The camp is described as "the [refugee] camp that avenges the honor of Tal-al-Zaʿtar . . . the camp which is surrounded by the mountain of fire . . . the camp of martyrs . . . "

50. Gerard Chailand, *The Palestinian Resistance* (Harmonsworth, England: Penguin Books, 1972), 10; Yehoshufat Harkabi, *Fedayeen Action and Arab Strategy* (London: Institute for Strategic Studies, 1968), 18–19.

51. Y. Harkabi, *Palestinians and Israel* (Jerusalem: Keter, 1974), 108–9.

52. For a detailed discussion, see Alain Gresh, *The Quest Within: Towards a Palestinian State* (London: Zed Books, 1985); see also Dr. Nabil Shaʿth, "Filastin al-Ghad," *Shu'un Filastiniya* 2 (May 1971): 5–23; ʿIsam Sakhnini's "Al-Kiyan al-Filastini," *Shu'un Filastiniyya* 41–42 (1975): 46–74; Sabri Jiryis, "Al-Majlis al-Watani al-Filastini, Nahwa Dawla Filastiniyya Mustaqilla," *Shu'un Filastiniyya* 66 (1977): 18–29. None of these articles discuss the state formation process but rather emphasize either the broad characteristics of the future regime principally in relation to the

Jewish population or the political history of the idea of statehood as it developed in PLO ideology and policies. The only exception is Samir ʿAyub's analysis of ʿIsi Shuʿaybi's book *Al-Kiyaniyya al-Filastiniyya: Al-Waʿi al-Thati wal-Tatawwur al-Muʾassasati 1947–1977* in *Shuʾun Filastiniyya* 102 (1979): 138–48. Shuʿaybi is the only diaspora thinker who clearly perceived the need to develop a central territorial political authority and analyzed its progressions and setbacks.

53. Naseer H. Aruri, *Jordan: A Study in Political Development (1921–1965)* (The Hague: Martinus Nijhoff, 1972), 67.

54. The national urban rate of growth was 25.3 percent between 1952 and 1961. Jerusalem's stood at 24.4 percent. Ibid., 28.

55. *IBRD, The Economic Development of Jordan* (Baltimore: Johns Hopkins University Press, 1957), 237.

56. Michael P. Mazur, *Economic Growth and Development of Jordan* (Boulder, Colo.: Westview Press, 1979), 8–9.

57. Amnon Cohen, *Political Parties in the West Bank under the Jordanian Regime, 1948–1967* (Ithaca, N.Y.: Cornell University Press, 1982), 30–31.

58. Robert Bachi, *The Population of Israel* (Jerusalem: Institute of Contemporary Jewry, Hebrew University of Jerusalem, 1974), table 18–5, p. 333.

59. Daniel Rubinstein, "The Jerusalem Municipality under the Ottomans, British, and Jordanians," in Joel L. Kramer, ed., *Jerusalem: Problems and Prospects* (New York: Praeger Publishers, 1980), 84.

60. Ibid. Furthermore, in 1965, the regime closed down four newspapers in East Jerusalem, including Filastin, dealing a blow to both Palestinian state building and the retention of an identity around which it could crystallize. *Middle East Record—1967*, vol. 3 (Tel Aviv: Israel Universities Press, 1971), 396.

61. Rubinstein, "Jerusalem Municipality," 82.

62. *Al-Quds*, February 9, 1969.

63. David Farchi, "HaHaluka haAdministrativit shel Yehuda veShomron," in Israel Raphaeli, ed., *Eser Shnot Shilton be Yehuda veShomron*, (Jerusalem: Magnes, 1980), 186.

64. Ibid., 187.

65. Rachel Simon, *Agudot veMohadonim baGada haMaaravit be Tequfat haShilton haHashemi* (Jerusalem: HaMachon leLimudei Asia veAfrica, 1974), 14.

66. Ibid., 15–16.

67. Ibid., 189. On the disturbances in Nablus, see Shlomo Gazit, *Hamakel veHagezer* (Tel Aviv: Shrafim, 1985), 179.

68. Farchi, *Ha Haluka*, 190.

69. Meron Benvinisti and Shlomo Khayat, *The West Bank Data Atlas* (Jerusalem: The West Bank Data Project, 1988), 36.

70. In 1984, urban inhabitants comprised the following percentages of the total population in states in the area: Israel, 88%; Iraq, 67%; Jordan, 55%; Lebanon, 80%; Syria, 49%. See Gerald Black, John Dewdney, and Jonathan Mitchell, *The Cambridge Atlas of the Middle East and North Africa* (Cambridge: Cambridge University Press, 1987), 53.

71. Benvinisti and Khayat, *West Bank Data Atlas*, 30.

72. Moshe Braver, *"HaKav haYarok" keGvul BeYehuda uveShomron:—Hearcha Geographit ke Rekqa le Shinuyim ve Tikkunim* (Tel Aviv: Tel Aviv University Research Project for Peace, 1980), 6, 24–25.

73. During the years 1961–67, while the population declined by 0.65% annually, building space increased by 3.70% annually as emigrants invested in their hometown. See Amnon Shinar, "Shchem: Hitpatchut haShetach haBanui beIr Aravit," in Avshalom Shmueli, David Grosman, Rehavam Zeevi, eds., *Yehuda veShomron: Prakim beGeographia* (Tel Aviv: Cnaan, 1977), 277.

74. Salim Tamari, "Building Other People's Homes," *Journal of Palestine Studies* 2.11 (Autumn 1981): 40.

75. Don Peretz, *Palestinian Refugees and the Middle East Peace Process* (Washington, D.C.: United States Institute of Peace Press, 1993), table 1. Figure includes budget for Extraordinary Measures in Lebanon and the Occupied Territories. The 1993 budget of the civil administration appeared in *Ha᾿aretz*, September 2, 1993. The civil administration in the past has reported its budgets erratically, hence the need to compare different years.

76. Meron Benvinisti, *US Government Funded Projects in the West Bank and Gaza (1977–1983) (Palestinian Sector)*, working paper no. 13, The West Bank Data Project, 1984, pp. 10–11.

77. See remarks by Hebron mayor Fahd Qawasmi in Leopold Yehuda Laufer, *U.S. Aid to the West Bank and Gaza: Policy Dilemmas* (Jerusalem: Leonard Davis Institute for International Relations, Policy Studies No. 12, May 1985), 15. Qawasmi was a member of the National Guidance Committee that led the political protest against the Camp David peace process.

3. Territorializing the PLO

1. On an elaboration of different mixes of repression and coaptation in the relationship between regime and opposition, see Charles Tilly, *From Mobilization to Revolution* (Reading, Mass.: Addison-Wesley, 1978), 6–8.

2. Shaul Mishal, "Ha Konflikt Bayn haGada haMaaravit laMizrahit beTkufat haShilton haYardeni veHashlachotav alDfusay haMimshal vehaMinhal baGada

haMaaravit (1949–1967)," (Ph.D. diss. Hebrew University, Jerusalem, 1972), 4–5.

3. The analysis is based heavily on rational actor theory. See Mark Irving Lichbach, *The Rebel's Dilemma* (Ann Arbor: University of Michigan Press, 1996), chapter 2 "Markets"; Michael Taylor, "Rationality and Revolutionary Collective Action," in Michael Taylor, ed., *Rationality and Revolution* (Cambridge: Cambridge University Press, 1988).

4. Munir Shafiq distinguishes between five subgroups among the advocates of the Palestinian entity.

1. A call for a Palestinian state in the West Bank and Gaza based on the partition plan independent of Jordan within a possible solution associated with Hamdi al-Taji al-Faruqi
2. ʿAziz Shahada's suggestion that the occupied territories be placed under UN trusteeship for five years and then allow the public by popular referendum to decide their fate
3. Muhammad ʿAli al-Jaʿbari's proposal to place occupied territories including Arab Jerusalem under protectorate of a neutral country for five years and then conduct a referendum
4. Hamdi Kanʿan's suggestion that a Palestinian state be formed which will then evolve into a confederacy with Jordan contingent on the democratization of the latter
5. A group of youth with plans of their own to replace a traditional leadership. Many appeared in the local election lists.

Munir Shafiq, "Limadha Yarfudun al-Filastiniyyun Mashruʿ al-Dawla fi al-Diffa al-Gharbiyya wa-Qutaʿ Ghazza," *Shuʾun Filastiniyya* 7 (March, 1972): 65–79.

5. See, for example, Muhammad Qarsh, "Ittihad al-Jamʿiyin: Hasan al-Waqt li-Tashkilihi," *Al-Fajr*, June 6, 1972; rejoinder of Salim Tamari, July 1, 1972; and another article by Qarsh on job creation on September 9, 1972.

6. *Al-Quds*, May 11, 1969, August 7, 1969; and June 23, 1970. See articles by Muhammad Abu Shilbaya, *Al-Quds*, August 10, 1970, and August 24, 1971. At least 100 articles supporting the Palestinian entity idea appeared in the newspaper between the years 1968–72.

7. See, for example ʿAziz Shahada's article "Al-Kiyan al-Filastini," *Al-Quds*, December 6, 1968; articles by Muhammad Abu Shilbaya, December 12 19, 1968, and May 16, 1969.

8. *Al-Quds*, March 13, 1969.

9. *Al-Difaʿ*, June 1, 1969.

10. *Al-Quds*, March 13, 1969.

11. *Al-Quds*, August 1, 1971.

12. *Al-Quds*, November 27, 1971.

13. Shemesh, "The West Bank," 312.

14. *Al-Quds*, March 21, 1972.

15. *Al-Quds*, March 10, 1970, and March 17, 1970.

16. See *Al-Quds*, March 24, 1970, and October 24, 1970. At the third meeting of the committee for public affairs, al-Ja^cbari denied that he was aiming at achieving self-determination for Palestinians in the occupied territories.

17. Muhammad Abu Shilbaya, perhaps the most outspoken and prolific advocate of the Palestinian entity, argued that although proponents of the idea of entity comprised the majority in that period, they lacked "leadership, organization and money." *Al-Anba*, December 19, 1972.

18. Shemesh, "The West Bank," 312.

19. *Al-Quds*, April 30, 1972.

20. *Ha^ɔaretz*, October 14, 1972.

21. *Al-Fajr*, November 25, 1972; on his inability to defend the Ibrahimi mosque from settler encroachment, see *Al-Fajr*, September 15, 1972.

22. See, for example, Jamil Hamad's "Wait a Minute: This is a Plot," *Al-Fajr*, August 6, 1972.

23. See ʿAdil Samra's articles on cooperatives in *al-Fajr*, July 7, 8, 9, 1974: Salim Tamari's retrospective comments on his "naive" institution-building conception in *Birzeit Research Review* 4 (Spring 1986): 79; see also Muhammad al-Yunis, "Tariq al-Khilas," *Al-Fajr*, May 26, 1973.

24. *Al-Fajr*, May 19, 1972. See, for example, the article by Aziz Shahada in which he emphasizes the representatives' unsuitability to represent the population on the grounds that only one-fourth of the urban adult population chose them.

25. Shemesh, "The West Bank," 309.

26. A. D. Smith, *Nationalist Movements* (London: Macmillan, 1976), 5.

27. *Al-Quds*, August 10, 1971.

28. Text of communiqué appears in *Arav ve-Israel*, 91–92.

29. *Al-Quds*, June 15, 1970, and August 19, 1970. See the decisions of the seventh session of the Palestinian National Council from late May to mid-June in which the idea of an entity is condemned and armed struggle is again emphasized as the only means to liberation, in *Al-Quds*, April 27, 1971.

30. *MERIP Report* 25 (February 1974): 22–23.

31. "Al-Jabha al-Wataniyya al-Filastiniyya fi al-Manatiq al-Muhtalla wa-Hamlat al-Iʿtiqalat Didaha," *Shuʾun Filastiniyya* 38 (October 1974): 207–11.

32. *Al-Fajr*, November 8, 1975.

33. On the establishment of the first student council in an UNRWA postsecondary institution, see *Al-Fajr*, June 10, 1975; in an article by Sami Husayn, July 1, 1976, a comparison is made between the mobilizing trips in the Zionist school system compared to the leisure parties in the schools of the West Bank; also see Muhammad Yunis's article on the need to build institutions toward the establishment of the state in *Al-Fajr*, May 26, 1973.

34. See Galia Golan, *The Soviet Union and the PLO* (New York: Praeger, 1980), 165–67; Ibrahim Daqqaq, "Back to Square One: A Study in the Reemergence if the Palestinian Identity in the West Bank 1967–1980," in Alexander Schölch ed. *Palestinians Over the Green Line: Studies in the Relations Between Palestinians on Both Sides of the 1949 Armistice Line Since 1949* (London: Ithaca Press, 1983), 78–80. Daqqaq was for a long time the president of the Union of Engineering Professions in the West Bank and one of the founding members of the Council of Higher Education. He was well known as a man of the left.

35. Interview with Hana Siniora, January 5, 1986.

36. Ghazzi al-Khalili, "Raʾi: Baʿda al-Intikhabat: Ma Huwa al-Mawqif," *Shuʾun Filastiniyya* 58 (June 1976): 72.

37. *Al-Fajr*, May 22, 1976; a similar call was issued on April 29, 1976, as well. The mayors also performed roles as traditional conciliators, see *Al-Fajr*, June 28, 1976, and April 9, 1978.

38. Some 1,640 files were opened against violators against the peace in 1974, rising to 2,107 in 1975, declining to 1,982 in 1976 and 1,925 in 1977. See *Annual Report—1974—The Israel Police Force* (Tel Aviv, 1975), 50; *Annual Report—1976—The Israel Police Force*, 24; *Annual Report—1976—The Israel Police Force*, 36.

39. A good example of such cooperation is Bassam al-Shakʿa's meeting with the military commander of the area in the middle of the Litani operation during which the Israeli army attacked head on PLO positions in Lebanon. See *Al-Fajr*, March 20, 1978.

40. *Davar*, May 9, 1980.

41. For a comprehensive overview of the use of these funds by the Jordanian-PLO Joint Committee, see Dr. Fuad Basisu, "Al-Tharwa al-Naftia wal-Musahama al-Qawmiyya fi Daʿam al-Sumud al-Filastini fi al-Aradi al-Muhtalla," *Samid al-Iqtisadi* 7.56 (July/August 1985): 8–23.

42. Daqqaq, "Back to Square One," 78–80.

43. See, ʿAbd al-Jawad Salih, *Al-Hadaf*, March 30, 1981, p. 15.

44. Walid Salim, "Dirasat Awaliyya fi Bahth Barnamij al-Lajna al-Mushtaraka," *Al-ʿAhd* 24 (September 1984): 1.

45. *Al-Hadaf*, September 22, 1981, p. 18.

46. *Al-Hadaf*, May 12, 1979; December 19, 1981; *Al-Hurriyya*, April 26, 1982.

47. For a powerful case against the subordination of the territories by the diaspora PLO for its own political purposes by a senior leftist politician, see Jamil Hilal, "Lahazat Hasima fi-Ta᾿rikh al-Nidal al-Watani al-Filastini," *Al-Fikr al-Dimuqrati* 4 (Winter 1988): 4–13, esp. 4–7. (Hilal is a member of long standing of the central committee of the DFLP and presently serves as spokesman of the PLO.)

48. *Shu᾿un Filastiniyya* 52 (December 1975): 234.

49. Galia Golan, *The Soviet Union and the PLO* (New York: Praeger, 1980), 108–10.

50. *Al-Hadaf*, December 9, 1979.

51. *Al-Taliʿa*, July 17, 1982.

52. For a more detailed account of the leftist unions and youth volunteer committees, see chapter 6 in Hillel Frisch, "Binui Mosdot baShtachim 1967–1985" (Ph.D. diss., Hebrew University of Jerusalem, 1989), 197–224.

53. *Al-Taliʿa*, July 24, 1980.

54. *Al-Hurriyya*, July 16, 1979; see also Rita Giacaman, "Palestinian Women and Development in the Occupied West Bank," *Palestine Cultural Week*, November 28–December 1, 1983 (stencil), p. 17.

55. Mustafa Salama, "Al-Tabaqa al-ʿAmila al-Filastiniyya fi al-Diffa wal-Qitaʿ," *al-Hurriyya*, May 7, 1978, pp. 48–55.

56. Hillel Frisch, *Stagnation and Frontier: Arab and Jewish Industry in the West Bank* (Jerusalem: The West Bank Data Project, 1983), 54–55.

57. Khalil Mahshi and Ramzi Rihan, "Education: Elementary and Secondary," in Emile A. Nakhleh, ed., *A Palestinian Agenda in the West Bank* (Washington, D.C.: American Enterprise Institute, 1979), 47; Ihsan ʿAtiyya, Samir Jibril and Jamal Talab, *Nashra Ihsa᾿iyya ʿan al-Manatiq al-ʿArabiyya al Muhtalla-Haqa᾿iq wa Arkam*, (Jerusalem: Al-Jamʿiyya lil-Dirasat al-ʿArabiyya, 1985), 155, 157.

58. *Statistical Abstract of Israel—1971* (No. 22), p. 647; *Statistical Abstract of Israel–1976* (No. 27), p. 729.

59. Computed from data in *Statistical Abstract of Israel—1985* (No. 36), p. 724.

60. Joshua D. Angrist, "Wages and Employment in the West Bank and Gaza Strip, 1981–1991," The Hebrew University of Jerusalem, June 1992, unpublished ms, pp. 13–14.

61. Figures from Frisch, "Binui Mosdot Filistinaim," table 2, p. 24.

62. Abdel-Khalek and Robert Tignor, "Introduction," in Gouda Abdel-Khalek and Robert Tignor, eds., *The Political Economy of Income Distribution in Developing Countries* (London: Holmes and Meier, 1982), 11–12; see also N. Gemell, "The Growth of Employment in Services in Egypt, 1960–75," *The Developing Economies* 23.1 (1985): 56; in Syria, over 50 percent of the university-educated work in the

public sector. Computed from *Al-Jumhuriyya al-Arabiyya al-Suriyya—1987* (Damascus: Riyasat Majlis al-Wuzara, al-Maktab al-Markazi lil-Ihsa$^{\supset}$, June 1986), 82–83, 108.

63. See Walid Salim, "Muqaddamat Awliyya li-Dirasat Mashari$^{\supset}$ al-Lajna al-Mushtaraka," *Al-$^{\supset}$Ahd*, September 1, 1984, pp. 6–8.

64. Munir Ahmad ʿAwad, "Al-Ta^{c}lim al-ʿAli fi al-Diffa al-Gharbiyya wa Qita^{c} Ghazza-Tatawwuruhu wa Asasuhu," *Al-Bayadir al-Siyasi*, June 11, 1983, pp. 33–34.

65. On the Shabiba victory in the first elections ever held in the Modern Community Colleges, see *Al-Fajr*, July 17, 1984, August 20, 1984; in al-Ibrahimiyya College, see *Al-Shira^{c}*, March 1, 1983, p. 37.

66. *Al-Fajr*, December 7, 1985.

67. *Al-Fajr*, January 8, 1985.

68. From questionnaires of a representative sample of 271 students in the university in 1981, only four students (1.5%) were Christian. See H. Fahmi Masri, "A Study of the Student Personnel Program of Ah-Najah National University-Nablus" (Ph.D. diss., Ann Arbor, Mich.: University Microfilms, 1983), 113.

69. *Al-Fajr*, December 16, 1985.

70. Interview with Musa Darwish, in charge of public relations, and a senior official, August 8, 1986.

71. On the first Shabiba-led victory at Birzeit University, see *Al-Fajr*, December 19, 1982. In al-Najah, the Shabiba had yet to be identified as such but both the president and vice-president of the winning coalition, ʿAdnan Damiri and Samir al-ʿAtili, were founders of the movement in the university. See *Al-ʿAwda*, December 11, 1982, pp. 44–45; the same situation prevailed at Hebron University, a former fundamentalist stronghold. See *Al-Bayadir al-Siyasi*, January 15, 1983, p. 38.

72. *Al-Fajr*, July 27, 1981; *Al-Bayadir al-Siyasi*, November 15, 1982.

73. Some of the prominent students who were released prisoners were Shabiba activist Ghassan ʿAli al- Masri, who was released in 1979, only to be elected to the al-Najah University Student Council a year later (*Ma$^{\supset}$ariv*, January 12, 1988); ʿAdnan Damiri; Ahmad al-Diq; and Ahmad Jabr Sulayman, imprisoned several times for terrorist activity as a member of DFLP and then activist at Bethlehem University. *Ha$^{\supset}$aretz*, April 12, 1988.

74. *Annual Report—1974—The Israel Police* (Tel Aviv, 1975), 50; *Annual Report—1976—The Israel Police*, 24.

75. Out of a random sample of 492 Palestinians tried by Israeli military tribunals between 1978 and 1983 for guerrilla activities, only 15 percent were sentenced to three years or more, as "most were caught at an early stage of involvement in the underground." Quoted in Eliezer Ben-Rafael, *Israel-Palestine: A Guerrilla Conflict in International Politics*, (Westport, Conn.: Greenwood Press), 111.

76. Ibrahim Muhammad Sha^{c}aban, *Al-Intifada al-Filastiniyya fi ʿAmiha al-Awwal* (Jerusalem: n.p., 1989), 207–20.

77. Moshe Ma^{c}oz, *Palestinian Leadership on the West Bank: The Changing Role of the Arab Mayors under Jordan and Israel* (London: Frank Cass, 1984), 199.

78. *Amnesty International Report on Restriction Orders in Israel and the Occupied Territories* (New York: Amnesty International, October 19, 1982), 51.

79. Ibid.

80. Amnon Cohen, "The Changing Patterns of West Bank Politics," *Jerusalem Quarterly*, Fall 1977, 111.

81. *Arav ve Israel* (3–4), 216, 218. Three of these personalities, former al-Bireh mayor ʿAbd al-Jawad Salih, ʿAbd al-Muhsin Abu Mayzar, a Jerusalem lawyer and member of the Supreme Muslim Council, and Walid Qamhawi were rewarded for leading the Palestinian National Front. *MERIP Report* 25 (February 1974): 22–23.

82. *Middle East Contemporary Survey—1987*, vol. 11 (Boulder, Colo.: Westview Press, 1989), 210–11.

83. *Shu$^{\supset}$un Filastiniyya* 191 (February 1989): 103.

84. Tunis Domestic Radio, August 9, 1989. FBIS-NES 89-152, August 9, 1989, 4; Baghdad Voice of the PLO, August 9, 1989. FBIS-NES 89-153, August 10, 1989, 4.

85. Haniya was former editor of *al-Sha^{c}b* while Shahin, a former prisoner, was a Fath commander in Gaza in the early 1980s and founder of the Shabiba movement there. Sana^{c}a-Voice of Palestine Radio, August 11, 1989. FBIS-NES 89-155, August 14, 1989, p. 4.

86. Guy Bechor, *Lexicon Ashaf* (Tel Aviv: Misrad Habitachon, 1991), 120–21.

87. *The Jerusalem Post*, August 7, 1988.

88. *Ha$^{\supset}$aretz*, November 26, 1989.

89. *Al-Nahar*, August 26, 1988.

90. This is not to say that organizational leadership was not represented in this list. Many—such as Shahir Sa^{c}ad, the secretary general of the Fath, who supported Federation of Labor Unions in the West Bank; Muharram Barghuthi, the head of the Communist Voluntary Work Committees; and Zuhayra Kamal of the DFLP's Women Action Committees—were designated as members of the proposed provisional council, but these cannot be regarded as top leadership.

91. Rab^{c}i al-Madhum, "Al-Intikhabat: Madiyyan wa Hadiran," *Shu$^{\supset}$un Filastiniyya*, no. 186 (September 1988): 17–18.

4. Education and State Building

1. *Al-Fajr*, October 7, 1972. Aziz Shahada discusses the topic of the proposed university.

2. *Ma^cariv*, April 2, 1971.

3. *Ma^cariv*, April 2, 1971.

4. *Al-Quds*, April 5, 1971. See article by Suni al-Bitar that stated that the conference would establish a permanent council for matters concerning education in cities and villages and address the establishment of a Palestinian national university.

5. *Al-Quds*, April 19, 1971.

6. See *Al-Quds*, July 31, 1971.

7. *Al-Anba*, October 14, 1972.

8. *Al-Anba*, September 8, 1972; September 29, 1972.

9. *Al-Quds*, June 12, 1972.

10. *Al-Quds*, September 22, 1972.

11. *Al-Quds*, December 11, 1981.

12. *Al-Quds*, September 24, 1972.

13. *Al-Fajr*, June 19, 1972.

14. *Al-Quds*, May 9, 1972.

15. *Al-Quds*, October 29, 1972.

16. *Al-Quds*, October 1, 1972.

17. *Al-Quds*, September 26, 1972.

18. Ibid.

19. *Al-Quds*, October 1, 1972.

20. *Al-Fajr*, October 5, 1972.

21. *Al-Quds*, October 17, 1972; *Al-Anba*, October 17, 1972.

22. *Al-Anba*, September 15, 1972.

23. *Al-Quds*, October 23, 1972.

24. Ibid.

25. Ibid.

26. *Al-Quds*, October 30, 1972.

27. "Jami^cat Bayt-Lahm: Ma Laha wa Ma ^cAlayha," *Shu'un Filastiniyya* 50/51 (October/November 1975): 410; *Shu'un Filastiniyya* 15 (November 1972): 233–34.

28. For the preliminary development of this idea, see Ibrahim Abu Nab, "Al-Jamiʿa al-Filastiniyya al-Muqtaraha . . . Ila ʿAyna Wasalat?" *Shuʾun Filastiniyya* 13 (June 1972): 226–29; on the participation of UNESCO, see Dr. Hisham al-Khatib, "Nadwa: Al-Jamiʿa al-Shaʿbiyya al-Maftuha," *Shuʾun Filastiniyya* 100 (March 1980): 141–46; on the curriculum of this university, see "Hiwar maʿa Duktur Ibrahim Abu Lughod hawla al-Jamiʿa al-Filastiniyya al-Maftuha," *Shuʾun Filastiniyya* 101 (April 1980): 21–33.

29. *Al-Quds*, October 5, 1972.

30. The term is taken from Hanna Nasir, "Jamiʿa Arabiyya fi Filastin: Dirasa Awwaliyya," *Shuʾun Filastiniyya* 55 (March 1976): 144.

31. Ibrahim Daqqaq, "Back to Square One," p. 76.

32. *Al-Fajr*, December 18, 1977.

33. Ibid.

34. Ibid.

35. ʿAbd al-Jawad Salih, *Al-Mushkilat al-Thatiyya li-Muʾasasat al-Taʿlim al-ʿAli fi al-Diffa wa Qitaʿ Ghazza* (Nicosia, Cyprus: Markaz al-Quds liʾl-Ibhath, 1982), 108.

36. Ibid., 138.

37. Al-Ard al-Muhtalla: Taqrir ʿan Maʿahid al-Taʿlim al-ʿAli fi al-Diffa al-Gharbiyya," *Shuʾun Filastiniyya*, 13 (September 1972): 231.

38. *Al-Nahar*, July 18, 1991.

39. Beyond the CHE's oversight, but certainly important in other respects, were institutions of higher learning that the military administration inherited from the Jordanian government. These consisted of a teachers college in Ramallah, agricultural institutes in Tulqarem and al-ʿArub, and two teachers colleges in Gaza. Salih, *Al-Mushkilat al-Thatiyya*, 99.

40. Samuel P. Huntington, *Political Order in Changing Societies* (New Haven, Conn.: Yale University Press, 1968), 11.

41. Salih, *Al-Mushkilat al-Thatiyya*, 99.

42. Daqqaq, "Back to Square One," 74.

43. Salih, *Al-Mushkilat al-Thatiyya*, 99.

44. *Al-Fajr*, October 22, 1977, October 25, 1977, October 28, 1977, and October 30, 1977; see *Al-Fajr*, October 26, 1977, and October 29, 1977 which contain the declarations of the Academic Council of Birzeit University declaring that henceforth Arabic will be the major teaching language in Birzeit University.

45. ʿAdil Samara, *Al-Fajr*, July 4, 1975. Samara analyzes the university student council's demand for a course on Palestinian history and politics, and its desire to coordinate activities with the Bir Zeit student council. The level of politicization in the university in the period after the establishment of the Council for Higher Education

is reflected in the ejection of Bethlehem mayor Elias Freij from the university by students at the opening of the new library to which he had been invited to speak by the university authorities. *Al-Fajr*, April 30, 1978.

46. Salih, *Al-Mushkilat al-Thatiyya*, appendix.

47. *Al-Fajr*, December 18, 1977.

48. *Al-Fajr*, June 2, 1978.

49. Ibid.

50. Salih, *Al-Mushkilat al-Thatiyya*, 102 (fn. 2).

51. *Al-Fajr*, July 14, 1979.

52. In 1983–84, 58.2 percent of students of higher education in Jordan studied in two year junior colleges. *The Hashemite Kingdom of Jordan: The Statistical Yearbook 1983/84* (n.p., n.d.).

53. *Al-Quds*, November 15, 1979.

54. *Al-Fajr*, April 7, 1979.

55. *Al-Fajr*, April 7, 1979, April 8, 1979, April 10, 1979, April 21, 1979, April 22, 1979; *Al-Quds*, April 7, 1979.

56. *Al-Fajr*, December 20, 1979.

57. Ibid.

58. Salih, *Al-Mushkilat al-Thatiyya*, 173–75.

59. Ibid., 137, and n. 112.

60. *Al-Quds*, February 16, 1980; an article in *Al-Fajr* (February 20, 1980) even details the changes that would occur.

61. *Al-Quds*, February 21, 1980, and February 22, 1980.

62. *Al-Quds*, February 28, 1980.

63. *Al-Fajr*, March 1, 1980.

64. *Al-Fajr*, March 12, 1980.

65. *Al-Quds*, February 26, 1980.

66. *Al-Quds*, February 26, 1980; *Al-Fajr*, February 26, 1980; *Al-Anba*, February 26, 1980.

67. *Al-Quds*, March 2, March 3, 1980.

68. See announcement by al-Jam[c]iyya al-Islamiyya in *Al-Quds*, March 5, 1980; Committee of the Great Mosque in Nusayrat (Refugee Camp), *Al-Quds*, March 8, 1980.

69. *Al-Quds*, March 12, 1980.

70. *Al-Quds*, March 16, 1980.

71. *Al-Quds*, March 24, 1980. See on same day Hafiz Tuqan's attacks on the composition of the council on the grounds that neither the CHE nor the Baramki proposal to revise it, remedied the unfair geographic distribution of its membership or more important, the small number of educators. These criticisms parallel those he voiced against the Palestinian Arab University scheme. Note the protest of the mayors of Bethlehem, Tulkarem, Salfit, and Qalqilya, and of the Council for Higher Education in *Al-Quds*, March 6, 1980.

72. *Al-Quds*, March 20, 1980.

73. *Al-Quds*, April 10, 1980.

74. Salih, *Al-Mushkilat al-Thatiyya*, 105.

75. Interview with Ibrahim Abu Sitta, *Al-Fajr*, May 31, 1987. Abu Sitta was among the founders of the PLO and responsible for training programs for university graduates in Gaza in 1980–81 that were funded by the Jordanian-Palestinian Committee. In the interview he complains of the aid package to the Islamic University by parties in the PLO despite its antinationalism and refusal to cooperate with the Council for Higher Education during a period of years. Thus, he attacks the behavior of Muhammad Saqr, president of the university, exiled in 1982, and his assistant in Gaza, Acting President Shaykh Muhammad Siam, both of whom were known for their affiliation to the Muslim Brotherhood. The ousted president, Riad al-Agha, had declared during his brief tenure in office his willingness to abide by CHE decisions. See interview, *Al-Quds*, May 13, 1981.

76. *Al-Fajr*, March 20, 1980.

77. Munir Ahmad ʿUd, *Nashra Ihsaʾiyya ʿan al-Taʿlim fi al-Diffa al-Gharbiyya wa Qitaʿ Ghazza* (Nablus: Jamiʿat al-Najah al-Wataniyya, Markaz al-Dirasat al-Rifiyya wa Jamʿiyyat al-Dirasat al-ʿArabiyya, n.d.), 26.

78. At least eight other faculty members took part in the rebellion, and school faculty and students also figured prominently in the reports of the Jordanian intelligence services. See Yehoshua Porath, *The Palestinian Arab Nationalist Movement, 1929–1939* (London: Frank Cass, 1977), 235, 248.

79. *Al-Fajr*, October 11, 1977.

80. *Al-Fajr*, September 25, 1978.

81. *Al-Fajr*, April 4, 1978.

82. *Al-Fajr*, August 2, 1978. See also *Al-Quds*, April 13, 1980, on the president of the university's meetings with his colleague from the University of Jordan and with senior officials in the Jordanian Ministry of Education with regard to the development of the university.

83. *Al-Fajr*, May 23, 1978.

84. *Al-Fajr*, October 4, 1978.

85. *Al-Fajr*, November 8, 1978.

86. *Al-Fajr*, June 3, 1979.

87. *Al-Fajr*, November 9, 1978.

88. See, for example, details on the visit of the student council of the theological college and religious tenets in *Al-Quds*, February 13, 1980. On ties with the Shari^ca college in Hebron, see *Al-Quds*, May 14, 1980.

89. *Al-Tali^ca*, February 15, 1979.

90. *Al-Fajr*, April 20, 1980.

91. Ibid.

92. *Al-Quds*, May 4, 1980.

93. *Al-Fajr*, May 14, 1980.

94. *Al-Fajr*, May 21, 1980.

95. *Al-Fajr*, May 20, 1980.

96. *Al-Quds*, June 20, 1980.

97. *Al-Quds*, June 24, 1980.

98. *Al-Quds*, June 21, 1980. Interview on May 1, 1988, with Dr. Sulayman Bashir, a member of the university staff during that period and vice-president of the university in 1984–85.

99. *Al-Quds*, July 1, 1980.

100. *Al-Fajr*, July 4, 1980.

101. *Al-Quds*, July 1, 1980.

102. *Al-Fajr*, July 3, 1980.

103. *Al-Fajr*, July 4, 1980.

104. The faculty and administrative employee unions at Birzeit University, each a distinct body, strongly supported the strike. Although both unions had refrained from integrating into the al-Najah union, they were represented at the emergency meeting by their chairmen, one of whom was Sari Nusseibeh.

105. *Al-Quds*, July 8, 1980.

106. *Al-Fajr*, July 15, 1980.

107. *Al-Fajr*, August 25, 1980.

108. *Al-Fajr*, July 22, 1980.

109. *Al-Fajr*, September 23, 1980.

110. See "Report on Higher Education and the Council for Higher Education in the Occupied Territories," March 12, 1981, by Muhammad al-Hallaj, the director of

the Council for Higher Education. This report appears in Salah's book, *Al-Mushkilat al-Thatiyya*, 176–79.

111. *Al-Fajr*, July 1, 1981.

112. Declaration by the student council of al-Najah National University, June 27, 1981, noted in Salih, *Al-Mushkilat al-Thatiyya*, 85 (n. 56).

113. *Al-Taliᶜa*, July 23, 1981.

114. *Al-Fajr*, June 24, 1981.

115. *Al-Fajr*, July 11, 12, 13, 1981.

116. *Al-Fajr*, July 8, 1981.

117. Excerpt from declaration read at the Assembly of Teachers and Workers of al-Najah University in Salih, *Al-Mushkilat al-Thatiyya*, 65; *Al-Fajr*, July 13, 1981.

118. Ibid., 157.

119. *Al-Quds*, September 29, 1981.

120. *Al-Fajr*, September 29, 1981.

121. Ibid.

122. *Al-Fajr*, October 27, 1981.

123. *Al-Fajr*, November 17, 1981.

124. *Al-Fajr*, October 21, 1981.

125. *Al-Fajr*, October 16, 1981.

126. Ibid.

127. *Al-Fajr*, October 17, 1981.

128. *Al-Fajr*, October 29, 1981.

129. Ibid.

130. *Al-Fajr*, November 9, 1981.

131. *Al-Quds*, October 31, 1981.

132. *Al-Fajr*, October 31, 1981.

133. *Al-Taliᶜa*, October 1, 1981.

134. *Al-Taliᶜa*, November 19, 1981.

135. *Al-Shaᶜb*, November 22, 1981.

136. Ibid.

137. *Al-Fajr*, November 22, 1981.

138. *Al-Quds*, November 21, 1981.

139. *Al-Tali ʿa*, November 26, 1981.

140. *Al-Fajr*, January 9, 1982.

141. *Al-Quds*, November 11, 1981.

142. *Al-Fajr*, January 10–12, 1982.

143. Announcement by the Council of the Friend's Committee on the events of January 9, 10, and 11, based on the report of the investigative committee that was submitted on January 31, 1982. *Al-Fajr*. February 16, 1982.

144. *Al-Fajr*, January 20, 1982.

145. Announcement by the United National Students Committee, *Al-Fajr*, February 2, 1982.

146. *Al-Fajr*, January 20, 1982.

147. *Al-Quds*, September 27, 1982.

148. *Al-Fajr*, February 5, 1982.

149. *Al-Hurriyya*, January 18, 1982.

150. Ibid.

151. *Al-Hurriyya*, January 25, 1982.

152. Interview with Dr. Mundhir Salah, *Al-Fajr*, July 17, 1982.

153. *Al-Fajr*, November 30, 1982.

154. *Al-Fajr*, January 23, 1983.

155. *Al-Fajr*, March 1, 1983.

156. *Al-Shira ʿ*, March 1, 1983.

157. *Al-Shira ʿ*, April 15, 1983.

158. Ibid.

5. The Intifada and State Building

1. Communiqué 2, Unified National Command, January 10, 1988. Communiqué 1 had been circulated by the DFLP around January 7 and was signed by "al-quwat al-filastiniyya."

2. Samih K. Farsoun and Jean M. Landis, "The Sociology of an Uprising: The Roots of the Intifada," in Jamal R. Nassar and Roger Heacock, eds., *Intifada: Palestine at the Crossroads* (New York: Praeger, 1990), 29.

3. Ibrahim Abu-Lughod, "Introduction: On Achieving Independence," in Nassar and Heacock, *Intifada*, 2.

4. Farsoun and Landis, "The Sociology of an Uprising," 15–37; Joost R. Hiltermann, *Behind the Intifada: Labor and Women's Movement in the Occupied Territories* (Princeton, N.J.: Princeton University Press, 1990); Rita Giacaman and Penny Johnson, "Palestinian Women: Building Barricades and Breaking Barriers," in Zachary Lockman and Joel Beinin, eds., *Intifada: The Palestinian Uprising against Israeli Occupation* (Boston: South End Press, 1989), 155–70; Husain Jameel Bargouti, " Jeep versus Bare Feet: The Villages in the Intifada," in Nassar and Heacock, *Intifada*, 107–9; Islah Jad, "From Salons to the Popular Committees: Palestinian Women, 1919–1989," in ibid, 131; Hanan Mikhail Ashrawi, "The Politics of Cultural Revival," in Michael C. Hudson, ed., *The Palestinians: New Directions* (Washington, D.C.: Center for Contemporary Arab Studies, 1990), 77–83.

5. Communiqué 10, March 11, 1988.

6. Communiqué 14, Unified National Command, April 20, 1988.

7. Communiqué 13, April 2, 1988.

8. April 20, 1990.

9. Salim Tamari, "The Palestinian Movement in Transition: Historical Reversals and the Uprisings," *Journal of Palestine Studies* 20.2 (Winter 1991): 57–70.

10. See Communiqué 2, January 9, 1988, and Communiqué 6, February 3, 1988.

11. In Communiqué 18 (May 28, 1988), Communiqué 20 (June 24, 1988), and Communiqué 26 (September 27, 1988).

12. Communiqué 27, Unified National Command, October 9, 1988.

13. Barry Rubin, *Revolution until Victory* (Cambridge, Mass.: Harvard University Press, 1994), 114.

14. "The fighting arm of the PLO" appeared at the end of almost all the communiqués after Communiqué 3.

15. *Jerusalem Post*, July 31, 1988.

16. *Al-Fajr*, August 6, 7, and 8, 1988.

17. Communiqué 24, Unified National Command, August 24, 1988.

18. Communiqué 32, Unified National Command, January 9, 1989.

19. Communiqué 23, Unified National Command, August 5, 1988.

20. Communiqué 42, Unified National Command, July 3, 1989.

21. Uri Nir, *Ha'artez*, March 1, 1989.

22. Communiqué 27, Unified National Command, October 9, 1988; Communiqué 28, October 30, 1988; Communiqué 29, November 20, 1988; Communiqué 30, December 6, 1988.

23. Communiqué 28, October 30, 1988.

24. Ahmad Jabr, *Al-Hurriyya*, December 25, 1988, 45; Sari Nusseibeh, "Time for Palestinian Offensive," *Middle East International*, December 2, 1988, p. 18.

25. Daud Kuttab, "The Ups and Downs of the Second Year," *Middle East International*, December 15, 1989, 16.

26. See interview in Moscow with Shahir Saʿad and George Hazbun, secretary-general and vice secretary-general respectively of the Federation of Unions in the West Bank, in *Haʾaretz*, November 25, 1990.

27. Interview with Ahmad Jabr, *Al-Hurriyya*, December 25, 1988.

28. *Jerusalem Post*, January 7, 1988.

29. *Al-Hurriyya*, January 17 and 24, 1988.

30. *Jerusalem Post*, January 15, 1988.

31. *Al-Hadaf*, February 21, 1988; March 13, 1988.

32. Communiqué 33, January 22, 1989—First day in honor of the foundation of the Palestinian Communist Party; Communique 39, April 30, 1989—Commemoration of Arab Liberation Front and Palestinian Liberation Front; Communiqué 43, July 25, 1989, Fath.

33. Ahmad Jabr, *Al-Hurriyya*, December 25, 1988.

34. *Al-Ittihad*, January 11, 1989.

35. *Haʾaretz*, March 21, 1988.

36. Communiqué 12, April 2, 1988.

37. Communiqué 2, Unified National Command, January 10, 1988.

38. Communiqué 10, Unified National Command, March 11, 1988.

39. Communiqué 18, Unified National Command, August 5, 1988.

40. Communiqué 27, Unified National Command, December 1988.

41. Communiqué 23, Unified National Command, June 15, 1988.

42. Communiqué 28, Unified National Command, October 30, 1988.

43. Communiqué 10, Unified National Command, March 10, 1988.

44. Communiqué 44, Unified National Command, August 17, 1988; Communiqué 45, September 5, 1989; Communiqué 55, April 20, 1990.

45. Communiqué 54, Unified National Command, March 27, 1990.

46. Bashir al-Barghuthi, the editor of the Communist weekly *Al-Taliʿa* in an interview in March 1990 in *Al-Hurriyya*, May 13, 1990.

47. Hasan Sulayman, "Al-Intifada wa al-Masʾala al-Ziraʿiyya Fi Filastin-Dirasa Madaniyya Fi Qarya Kafr Nuʿma, Qadaʾ Ramalla," in *Al-Intifada: Mubadara Shaʿbiyya* (Jerusalem: n.p., 1990), 293.

48. Communiqué 25, Unified National Command, September 9, 1988, p. 143.

49. See Lustick's discussion of the appropriateness of rational actor theory to understanding the intifada in "Writing the Intifada: Collective Action in the Occupied Territories," *World Politics* 45 (July 1993): 586–94. It seems to me that rational actor theory explains the nature of the organization of the intifada and its persistence rather than its outbreak. In the latter case, psychological causes perhaps play the crucial role. Recall that the political organization of the intifada—namely the formation of the UNC occurred one month after the outbreak of unprecedented mass violence. As late as January 1, 1988, the public failed to respond to Fath's call for violence on its anniversary date commemorating its establishment in 1965. *Haʾaretz*, January 2, 1988. Moreover, Schiff and Yaʾari also make reference to studies conducted by the Israel General Security Services in which they found that most of those apprehended in the first month of the intifada had no past political record and as such did not appear in their computerized databases. Extensive interrogations with hundreds of such participants revealed that most participated to vent their rage at racial discrimination and economic exploitation as a result of work within Israel, were not motivated by coherent political goals, and expected no payoffs. Ehud Yaari and Zeev Schiff, *Intifada: The Palestinian Uprising—Israel's Third Front* (New York: Simon & Schuster, 1989), 81–82. I argue that the longer the intifada continued, the more "rational" were the actors involved in the intifada. Organization became critical to apply sanctions to those who did not participate and structure rewards to those who did.

50. *Al-Hadaf*, October 10, 1988.

51. Interviews with Ahmad Jabr and Jamal Zaqut, two leading DFLP activists and faction representatives in the first UNC. *Al-Hurriyya*, January 24, 1989.

52. *Al-Anba* (Kuwait), January 19, 1989.

53. Communiqué 57, Unified National Command, May 26, 1990.

54. Communiqué 75, Unified National Command, October 6, 1991.

55. Communiqué 78, Unified National Command, January 1, 1992.

56. On the nature of the problem, see Muhammad Abu al-Muhnid "Hal Yumkin Manʿ Zahirat al-Ghash fi al-Imtihanat," *Al-Bayadir al-Siyasi*, June 16, 1990, pp. 54–55. On the success of the intervention of political and civil organizations in combating the phenomenon, see *Al-Nahar*, April 4 and 26, 1991; *Al-Quds*, June 21, 1992.

57. Communiqué 82, Unified National Command, May 30, 1992.

58. The exact categories involve refraining from work in Israel, refraining from work in the settlements, boycott of Israeli goods, withdrawing deposits from Israeli banks, resignations of local workers from the civil administration, developing the home economy, expanding industry and absorbing local workers, increasing the number of all types of committees, and matters relating to popular education.

6. The Madrid Peace Process and the Challenge of the Inside

1. Camille Mansour, "The Palestinian-Israeli Peace Negotiations: An Overview and Assessment," *Journal of Palestine Studies* 12.3 (Spring 1993): 5–6. To understand just how radical a change the Madrid format presented, Hanan ʿAshrawi, the prominent member of the delegation, recalls how territorialists were forbidden by the PLO to meet with diplomats abroad unaccompanied by a PLO official. *This Side of Peace: A Personal Account* (New York: Simon & Schuster, 1995), 201.

2. *Al-Fajr* (English), August 29, 1991.

3. Amman TV, October 31, 1991, in FBIS-NES 91–212, November 2, 1991, p. 2.

4. Madrid TVE International Television, November 5, 1991, FBIS-NES 91–215, November 6, p. 5.

5. IDF Radio, October 22, 1991, FBIS-NES October 23, 1991, 91–207, p. 43.

6. Ashrawi, *This Side of Peace*, 182.

7. Ibid., 182.

8. Ibid., 183.

9. Full text of Palestinian Self-Rule Plan, *Jordan Times*, March 5, 1992, in FBIS-NES 92-044, March 5, 1992, p. 4.

10. Ibid., 3.

11. Even in the 21st Palestinian National Council that took place on April 24–27, 1996, nearly two years after the territorialization of the major PLO leadership, the ratio between diaspora and territorial members remained approximately the same; 191 members located in the territories of a total of 669, of which 536 attended. *Haʾaretz*, April 25, 1996. It was only then that six new members from the territories were included in the eighteen-person Executive Committee, thus, maintaining the ratio between territorialists and diaspora and former diaspora-based leaders. *Al-Hayat al-Jadida*, April 26, 1996.

12. Camille Mansour, "The Palestinian-Israeli Peace Negotiations," 14.

13. AFP Radio (Paris), October 20, 1991, FBIS-NES 91-205, October 20, 1991.

14. *Sawt al-Kuwayt al-Dawli*, April 12, 1991, FBIS-NES 91-074, April 17.

15. Interview with Sari Nusseibeh in *Al-Hayat*, October 22, 1991, FBIS-NES 91-207, October 23, 1991, p. 3.

16. Interview with Dr. Haydar ʿAbd al-Shafi in the Arabic journal of the Institute for Palestine Studies, *Majallat al-Dirasat al-Filastiniyya* on August 2, 1992, in Gaza, p. 69.

17. Ibid.

18. Ibid., 73.

19. Ibid., 67.

20. Ibid.

21. Interview with Husayni in *Al-Hamishmar*, December 6, 1991, FBIS-NES, 91–235.

22. Ibid.

23. *Al-Fajr* (English), March 6, 1991.

24. *Al-Hurriyya*, December 27, 1993.

25. For an excellent but bitter critique on the gap between the way the leftist factions conduct their internal affairs and their demands for reform within the PLO, see Rasim ʿAbidat, "Al-Matlub min al-Muʿarada al-Yasariyya: al-Intilaq min al-Waqiʿ wal-Waqaʾiʿ—La min al-Shiʿarat al-Kabira," *Al-Quds*, December 15, 1993.

26. Radi al-Jaraʿi's proposal of March 1991 was the most serious of its kind. Al-Jaraʾi was an editor in *al-Fajr*, a former Fath member who had spent a total of twelve years in prison, the most recent term in prison having ended three weeks before making the proposal. Michal Sela, *Davar*, March 31, 1991. He was first freed in the PFLP–General Command prisoner exchange in 1985. In his article, he called for the dissolution of the PNC and its replacement by representatives elected democratically on a proportional basis both in the West Bank and in the diaspora, so that a government in exile would then be formed of members elected to the PNC. Such a government would then supervise the national institutions in the territories. Radi al-Jaraʾi, *Al-Fajr*, March 24, 1991. See also Salim Tamari, "Bayna al-Khitab al-Dimuqrati wal-Mumarasa al-Nakhbawiyya," *Al-Quds*, December 19, 1993.

27. Sari Nusseibeh, "Time for a Palestinian Offensive," *Middle East International* 339 (December 2, 1988): 17.

28. This was evinced in the controversy over early empowerment of territorial Palestinians by placing some functions under their jurisdiction before the interim agreement was terminated. Officials on the "outside" such as Yasir ʿAbd Rabbu rejected proposals for early empowerment of territorial Palestinians on the grounds that "early assumption of authority is an indirect way for the U.S. to separate Jerusalem from the rest of the occupied territories" during the interim government period. Yet one month later, they accepted those conditions once Israel agreed to negotiations directly with the PLO "outside." See *Jordan Times*, August 3, 1993; FBIS-NES, 93-147, August 4, 1993, p. 1.

29. *Al-Fajr*, March 31, 1991; FBIS-NES, 91-065, p. 4.

30. Israel Television, November 7, 1991, Jerusalem; FBIS-NES November 8, 91-217.

31. Israel Radio, November 12, 1991; FBIS-NES, 91-220, November 12, 1991.

32. Israeli Television, November 11, 1991; FBIS-NES 91-220, November 12, 1991.

33. Israeli Television, November 12, 1991; FBIS-NES 91-221, November 13, 1991.

34. Ibid.

35. *Ha'aretz*, November 13, 1991; FBIS-NES, 91-220, November 14, 1991.

36. Israel Radio, November 12, 1991; FBIS-NES, November 12, 1991, 91-220.

37. Kol Yisrael, November 13, 1991; FBIS-NES, 91-220, pp. 8–9.

38. *Al-Hamishmar*, November 15, 1991, FBIS-NES, 91-221, pp. 8–9.

39. *Ha'aretz*, November 4, 1991.

40. Interview with ʿAbd al-Shafi in *Al-Ra'i*, November 28, 1991; FBIS-NES, 91-230, November 29, 1991.

41. Israeli Television, December 28, 1991; FBIS-NES 91-249, December 29, 1991.

42. They included Asʿad al-Siftawi, a Fath activist from the Egyptian era who attained prominence when he published a peace plan not to the PLO's liking in 1989; a former prisoner, Faris Hasuna; and a third unnamed activist who was being interrogated for a violent incident in which he was involved. Israeli TV, December 29, 1991; FBIS-NES 92-002, January 2, 1992.

43. *Ha'aretz*, January 15, 1992; FBIS-NES 92-010, January 15, 1992.

44. AEP Radio (Paris), November 17, 1991; FBIS-NES 91-225, November 17, 1991.

45. Sari Nusseibeh, the head of the technical committees, categorically denied that they were "the nucleus of future ministries." *Al-Fajr*, August 7, 1992.

46. *Al-Fajr* (English), October 26, 1992.

47. Jerusalem Radio, November 29, 1992; FBIS-NES 92-230, November 30, 1992.

48. Ephraim Reiner Autonomia Kalkalit MeReshita," *Ha'aretz*, April 30, 1993.

49. *Al-Fajr* (English), April 19, 1993.

50. Ibid.

51. *Ha'aretz*, December 18, 1992.

52. *Ha'aretz*, March 30, 1993.

53. Voice of Palestine (Algiers), April 25, 1993; FBIS-NES 93-079, April 25, 1993.

54. *Al-Fajr*, June 14, 1993.

55. *Al-Fajr* (English), June 14, 1993.

56. Mark Perry and Daniel Shapiro, "Navigating the Oslo Channel—How An Unusual Cast of Characters Found Peace in an Unexpected Place," *Middle East Insight*, September–October 1993, p. 16.

57. U.S. Draft of "Israeli-Palestinian Joint Statement," Washington, D.C., May 12, 1993. Reprinted in *Journal of Palestine Studies* 22.4 (Summer 1993): 158–59.

58. Palestinian Delegation to Peace Talks, "Ten-Point Statement on Peace Process, May 28, 1993," *Journal of Palestine Studies* 23.1 (Autumn 1993): 107–9.

59. "U.S. Draft of "Israeli-Palestinian Joint Declaration of Principles," Washington, D.C., June 30, 1993, in *Journal of Palestine Studies* 23.1 (Autumn 1993): 111–13.

60. Al-Quds Palestinian Arab Radio, August 5, 1993; FBIS-NES 93-150, August 6, 1993.

61. Interview, *Al-Fajr* (English), July 5, 1993.

62. *Sawt al-Sha*ʿ*b*, August 5, 1993; FBIS-NES 93-149, August 5, 1993.

63. PLO Delegation to Peace Talks, Draft of Israeli-Palestinian Statement of Principles, Jerusalem, August 5, 1993, in *Journal of Palestine Studies* 23.1 (Autumn 1993): 113–14.

64. Hanan ʿAshrawi in interview on Amman Jordan TV, August 8, 1993 FBIS-NES, 93-151, August 9, 1993.

65. *Al-Quds*, August 13, 1993.

66. Hanan ʿAshrawi in interview with the Voice of Israel Radio, August 5, 1993; FBIS-NES 93-149, August 5, 1993, p. 1.

67. Ibid.

68. *Al-Quds*, August 14, 1993.

69. *Al-Katib* 152 (September 1993): 33–34.

70. *Ha*ʾ*aretz*, August 24, 1993.

71. *Al-Quds*, August 25, 1993.

72. BBC Radio in Arabic, August 28, 1993.

73. Walid al ʿAmry, *Al-Quds*, August 17, 1993.

74. Jamil al-Tarifi, "Li Maslaha Man Hatha al-Tajawwuzat," *Al-Quds*, August 10, 1993.

75. Danny Rubinstein, *Ha*ʾ*aretz*, September 2, 1993.

7. Countdown to Statehood

1. Zeev Sharef, *Three Days* (London: W. H. Allen, 1962), 13.

2. Ruth Weiss, *Zimbabwe and the New Elite* (New York: British Academic Press, 1994), 60; William B. Quandt, *Revolution and Political Leadership: Algeria, 1954–1968* (Cambridge, Mass.: M.I.T. Press, 1969), pp.149–54; John Hatchard, *Industrial Freedoms and State Security in the African Context* (Harare, Zimbabwe: Baobab Books, 1993), 31–32.

3. See compilation of papers by ʿAzmi Bishara, Ghazi Abu Jiab, and ʿAbd al-Jawad Salih on this point in *Azmat al-Hizb al-Siyasi al-Filastini—Waqaʾiʿ Muʾtamar Muʾassasat Muwatin bi-Taʾrikh 24/11/95* (Ramallah: Muwatin-The Palestinian Institute for the Study of Democracy, 1995).

4. *Al-Quds*, August 22 and 23, 1993.

5. Bayan al-Hut, "Wujub IjraʾTaʿdilat Jawhariyya ʿAla al-Mithaq," *Al-Hayat*, October 19, 1993.

6. Guy Bechor, *Lexicon Ashaf* (Tel Aviv: Misrad Habitachon, 1991), 206.

7. *Al-Quds*, October 10, 1993.

8. *Al-Nahar*, October 12, 1993.

9. *Al-Quds*, October 10, 1993.

10. *Al-Quds*, October 17, 1993.

11. *Al-Quds*, October 13, 1993.

12. *Al-Nahar*, October 15, 1993.

13. *Al-Quds*, October 11, 1993.

14. Ostensibly, Abu-Sharif disappeared from the limelight for his profligate expenses. *Al-Quds*, October 10, 1993.

15. London BBC Television in Arabic, October 8, 1993; FBIS-NES, 93-199, p. 21.

16. This was sharply denied by Ahmad Qariʿ (Abu ʿAlaʾ), director of the PLO economic department in an interview with *Al-Hayat*, October 25, 1993 (FBIS-NES-93-207, October 28, 1993, p. 6).

17. One reason that these parties' influence was never great was that they rarely practiced what they preached. While the PFLP inveighed against Arafat's *fardiyya* (individualism), the personality cult surrounding George Habash as "al-Hakim," continued unabated. Nor did these factions seem to be more institutionalized than Fath, the faction they derided. Both the PFLP and the DFLP convened their general assemblies three times only over a period of over twenty-two years. Fath convened its general council five times over a slightly longer period (1964–89).

18. See, for example, articles in this journal by Bilal Jamal, "Al-Daman al-Ijitimaʿi fi al-Dawla: Al-Baramij wal-Ahdaf," 13 (April 1992): 15–21; Adib Abu

Khalil, "Jihaz al-Shurta al-Filastini," in ibid., 5–10; Hani ʿArafat, "Dawla Bidun ʿUnf," 17 (September 1992): 6–11; and by same author "Al-Dimuqratiyya wal-Siyada: Al-Qanun fi al-Dawla al-Filastiniyya," 21 (January 1993): 19–24.

19. On ʿArafat, see "Abu ʿAmmar: Al-Qadiya wa Rajul al-Qarar al-Filastini," 21, 5–10.

20. *Al-Fajr* (English), August 2, 1993.

21. According to Jean-Luc Renaudie of AFP Radio, PLO aid declined from $300–310 million annually in 1991 to $90 million in 1992. Prisoners stopped receiving $75–105 stipends, aid to educational and cultural organizations declined by 80 percent, and universities that received $20–22 million, now received $2 million. August 18, 1993, FBIS-NES, 93-158, p. 6.

22. Muhammad Shakir Saif al-Din, "Bayna al-Khass wal-ʿAmm fi al-ʿAlaqat al-Filastiniyya," *Al-Quds*, October 16, 1993.

23. Asad al-Asʿad, "Liʾla yatahawala al-Watan ila Suq al-Mal," *Al-Quds*, October 13, 1993.

24. On preparation for the establishment of Fida, see *Al-Quds*, February 4, 1992.

25. Interview with George Habash, *Vienna News* (German), October 28, 1993, 62; FBIS-NES 93-208, October 29, 1993, p. 5.

26. *Al-Hurriyya*, August 22, 1993, 4. Since there was no consistency in these charges amongst the opposition, they must be treated with caution.

27. On one of the latest analyses of the PLO's financial situation, see Stephen Rodan's article in the *Jerusalem Post* and translated in full in *Al-Quds*, June 24, 1994.

28. Sharef, *Three Days*, 45.

29. See communiqués in *Al-Quds*, October 13, 1993.

30. *Al-Quds*, October 10, 1993.

31. *Al-Quds*, November 6, 1993.

32. Even Marwan al-Barghuthi, the leading figure behind the democratization of Fath, was opposed to its transformation into a political party. See interview with Marwan al-Barghuthi in *Majallat al-Dirasat al- Filastiniyya*, Winter, 1995, p. 66.

33. Dr. Sari Nusseibeh, "Al-Tawaqim al-Fanniyya Satuʿid Siyaghaha Qariban baʿd Istiqmal Mahammiha," *Al-Quds*, September 20, 1993.

34. *Al-Quds*, October 10, 1993.

35. As reported in *Al-Nahar*, November 5, 1993.

36. Dr. Sari Nusseibeh, interview, *Al-Quds*, September 9, 1993.

37. *Al-Nahar*, September 24, 1993.

38. *Al-Nahar*, September 30, 1993.

39. *Al-Quds*, September 28, 1993.

40. *Al-Nahar*, October 1, 1993.

41. Danny Rubinstein, "Anachnu Lo Merutzim, Mar Yoshev Rosh," *Ha'aretz*, November 22, 1993.

42. *Al-Quds*, January 12, 1994.

43. Israel TV Channel 1, December 27, 1993.

44. George T. Abed, assistant director of general finance of the International Monetary Fund, as reported in *Al-Quds*, May 31, 1995.

45. For Muhammad Dahlan—the deported Shabiba leader from Gaza who, after deportation, was a high ranking internal security official in Fath in Tunis—such personalism would also characterize future nominations in the general security apparatus. When asked in an interview with *Ha'aretz* who would nominate, from among the Fath Hawks, members in the future general security services, he responded: "Abu ʿAmmar would place men in positions like these. Who else? Who appoints positions like these in the Third World?" Dahlan at the time was negotiating with Israeli officials in Rome the cessation of pursuit of Fath Hawks in Gaza. *Ha'aretz*, January 12, 1994. He later became the head of the Preventative Security Service (*Jihaz al-'Amn al-Wiqa'i*) in Gaza.

46. This revolutionary military image also extended to structural arrangements. Arafat has effectively stopped a process of holding district elections in Fath that was meant to transform the faction he controlled within the PLO into a political party. Interview with Marwan al-Barghuthi, chairman of the Fath Central Political Committee in the West Bank, November 23, 1994.

47. *Al-Quds*, January 17, 1995.

48. The term *juridical state* was coined by Robert H. Jackson and Carl J. Roseberg in their article, "Why African States Persist: The Empirical and Juridical Statehood," *World Politics* 35.1 (1982): 1–25. It refers to a state that is ineffective domestically but nevertheless recognized and often maintained artificially by the international community. The fact that states no longer have to fight for their survival in the face of external foes makes for bad leadership at home and often for disastrous government performance.

49. Prem C. Garg and Samir el-Khouri, "Aiding the Development Effort for the West Bank and Gaza," *Finance and Development*, September 1994, pp. 7–9.

50. Data provided by Dina Abu-Ghaida, Consultant to the World Bank and various written material of the World Bank.

51. George T. Abed, assistant director of general finance in the IMF, as reported in *Al-Quds*, May 31, 1995.

52. See Elizabeth Picard, "Arab Military in Politics: From Revolutionary Plot to Authoritarian State," in Adeed Darwisha and William I. Zartman, eds., *Beyond Coercion* (London: Croom Helm, 1988), 154–71.

53. Yossi Torfstein, *Haʾaretz*, January 7, 1994.

54. *Al-Quds*, December 7, 1993.

55. Torfstein, *Haʾaretz*, January 7, 1994.

56. *Majallat al Dirasat al Filastiniyya,* Winter 1995, p. 66.

57. Ibid., 65.

58. Ibid., 78.

59. *Al-Quds*, October 29, 1995.

60. *Al-Hayat al-Jadida*, November 21, 1995. The committee heads were Mahmud ʿAbbas, the political committee; Nabil Shaʿth, media; Faysal al-Husayni, the organizational committee in the West Bank; Zakariya al-Agha, the organizational committee in Gaza; Ahmad Qariʿ, the financial committee; and Intisar al-Wazir, the women's committee.

61. For one of the earliest and most powerful critiques of this division of labor, see Ibrahim Daqqaq, "Back to Square One," 64–101.

62. See Hillel Frisch, "The Palestinian Movement in the Territories: The Middle Command," *Middle Eastern Studies*, 29 (1993): 254–74.

63. For a poignant analysis of the effects of politicization and the struggle over institutions, see Sara M. Roy, "Gaza: New Dimensions of Civic Disintegration," *Journal of Palestine Studies* 22.4 (Summer 1993): 24–25. "Acquiring control over established institutions," she states, "is increasingly achieved through intimidation. There are already many examples of how a given faction will approach the head of an institution and demand that certain of its members be hired. Refusal to do so has sometimes resulted in personal threats to the organization head and his or her family as well as property damage to the targeted institution" (p. 24). Perhaps the most telling indication of the fear of predatory activities is the fact that not one of the many people she interviewed was willing to be identified by his real name and title. She concludes that section by saying that "the creation of *structures*, once a prominent feature of the uprising, is steadily giving way to the creation of *constituencies* in institutional guise." As my analysis on the intifada would indicate, I would seriously question the veracity of the first part of the statement. The creation of organs, perhaps, but not structures.

64. Birzeit University lecturer George Giacaman, for example, called for a thorough depoliticization of all national institutions, future government ministries as well as voluntary organizations. "The nationalism of the institutions in the future," he stated, "resides specifically in their ability in performing their tasks as specifically stated." Dr. George Giacaman, "Wataniyyat al-Muʾassasat al-Wataniyya fi al-Marhala al-Qadima," *Al-Quds*, November 3, 1993.

65. ʿAbd al-Fattah Hamid, "Lijan al-Islah fi Qitaʿ Ghazza," *Al-Quds*, June 12, 1994. Hamid suggests ways of integrating semitraditional and traditional arbitration structures into an emerging civil-legal system. Note many of these structures comprised political and modern professionals in addition to experts of customary law and

men of high social standing. According to Dr. Ali H. Qleibo, a Palestinian anthropologist, "in the Occupied Territories, in the West Bank and in the Gaza Strip because of the refusal of the Palestinians to recognize and normalize relations with the Israeli legal system and in effect in the absence of a Palestinian legal apparatus, ʿatwah or sulhʿashaʾiry has become par excellence the major method by which intra-Arab conflicts are resolved." See his "Tribal Methods of Conflict Resolution—The Palestinian Model: ʿAtwah or Sulh ʿAshaʾiry," in *Practicing Conflict Resolution in Divided Societies* (Jerusalem: Leonard Davis Institute, July 1993), 58.

66. Analysis of *Al-Quds*, September 14–16, 1993.

67. Three announcements that appeared in *al-Quds* in June 26, 1994, one month after the establishment of the Palestinian National Authority, vividly reflect the durability of embedded social groups in local Palestinian society. In the first, the family council of the al-Dajani family congratulate Mundhir ʿIzz al-Din al-Dajani, PLO ambassador to Algeria, on his arrival to the country; in the second, the Bandak family of Bethlehem, who own one of the biggest manufacturing plants in the West Bank, condemn the attack on two members of the family relating to a land feud, and ask that the Palestinian National Authority intervene "with on iron hand on their behalf"; a third thanks Nabil Shaʿth for his attendance at the "diwan" of Mukhtar Fuad Shaʿth of Khan Yunis. The killing of Nasr Ishaq Salwaha, a twenty-two-year-old Hamas activist in Gaza, reflects this reality from a different perspective. Presumably, he was killed by family members of a man whom the Hamas suspected of collaboration and killed during the intifada. See *Al-Quds*, June 24, 1994.

68. *Al-Quds*, February 21, 1994.

69. *Al-Quds*, November 5, 1995.

70. *Al-Quds*, December 7, 1995.

71. *Al Quds*, October 26, 1995.

72. Interview with Khalid al-Qidra, attorney general of the PA (Gaza, May 28, 1995).

73. *Al-Quds*, October 24, 1995.

74. *Al-Quds*, November 2, 1995.

75. *Al-Quds*, October 17, 1995.

76. Hisham Sharabi, *Neopatriarchy: A Theory of Distorted Change in Arab Society* (Oxford: Oxford University Press, 1988).

77. *Al-Intikhabat wal-Nizam al-Siyasi al Filastini* (Nablus: Center for Palestine Research and Studies, February 1995), 45.

78. Naseer Aruri and John Carroll, "The Palestinian 'constitution' and the 'old regime,' " *Middle East International*, April 15, 1994, p. 16.

79. *Al-Intikhabat*, 152.

80. Ibid., 45.

81. *Le Figaro*, May 26, 1994; FBIS-NES, 94-105, June 1, 1994, p. 10.

82. Ibid.

83. *Haʾaretz*, May 27, 1995.

84. *Haʾaretz*, May 25, 1995.

85. *Al-Intikhabat*, 26.

86. *Al-Quds*, February 4, 1996. Other members included Salim Zaʿanun, Nabil Shaʿath, Furayk Abu Middayn, Ibrahim al-Daghma, Eugine al-Qasim, Kamil Mansur, Fatih ʿAzzam, and Farid al-Jallad.

87. Wizarat al-Takhtit wal-Taʿawwun al-Dawli, Waraqat ʿAmal Lil-Taʿammul maʿa al-Munazamat Ghair al-Hukumiyya, Muqaddama min al-Duktur Anis al-Qaq, Wakil Wizarat al-Taʿawwun al-Dawli [Ministry of Planning and International Cooperation, Working Paper Regarding Relations with the Nongovernmental Organizations. Presented by Dr. Anis al Qaq, Deputy Minister for International Cooperation] (n.p., n.d.).

88. *Al-Quds*, February 16, 1994.

89. Naseer Aruri, "Oslo and the Crisis in Palestinian Politics," *Middle East International*, 467 (January 1994): 17.

90. Hiba Husseini, "A Comparative Analysis of Legislation Regulating NGO Work in Various Country Contexts," unpublished manuscript, May 1995.

91. Interview with Rana Bishara, coordinator of the PNGO Network, June 22, 1995.

92. In the monthly polls conducted by the Center for Palestine Research and Studies in Nablus between November 1993 and February 1995, support for the DFLP and the PFLP ranged from 9 to 11 percent. See Lauren G. Ross and Nader Izzat Saʾid, "Palestinians: Yes to Negotiations, Yes to Violence," *Middle East Quarterly* 2.28 (June 1995): 16, table 1. For a qualitative analysis that draws the same conclusion, see Dr. Isama ʿAbd al Sitar al-Fara, "Al-Intikhabat al-Muqbila Sataʿidu al-Siyasiya al-Muqbila," *Al-Quds*, November 2, 1995.

93. Newsletter—*Perspectives on the PGNO Network*, May 1995, p. 2.

94. Risala Ikhbariyya Sadira ʿAn Shabakat al-Munazamat al-Ahliyya Al-Filastiniyya, *Al-Siyasa al-Filastiniyya* 2.7–8 (Summer–Fall 1995): 248–50.

95. For an extensive analysis of this law, see the two-part article by Tahir al Nimri, "Al-Qiraʾa fi Mashruʿ al-Jamʿiyyat al Khairiyya wal-Haiʾat al-Ijtimaʿiyya wal-Muʾassasat al-Khassa," *Al-Quds*, November 1 and 2, 1995.

96. *Haʾaretz*, July 13, 1994.

97. *Haʾaretz*, May 3, 1995

98. Ross and Saʾid, "Yes to Negotiations," p. 16, table 1.

99. *Haʾaretz*, November 19, 1995; January 2, 1996.

100. *Al-Intikhabat wal-Nizam al-Siyasi al Filastini* (Nablus: Center for Palestine Research and Studies, February 1995), 172–73.

101. Ibid., 199.

102. "Qanun Ruqm (15) li-Sana 1995 bi-Shaʾn al-Intikhabat," *Qanun al-Intikhabat al-Filastini li-ʿAm* 1995 (Al-Sulta al-Wataniyya -Lajnat al-Intikhabat al-Markazia, n.d.).

103. Nass Mashruᶜ Qanun al-Ahzab al-Siyasiyya al-Filastiniyya *Al-Siyasa Al-Filastiniyya* 2.7–8 (Summer–Fall 1995): 259–64.

104. Dr. Ahmad Majdalani, "Qiraʾat Naqdiyya li-Mashruᶜ Qanun al-Ahzab al-Siyasiyya al-Filastiniyya," *Al-Hayat al-Jadida*, January 10, 1995. Majdalani is a member of the political bureau of the Palestinian Popular Struggle Front.

105. *Haʾaretz*, January 22, 1996.

106. Ismaᶜil Haniya, Khalid al-Hindi, and Saᶜid al-Namruti, members of the Committee of National Accord (Lajnat al-Wifaq al-Watani) and of Hamas announced their decision to resign amidst considerable but veiled criticism leveled against the latter movement. In the announcement they published in the newspapers they wrote, "despite our conviction that participation in the elections is a choice that had it been carried out, would have served both our country and religion, we have weighed the scales in favoring the choice to withdraw our candidacies in order to put an end to the confusion and in the interest of maintaining the peace in the homeland." *Al-Nahar*, January 3, 1996.

107. Al-Najjar was even elected to represent Khan Yunis. *Al-Hayat*, January 23, 1996.

108. *Al-Nahar*, October 15 and 17, 1993.

109. Graham Usher, "Fath Tearing Itself Apart," *Middle East International*, February 18, 1994, pp. 4–5.

110. Nataʾij Istitlaᶜ lil-Raʾi al-ʿAmm al-Filastini—al-Diffa al-Gharbiyya wa-Qitaᶜ Ghazza Ab-Ilul, 1995 (Nablus: Center for Palestine Research and Studies, August/September 1995), 10.

Conclusion

1. Charles Tilly, "War Making and State Making as Organized Crime," in Peter B. Evans, Dietrich Rueschmeyer, and Theda Skocpol, eds., *Bringing the State Back In* (Cambridge: Cambridge University Press, 1985), 164.

2. Sheldon Gellar, "State-Building and Nation-Building in West Africa," in S. N. Eisenstadt and Stein Rokkan, eds. *Building States and Nations*, vol. 2, (Beverly Hills, Calif.: Sage, 1973), 384–426.

3. Patrick Chabal, *Amilcar Cabral: Revolutionary Leadership and People's War* (Cambridge: Cambridge University Press 1983), 95; John S. Saul, *The State and*

Revolution in Eastern Africa (New York: Oxford University Press, 1979), 71–72; Basil Davidson, "The Politics of Armed Struggle," in Davidson et al., *Southern Africa: The New Politics of Revolution* (Harmondsworth, England: Penguin, 1976), 75. Davidson in his latest book written from the perspective of the 1990s reiterates the theme regarding the former Portuguese colonies, blaming the civil war and catastrophic state consolidation in Angola, Mozambique, and Zambia on foreign state intervention and superpower regional rivalry. One can hardly question the veracity of his argument, but as we shall see, very violent conflicts that did not suffer such intervention might have averted civil war but did not achieve higher levels of state consolidation than less violent conflicts. See Basil Davidson, *The Black Man's Burden: Africa and the Curse of the Nation-State* (London: James Currey, 1993), 312–16.

4. Bard E. O'Neill, *Armed Struggle in Palestine: A Political-Military Analysis* (Boulder, Colo.: Westview, 1978), 232.

5. Ronald Weitzer, "In Search of Regime Security: Zimbabwe since Independence," *Journal of Modern African Studies* 22.4 (1984): 530.

6. Ibid., 554.

7. Leaders of national liberation movements in Africa in the 1970s were especially sensitive to the dangers of violence and the relationship between pre-independence militarism and post-independence consequences. "Hence their wartime slogan, repeated so often by Cabral: 'We are armed militants, not militarists'." Davidson, *Black Man's Burden*, 301.

8. Migdal, *Strong Societies.*

9. Ibid., 160.

10. On a very interesting exception, see Michael Crowder, "Bostwana and the Survival of Liberal Democracy in Africa," in Prosser Gifford and William Roger Lewis, eds., *Decolonization and African Independence: The Transfers of Power, 1960–1980* (New Haven, Conn.: Yale University Press, 1988), 461–77.

11. Joel Migdal, "The Crystallization of the State and the Struggles over Rulemaking: Israel in Comparative Perspective," in Baruch Kimmerling, ed., *The Israeli State and Society: Boundaries and Frontiers* (Albany: State University of New York Press, 1989), 1–5.

12. Ruth Berins Collier, *Regimes in Tropical Africa: Changing forms of Supremacy, 1945–1975* (Berkeley: University of California Press, 1982).

13. Ibid., 154.

14. Joshua Bernard Forrest, "A Promising Start: The Inauguration and Consolidation of Democracy in Namibia," *World Policy Journal* 9.4 (Fall/Winter 1992): 740–53.

15. Ibid., 743.

16. Reginald Green, Marja-Liisa Kiljunen, Kimo Kiljunen, eds., *Namibia: The Last Colony* (London: Longman, 1981), 155.

17. Forrest, "Promising Start," 743.

18. By way of example, "The A.N.C.'s success as spokesman for oppressed South Africans made its transformation into a democratic party much more difficult. It could not be both the mouthpiece of an entire people and just one of several contenders in the political fray. At some point, it would have to choose. Faced with the same alternatives, African liberation movements in the past chose the first: they proclaimed that unity was imperative and that the nation should continue to speak with one voice." Marina Ottaway, "Liberation Movements and Transition to Democracy: The Case of the A.N.C.," *The Journal of Modern African Studies* 29.1 (1991): 69.

19. ʿAzmi Bishara, "Waraqa ʿAwwaliyya Hawla Azmat al-ʿAmal al-Hizbi" (Preliminary Working Paper Regarding the Crisis of Political Action), in *Azmat al-Hizb al-Siyasi al-Filastini—Waqaʾiʿ Muʾtamar Muʾassasat Muwatin bi-Taʾrikh 24/11/95* (Ramallah: Muwatin-The Palestinian Institute for the Study of Democracy, 1995), 18.

20. Peter Evans, "The State as Problem and Solution: Predation, Embedded Autonomy, and Structural Change," in Stephen Haggard and Robert R. Kaufman, eds., *The Politics of Economic Adjustment: Internal Constraints, Distributive Conflicts, and The State* (Princeton, N.J.: Princeton University Press, 1992), 141.

21. Tilly, "War-Making and State-Making," 609.

22. Thomas M. Callaghy, *The State-Society Struggle: Zaire in Comparative Perspective* (New York: Columbia University Press, 1984), 97.

23. Robert Jackson and C. G. Rosberg, "Why African Weak States Persist—The Empirical and Juridical in Statehood," *World Politics* 35.1 (1982): 1–25.

24. Aristide Zolberg, "One-Party Systems and Government for the People," *Africa Today* 9.4 (May 1962): 4–7.

25. Victor Azarya and Naomi Chazan, "Disengagement from the State in Africa: Reflections on the Experience of Ghana and Guinea," *Comparative Studies in Society and History* 29.1 (1987): 107.

26. As Evans writes, "recognition of the importance of state capacity, not simply in the sense of the prowess and perspicacity of technocrats within the state apparatus but also in the sense of an institutional structure that is durable and effective, is characteristic of the third wave of thinking about the state and development." Peter Evans, "The State as Problem and Solution," 141. In fact, Evans juxtaposes Zairian predatory rent-seeking with the Japanese, Taiwanese, and Korean experiences in which rent-seeking was constrained by an intellectual and professional bureaucratic elite. Working backward, one would conclude that the creation of such an elite rather than its domination would facilitate successful state consolidation.

BIBLIOGRAPHY

ʿAbd al-Majid, Wahid. "Al-Intifada al-Flastiniyya: Al-Siyaq al-Taʾarihi—Al-Quwa al-Faʿila—Al-Masar wal-Mustaqbal" [The Palestinian Intifada: The Historical Course—The Path and the Future]. *Al-Mustaqbal al-ʿArabi* 11 (May 1988): 6–33.

Abu ʿAmru, Ziad. *Usul al-Harakat al-Siyasiya Fi Qitaʿ Ghazza 1948–1967* [The Origins of the Political Movements in the Gaza Strip 1948–1967]. Accre Israel: Dar al-Aswar, 1947.

Abukhalil, Asʿad. "Internal Contradictions in the PFLP: Decision Making and Policy Orientation." *Middle East Journal*, 41.3 (1987): 371–72.

Abu-Lughod, Ibrahim. "Introduction: On Achieving Independence." In Jamal R. Nassar and Roger Heacock, eds. *Intifada: Palestine at the Crossroads*. New York: Praeger, 1990, 2–11.

———. "Lebanon and Palestine: Some Contrasts in the Application of Principles of National Liberation." *Arab Studies Quarterly* 7.4 (Fall 1985): 78–88.

Abu Nab, Ibrahim. "Al-Jamiʿa al-Filastiniyya al-Muqtaraha . . . ila ʿAyna Wasalat?" [The Proposed Palestinian University . . . What Stage Has It Reached?]. *Shuʾun Filastiniyya* 13 (June 1972): 226–29.

Ageron, Charles-Robert. *Modern Algeria: A History from 1830 to the Present*. Trenton, N.J.: Africa World Press, 1993.

Al-ʿAzm, Sadik J. "Palestinian Zionism." *Die Welt des Islams* 28 (1988): 90–98.

ʿAlush, Naji. *Al-Masira ila Filastin* [The March to Palestine]. Beirut: Dar al-Taliʿa, 1964.

Amnesty International Report on Restriction Orders in Israel and the Occupied Territories. New York: Amnesty International, October 19, 1982.

Amos II, John W. *Palestinian Resistance: Organization of a Nationalist Movement*. New York: Pergamon Press, 1980.

Anderson, Lisa. "Absolutism and the Resilience of Monarchy in the Middle East," *Political Science Quarterly*, 106.1 (Spring 1991): 1–16.

Angrist, Joshua D. "Wages and Unemployment in the West Bank and Gaza Strip, 1981–1991." Unpublished ms, The Hebrew University of Jerusalem, June 1992.

Annual Report 1974. Tel Aviv: The Israel Police Force, 1975.

Annual Report 1976. Tel Aviv: The Israel Police Force, 1976.

ʿArafat, Hani. "Dawla Bidun ʿUnf" [A State without Violence]. *Al-Nashra al-Istratijiyya* 17 (September 1992): 6–11.

———. "Dimuqratiyya wa Siyada: Al-Qanun fi al-Dawla al-Filastiniyya" [Democracy and Sovereignity: Law in the Palestinian State]. *Al-Nashra al-Istratijiyya* 21 (January 1993): 19–24.

Arav ve-Israel [The Arab World and Israel] 3–4, Yehoshufat Harkabi, ed. Tel Aviv: Am Oved, 1975.

Aruri, Naseer H. *Jordan: A Study in Political Development (1921–1965)*. The Hague: Martinus Nijhoff, 1972.

——— "Oslo and the Crisis in Palestinian Politcs." *Middle East International* 467 (January 1994): 17.

Aruri, Naseer, and John Carroll. "The Palestinian 'Constitution' and the 'Old Regime.'" *Middle East International*, 473 (April 15, 1994): 16.

Ashrawi, Hanan Mikhail. "The Politics of Cultural Revival." In Michael C. Hudson, ed., *The Palestinians: New Directions*, Washington, D.C.: Center for Contemporary Arab Studies, 1990, 8.

——— *This Side of Peace: A Personal Account*. New York: Simon & Schuster, 1995.

ʿAtiya, Ihsan, Samir Jibril, and Jamal Talab. *Nashra Ihsaʾiyya ʿan al-Manatiq al-ʿArabiyya al-Muhtalla—Haqaʾiq wa Arqam* [Statistical Publication for Occupied Arab Territories—Facts and Figures]. Jerusalem: al-Jamiʿiyya lil-Dirasat al-Arabiyya, 1985.

Avineri, Shlomo. *The Makings of Modern Zionism: The Intellectual Origins of the Jewish State*. New York: Basic Books, 1981.

Ayub, Samir. "Al-Kiyaniyya al-Filastiniyya: Al-Waʿi al-Thati wal-Tatawwur al-Muʾassasati 1947–1977 [The Palestinian Entity: Self-Consciousness and Institutional Development]." *Shuʾun Filastiniyya* 102, (1979): 138–48.

ʿAwad, Munir Ahmad. "Al-Taʿlim al-ʿAli fi al-Diffa al-Gharbiyya wa Qitaʿ Ghazza-Tatawwuruhu wa Asasuhu" [Higher Education in the West Bank and Gaza Strip: Its Development and Foundations]." *Al-Bayadir al-Siyasi*, June 11, 1983, 33–34.

Azarya, Victor, and Naomi Chazan. "Disengagment from the State in Africa: Reflections on the Experience of Ghana and Guinea." *Comparative Studies in Society and History* 29.1 (1987): 106–31.

Azmat al-Hizb al-Siyasi al-Filastini—Waqaʾiʿ Muʾtamar Muʾasassat Muwatin bi-Taʾrikh 24/11/95 [The Problem of the Palestinian Political Party—The Proceedings of the Muwatin Institute Conference]. Ramallah: Muwatin—The Palestinian Institute for the Study of Democracy, 1995.

Bachi, Robert. *The Population of Israel*. Jerusalem: Institute for Contemporary Jewry, Hebrew University of Jerusalem, 1974.

Barghuthi, ᶜIyad. *Palestinian Americans: Socio-Political Attitiudes of Palestinian Americans toward the Arab American Conflict*. Occasional Paper Series No. 38. Durham, U.K.: Center for Middle Eastern and Islamic Studies, University of Durham, 1988.

Basisu, Fuad. "Al-Tharwa al-Naftia wal-Musahama al-Qawmiyya fi Daᶜam al-Sumud al-Filastini fi al-Aradi al-Muhtalla" [The Oil Wealth and (Pan-Arab) Nationalist Cooperation in the Support of Palestian Steadfastness in the Occupied Territories]. *Samid al-Iqtisadi* 7.56 (July/August 1985): 8–23.

Bechor, Guy. *Lexicon Ashaf* [Lexicon of the PLO]. Tel Aviv: Misrad Habitachon, 1991.

Beinen, Joel. "The Palestine Communist Party." *MERIP Report* 55 (1975): 3–17.

Beker, Michiel, and Roemer van Oordt. "The Palestinians in Lebanon: Contradictions of State-Formation in Exile." Occasional Paper, No. 10. Amsterdam: Middle East Research Associates, 1991.

Ben-Dor, Gabriel."The Institutionalization of Palestinian Nationalism." In Itamar Rabinovich and Haim Shaked eds., *From June to October*. New Brunswick, N.J.: Transaction Books, 1978, 245–48.

——— "Institutionalization and Political Development: A Conceptual and Theoretical Analysis." *Comparative Studies in Society and History* 17 (1975): 309–25.

Ben-Rafael, Eliezer. *Israel-Palestine: A Guerrilla Conflict in International Politics*. Westport, Conn.: Greenwood, 1984.

Benvinisti, Meron, and Shlomo Khayat. *The West Bank Data Atlas*. Jerusalem: The West Bank Data Project, 1988.

———. *US Government Funded Projects in the West Bank and Gaza (1977–1983) (Palestinian Sector)*. Working Paper No. 13. Jerusalem: The West Bank Data Project, 1984.

Bisharat, George. *Palestinian Lawyers and Israeli Rule: Law and Disorder in the West Bank*. Austin: University of Texas Press, 1989.

Black, Cyril E., Louis Dupree, Elizabeth Endicott-West, Daniel C. Matuszewski, Eden Naby, and Arthur N. Waldron, *The Modernization of Inner Asia*. Armonk, N.Y.: M.E. Sharpe, 1991.

Black, Gerald, John Dewdney, and Jonathan Mitchell. *The Cambridge Atlas of the Middle East and North Africa*. Cambridge: Cambridge Univeristy Press, 1987.

Brand, Laurie A. *Palestinians in the Arab World: Institution Building and the Search for State*. New York: Columbia University Press, 1988.

Braver, Moshe. *ᶜHa Kav haYarok keGvul BeYehuda uveShomron: Hearcha Geographit keReka leShinuyim veTikkunim* ["The Green Line" in Judea and Samaria: A Geographic Evaluation as a Background to Changes and Emmendations]. Tel Aviv: Tel Aviv Univeristy Project for Peace, 1980.

Breytenbach, Willie. "South Africa within the African Revolutionary Context." In Johannes Albertus Venter, ed. *Challenge: South Africa within the African Revolutionary Context*. Gilbraltar: Ashkanti Publishers, 1989, 63–88.

Brinton, Crane. *The Anatomy of Revolution*. New York: Vintage, 1965.

Brubaker, Rogers. *Citizenship and In France and Germany*. Cambridge, Mass.: Harvard University Press, 1992.

Brynen, Rex. *Sanctuary and Survival: The PLO in Lebanon*. Boulder, Colo.: Westview, 1990.

Callaghy, Thomas M. "Toward State Capability and Embedded Liberalism in the Third World: Lessons for Adjustment." In Joan M. Nelson, ed. *Fragile Coalitions: The Politics of Economic Adjustment*. New Brunswick: Transaction Books, 1989, 115–38.

——— *The State-Society Struggle: Zaire in Comparative Perspective*. New York: Columbia University Press, 1984.

Chabal, Patrick. *Amilcar Cabral: Revolutionary Leadership and People's War*. Cambridge: Cambridge University Press, 1983.

Chaliand, Girard. *The Palestinian Resistance*. London: Penguin Books, 1972.

Cliffe, L. "Forging a Nation: The Eritrean Experience." *Third World Quarterly* 11.4 (1993): 131–47.

Cobban, Helena. *The Palestinian Liberation Organization: People, Power, and Politics*. Cambridge: Cambridge University Press, 1984.

Cohen, Amnon. *Political Parties in West Bank under the Jordanian Regimes, 1949–1967*. Ithaca, N.Y.: Cornell University Press, 1982.

Cohen, Mitchell. *Zion and State: Nation, Class, and the Shaping of Modern Israel*. Oxford: Basil Blackwell, 1987.

Collier, Ruth Berins. *Regimes in Tropical Africa: Changing Forms of Supremacy, 1945–1975*. Berkeley: University of California Press, 1982.

Conner, Walker. "Nation-Building or Nation-Destroying." *World Politics*, 24.3 (April 1972): 319–55.

Crowder, Michael. "Bostwana and the Survival of Liberal Democracy in Africa." In Prosser Gifford and William Roger Lewis, eds. *Decolonization and African Independence: The Transfers of Power, 1960–1980*. New Haven, Conn.: Yale University Press, 1988, 461–77.

Danziger, Raphael. "Algeria and the Palestinians." In Gabriel Ben-Dor, ed., *The Palestinians and the Middle East Conflict*. Ramat-Gan Israel: Turtledove, 1979, 347–73.

Daqqaq, Ibrahim. "Back to Square One: A Study in the Reemergence of the Palestinian Identity in the West Bank, 1967–1980." In Alexander Schölch, ed., *Palestinians Over the Green Line: Studies in the Relationship Between Palestinians on Both Sides of the 1949 Armistice Line Since 1949*. London: Ithaca Press, 1983.

Davidson, Basil. *The Black Man's Burden: Africa and the Curse of the Nation-State*. London: James Currey, 1993.

——— "The Politics of Armed Struggle." In Davidson et al., *Southern Africa: The New Politics of Revolution*. Harmondsworth: Penguin, 1976.

Diskin, Avraham. "Trends in Intensity Variation of Palestinian Military Activity, 1967–1978." *Canadian Journal of Political Science* 16.2 (June/July 1983): 335–48.

Doyle, Michael. *Empires*. Ithaca, N.Y.: Cornell University Press, 1986.

Eisenstadt, Shmeul Noah. *The Transformation of Israeli Society: An Essay in Interpretation*, London: Weidenfeld and Nicolson, 1985.

——— *Traditional Patrimonialism and Modern Neopatrimonialism*. Beverly Hills, Calif.: Sage, 1973.

——— "Varieties of Political Development: Theoretical Challenge.," In S. N. Eisenstadt and Stein Rokkan, eds., *Building States and Nations*, vol. 1. Beverly Hills, Calif.: Sage, 1973, 41–72.

Evans, Peter. "The State as Problem and Solution: Predation, Embedded Autonomy, and Structural Change." In Stephen Haggard and Robert R. Kaufman, eds., *The Politics of Economic Adjustment: Internal Constraints, Distributive Conflicts, and the State*. Princeton, N.J.: Princeton University Press, 1992, 149–66.

Farchi, David. "HaHaluka haAdministrativit shel Yehuda veShomron" [The Administrative Division of Judea and Samaria]. In Israel Raphaeli, ed., *Eser Shnot Shilton beYehuda veShomron*. Jerusalem: Magnes, 1980, pp. 183–191.

Farsoun, Samih K., and Jean M. Landis. "The Sociology of an Uprising: The Roots of the Intifada." In Jamal R. Nassar and Roger Heacock, eds., *Intifada: Palestine at the Crossroads*. New York: Praeger, 1990.

Fieldhouse, D. K. *Colonialism 1870–1945: An Introduction*. New York: St. Martin's Press, 1988.

Forrest, Joshua Bernard. "A Promising Start: The Inauguration and Consolidation of Democracy in Namibia." *World Policy Journal* 9.4 (Fall/Winter 1992): 740–53.

Frisch, Hillel. "Between Diffusion and Territorial Consolidation in Rebellion: Striking at the Hard Core of the Intifada." *The Journal of Terrorism and Political Violence* 3.4 (Winter 1991): 39–62.

——— "The Palestinian Movement: The Middle Command." *Middle Eastern Studies* 29.2 (April, 1993): 254–74.

——— "Binui Mosodot Falestinaiim baShtachim 1967–1985" [Palestinian Institution-Building in the Territories 1967–1985]. Ph.D. dissertation, The Hebrew University of Jerusalem, February 1989.

——— *Stagnation and Frontier: Arab and Jewish Industry in the West Bank*, Jerusalem: The West Bank Data Project, 1983.

Gabriel, Stuart, and Eitan Sabatello. "Palestinian Migration from the West Bank and Gaza: Economic and Demographic Analysis." *Economic Development and Cultural Change* 34.2 (1986): 245–62.

Galnoor, Yitzchak, and Menachem Hophnung, *The Regime of the State of Israel: A Compilation of Sources*. Jerusalem: Navo Publishing, 1993.

Garg Prem C., and Samir el-Khouri. "Aiding the Development Effort for the West Bank and Gaza." *Finance and Development*, September 1994, 7–9.

Gazit, Shlomo. *Hamakel veHagezer* [The Stick and the Carrot]. Tel Aviv: Shrafim, 1985.

Gellar, Sheldon. "State-Building and Nation-Building in West Africa." In S. N. Eisenstadt and Stein Rokkan, eds., *Building States and Nations*, vol. 2. Beverly Hills, Calif.: Sage, 1973, 384–426.

Gemell, N. "The Growth of Employment Services in Egypt, 1960–1975." *The Developing Economies* 23.1 (1985): 53–68.

Giacaman, Rita. "Palestinian Women and Development in the Occupied West Bank." Palestinian Cultural Week, November 28–December 1, 1993 (stencil), p. 17

Giacaman, Rita, and Penny Johnson. "Palestinian Women: Building Barricades and Breaking Barriers." In Zachary Lockman and Joel Beinin, eds., *Intifada: The Palestinian Uprising against Israeli Occupation*. Boston: South End Press, 1989, 155–70.

Gibson, Richard. *African Liberation Movements: Contemporary Struggles against White Minority Rule*. New York: Oxford University Press, 1972.

Giddens, Anthony. *The Nation State and Violence*. Berkeley, Calif.: University of California, 1987.

Gifford, Prosser, and William Roger Lewis, eds., *Decolonization and African Independence: The Transfers of Power, 1960–1980*. New Haven, Calif.: Yale University Press, 1988.

Gilmour, David. *Dispossessed: The Ordeal of the Palestinians*. London: Sphere, 1980.

Golan, Galia. *The Soviet Union and the PLO*. New York: Praeger, 1980.

Gouda, Abdel Khalek, and Robert Tignor. "Introduction." In Gouda Abdel Khalek and Robert Tignor, eds., *The Political Economy of Income Distribution in Developing Countries* London: Holmes and Meier, 1982, 1–19.

Gresh, Alain. *The Struggle Within: Towards a Palestinian State*, London: Zed, 1985.

Haas, Ernest. "What is Nationalism and Why Should We Study It?" *International Organization* 40.3 (Summer 1986): 707–44.

Al-Hadi, ᶜIzzat ᶜAbd. *Al-Intifada wa baᶜdh Qadaya al-Tanmiyya al-Shaᶜbiyya* [The Intifada and Some Problems of Popular Development]. Ramallah: Bisan Press, 1992.

Al-Haj, Majid, Elihu Katz, and Shmuel Shye. "Arab and Jewish Attitudes: Toward a Palestinian State." *Journal of Conflict Studies* 37.4 (December 1993): 619–32.

Halpern, Ben. *The Idea of the Jewish State*. Cambridge, Mass.: Harvard University Press, 1969.

Harkabi, Yehoshafat. *Fedayeen Action and Arab Strategy*. London: Institute for Strategic Studies, 1968.

——— *Palestinians and Israel.* Israel: Keter, 1974.

Hatchard, John. *Industrial Freedoms and State Security in the African Context*. Harare, Zimbabwe: Baobab Books, 1993.

Heller, Mark, and Sari Nusseibeh. *No Trumpets, No Drums*. New York: Hill and Wang, 1991.

Hermassi, Elbaki. *Leadership and National Development in North Africa: a Comparative Study*. Berkeley: University of California Press, 1972.

Hertzberg, Arthur. *The Zionist Idea.* New York: Atheneum, 1977.

Herz, John L. "Rise and Demise of the Territorial State." *World Politics* 9.4 (July 1957): 473–93.

Hilal, Jamil. "Lahza Hasima fi-Taʾarikh al-Nidal al-Watani al-Filastini" [A Crucial Moment in the National Palestinian Struggle]. *Al-Fikr al-Dimuqra* 4 (Winter 1988): 4–13.

Hilterman, Joorst R. *Behind the Intifada: Labor and Women's Movement in the Occupied Territories*. Princeton, N.J.: Princeton University Press, 1990.

Hiwar maᶜa al-Duktur Ibrahim Abu Lughod hawla al-Jamᶜia al-Filastiniyya al-Maftuha [Conversation with Dr. Ibrahim Abu Lughud Concerning the Palestinian Open University]. *Shuʾun Filastiniyya* 101 (April 1980): 21–33.

Horowitz, Dan. "Dual Authority Polities." *Comparative Politics* 14.3 (Fall 1982): 329–49.

Huntington, Samuel P. *Political Order in Changing Societies*. New Haven, Conn.: Yale University Press, 1968.

Husseini, Hiba. "A Comparative Analysis of Legislation Regulating NGO Work in Various Country Contexts." Unpublished Manuscript, May 1995.

International Bank for Recontruction and Development: The Economic Development of Jordan. Baltimore: Johns Hopkins University Press, 1965.

Al-Intikhabat wal-Nizam al-Siyasi al Filastini [The Elections and the Palestinian Political Order]. Nablus: Center for Palestine Research and Studies, February 1995.

Islah, Jad. "From Salons to the Popular Committees: Palestinian Women, 1919–1989." In Jamal R. Nassar and Roger Heacock, eds., *Intifada: Palestine at the Crossroads*. New York: Praeger, 1990.

Jackson, Robert. *Quasi-States: International Relations, and the Third World*. Cambridge: Cambridge University Press, 1990.

——— "Sovereignty and Underdevelopment: Judicial Statehood in the African Crisis." *Journal of Modern African Studies* 24.1 (March 1986): 1–31.

Jackson, Robert, and Carl J. Rosberg. "Why African Weak States Persist: The Empirical and Juridical Statehood." *World Politics* 35.1 (1982): 1–25.

——— *Personal Rule in Black Africa: Prince, Autocrat, Prophet, Tyrant*. Berkeley: University of California Press, 1978.

Jamal, Bilal. "Al-Daman al-Ijitimaᶜi Fi al-Dawla . . . Al-Baramij wal-Ahdaf" [Social Security in the State . . . Programs and Goals]. *Al-Nashra al-Istratijiyya* 13 (April 1992): 15–21.

Jameel, Husain. "Jeep versus Bare Feet: The Villages in the Intifada." In Jamal R. Nassar and Roger Heacock, eds., *Intifada: Palestine at the Crossroads*, New York: Praeger, 1990, 107–24.

Al-Jarbawi, ᶜAli. *Al-Intifada wa al-Qiyadat al-Siyasiyya fi al-Diffa al-Gharbiyya wa Qitaᶜ Ghazza: Bahth fi al-Nukhba al-Siyasiyya* [The Uprising and Political Leadership in the West Bank and Gaza Strip: A Study of the Political Elite]. Beirut: Dar al-Taliᶜa, 1989.

The Jewish National Home. Binyamin, Eliav, ed., Jerusalem: Keter, 1976. (Hebrew)

Jiryis, Sabri. "Al-Majlis al-Watani al-Filastini: Nahwa Dawla Filastiniyya Mustaqilla" [The Palestinian National Council: Towards An Independent State]. *Shuʾun Filastiniyya* 66, (1977): 18–29.

——— "Hawar Min Nawᶜin Ahirin Hawla ᶜal-Hawarʾ wal-Wahda al-Wataniyya" [Another Type of Dialogue Surrounding "the Dialogue" and "National Unity"]. *Shuʾun Filastiniyya* 170–71 (May–June 1987): 3–32.

Johnson, Chalmers. *Revolutionary Change*. Stanford, Calif.: Stanford University Press, 1982.

Jowitt, Kenneth. *Revolutionary Breakthroughs and National Development*. Berkeley: University of California Press, 1971.

Kahler, Miles. *Decolonization in Britian and France*. Princeton, N.J.: Princeton University Press, 1984.

Khalaf, ᶜIsi. *Politics in Palestine: Arab Factionalism and Social Disintegration, 1939–1948*. Albany: State University of New York Press, 1991.

Khalidi, Rashid. *Under Siege: PLO Decision-Making during the 1982 War*. New York: Columbia University Press, 1986.

——— "The Palestinians in Lebanon: Social Repercussions of Israel's Invasion." *Middle East Journal* 38.2 (Spring): 255–66.

Khalil, Adib Abu. "Jihaz al-Shurta al-Filastini" [The Palestinian Police Force]. *Al-Nashra al-Istratijiyya* 13 (April 1992): 5–10.

Al-Khalili, Ghazi. "Raʾi: Baᶜda al-Intikhabat: Ma Huwa al-Mawqif?" [A Point of View: After the Elections: What Should the Position Be?]. *Shuʾun Filastiniyya* 58 (June 1976): 15–36.

Khashan, Hilal. "The Despairing Palestinians." *Journal of South Asian and Middle Eastern Studies* 16.1 (Fall 1992): 2–17.

Al-Khatib, Hisham. "Nadwa: Al-Jamiᶜa al-Shaᶜbiyya al-Maftuha" [Round Table: The Popular Open University]. *Shuʾun Filastiniyya* 100 (March 1980): 141–46.

Kiljunen, Reginald Marja-Liisa, and Kimo Kiljunen, eds. *Namibia: The Last Colony*. London: Longman, 1981.

Kimmerling, Baruch, and Joel S. Migdal. *The Palestinians: The Making of a People*. New York: Free Press, 1993.

Kuttab, Daud. "The Ups and Downs of the Second Year." *Middle East International*, December 15, 1989, p. 16.

Lambert, C. "From Citizenship to Negritude: 'Making a Difference' in Elite Ideologies of Colonized Fancophone in West Africa." *Comparative Studies in Society and History* 35.2 (April 1993): 247–51.

Laufer, Leopold Yehuda. *U.S. Aid to the West Bank and Gaza: Policy Dilemmas*. Policy Studies No. 12. Jerusalem: Leonard Davis Institute for International Relations, May 1985.

Lesch, Ann. *Political Perceptions of the Palestinians on the West Bank and the Gaza Strip*. Washington, D.C.: The Middle East Institute, 1980.

Lichbach, Mark Irving. *The Rebel's Dilemma*. Ann Arbor: University of Michigan Press, 1995.

Liebman, Charles. *Pressure without Sanctions*. Rutherford, N.J.: Fairleigh Dickinson University Press, 1966.

Lissak, M. and D. Horowitz. *The Origins of the Israeli Polity*. Chicago: University of Chicago Press, 1978.

Low, D. A. "The Asian Mirror to Tropical Africa's Independence." In Prosser Gifford and Wm. Roger Louis, eds., *The Transfer of Power in Africa: Decolonization 1940–1960*. New Haven, Conn.: Yale University Press, 1980, 1–29.

Lustick, Ian S. *Arabs in the Jewish State*. Austin: University of Texas, 1980.

——— "Israeli State-Building in the West Bank and the Gaza Strip: Theory and Practice." *International Organization*, 41.1 (Winter 1987): 151–71.

——— *Unsettled States, Disputed Lands: Britain and Ireland, France and Algeria, Israel and the West Bank-Gaza*. Ithaca, N.Y.: Cornell University Press, 1993.

——— "Writing the Intifada: Collective Action in the Occupied Territories," *World Politics* 45 (July 1993): 560–94.

Mack, Andrew J. "Why Big Nations Lose Small Wars: The Politics of Asymmetric Conflict." *World Politics*, 27 (January 1975): 175–200.

Maddy-Weitzmann, Bruce. "Conflict and Conflict Management in the Western Sahara: Is the Endgame Near?" *Middle East Journal* 45.1 (Autumn 1991): 594–607.

Al-Madhum, Rabᶜi. "Al-Intikhibat—Madiyyan wa-Hadiran" [The Elections—Past and Present]. *Shuᵓun Filastiniyya* 186 (September 1988): 17–18.

Mahshi, Khalil, and Ramzi Rihan."Education: Elementary and Secondary." In Emile A. Nakhleh, ed., *A Palestinian Agenda in the West Bank*, Washington, D.C.: American Enterprise Institute, 1979, 42–54.

Mansour, Camille. "The Palestinian-Israeli Peace Negotiations: An Overview and Assessment." *Journal of Palestine Studies*, 12.3 (Spring 1993): 5–31.

Maᶜoz, Moshe. *Palestinian Leadership on the West Bank: The Changing Role of the Arab Mayors under Jordan and Israel*. London: Frank Cass, 1984.

Marsi, Mustafa. ʿAbd al-ʿAziz. *Al-ʿArab fi Muftaraq al-Tariq: Bayna Darurat Tajdid al-Mahsruᶜ al-Qawmi wa-Makhatir al-Mashruᶜ al-Sharq al-Awsati* [The Arabs at the Crossroad: Between the Neccessity of Renewing the (Pan-Arab) National Plan and the Dangers of the Middle Eastern Scheme]. Cairo: al-Shuruq, 1995.

Masri, H. Fahmi. "A Study of the Student Personnel Program of An-Najah National University-Nablus." Ph.D. diss. Ann Arbor, Mich.: University Microfilms, 1983.

Matar, Philip. *The Mufti of Jerusalem: Al-Hajj Amin Al-Husayni and the Palestine National Movement*. New York: Columbia University Press, 1988.

Mayall, James. *Nationalism and International Society*. Cambridge: Cambridge Studies in International Relations, 1993.

Mazrui, Ali A., and Michael Tidy. *Nationalism and New States in Africa*. London: Heinemann, 1984.

Mazur, Michael P. *Economic Growth and Development of Jordan*. Boulder, Colo.: Westview Press, 1979.

McDowall, David. *Palestine and Israel: The Uprising and Beyond*. Berkeley: University of California Press, 1989.

Middle East Contemporary Survey-1987. Vol. 11. Boulder, Colo.: Westview Press, 1989.

The Middle East Record—1968. Jerusalem: Shiloa Institute for Middle Eastern and African Studies and Israel Universities Press, 1973.

Migdal, Joel. *Strong Societies and Weak States: State-Society Relations and State Capabilities in the Third World*. Princeton, N.J.: Princeton University Press, 1988.

——— "The Crystallization of the State and the Struggles over Rulemaking: Israel in Comparative Perspective." In Baruch Kimmerling, ed., *The Israeli State and Society: Boundaries and Frontiers*. Albany: State University of New York Press, 1989.

Miller, Aaron David. *The PLO and the Politics of Survival*. New York: Praeger, 1983.

Mishal, Shaul *HaKonflikt Bayn haGada haMaaravit laMizrahit beTkufat haShilton haYyardeni veHashlachotav alDfusay haMimshal veha Minhal baGada haMaaravit* [The Conflict between the East Bank and the West Bank and Its Influence on the Perceptions of Government and Administration in the West Bank (1949–1967)]. Ph.D. diss. Hebrew University, Jerusalem, 1972.

——— *West Bank/East Bank*. New Haven, Conn.: Yale University Press, 1978.

Mishal, Shaul, and Reuven Aharoni. *Avanim Ze Lo Hakol* [Not rocks alone]. Tel Aviv: Ha-Kibbutz Ha-Meuchad, 1989.

Moore Jr., Barrington. *Social Origins of Dictatorship and Democracy: Lord and Peasant in the Making of the Modern World*. Boston: Beacon, 1966.

Moore, Clement Henry. *North Africa: Algeria, Morocco, and Tunisia*. Boston: Little, Brown, 1970.

Muslih, Muhammad. "Palestinian Civil Society." *The Middle East Journal* 47.2 (Spring 1993): 258–74.

Nahas, Riad el-Rayyes, and Dunia Nahas. *Guerrillas for Palestine*. London: Croom Helm, 1976.

Al-Nashashibi, Nasir al-Din. *Tadhkirat al-ʿAwda* [The Return Ticket]. Beirut: Al-Maktab al-Tajari, 1962.

Nasr, Hana. "Jamiʿa Arabiyya fi Filastin: Dirasa Awwaliyya" [An Arab University in Palestine: Preliminary Report] *Shuʾun Filastiniyya* 55 (March 1976): 132–45.

Nassar, Jamil Raji. *The Palestine Liberation Organization: From Armed Struggle to Declaration of Independence*. New York: Praeger, 1992.

"Nass Mashruʿ Qanun al-Ahzab al-Siyasiyya al-Filastiniyya" [The Text of the Draft Law on Palestinian Political Parties]. *Al-Siyasa Al-Filastiniyya* 2.7–8 (Summer–Fall 1995): 259–64.

Nisan, Mordechai. "The PLO and Vietnam: National Liberation Models for Palestinian Struggle." *Small Wars and Insurgencies* 4.2 (Autumn 1993): 181–210.

Nusseibeh, Sari. "Time for Palestinian Offensive," *Middle East International*, December 2, 1988, p. 18.

O'Neill, Bard E. *Armed Struggle in Palestine: A Political-Military Analysis.* Boulder, Colo.: Westview Press 1978.

Ottaway, Marina. "Liberation Movements and Transition to Democracy: The Case of the A.N.C." *The Journal of Modern African Studies* 29.1 (1991): 61–82.

Peretz, Don. *Palestinian Refugees and the Middle East Peace Process.* Washington, D.C.: United States Institute of Peace Press, 1993.

Perry, Mark and Daniel Shapiro. "Navigating the Oslo Channel—How an Unusual Cast of Characters Found Peace in an Unexpected Place." *Middle East Insight,* September–October, 1993, pp. 11–16.

Picard, Elizabeth. "Arab Military in Politics: From Revolutionary Plot to Authoritarian State." In Adeed Darwisha and William I. Zartman, eds., *Beyond Coercion.* London: Croom Helm, 1988.

Pipes, Daniel. "Declaring Independence: Israel and the PLO." *Orbis* 33.2 (1989): 247–60.

Porath, Yehoshua. *The Palestinian Arab Nationalist Movement, 1929–1939.* London: Frank Cass, 1977.

"Qanun Ruqm (15) li-Sana 1995 bi-Shaʾn al-Intikhabat." *Qanun al-Intikhabat al-Filastini li-ʿAm 1995* [Law No. (15) for the Year 1995 Concerning the Palestinian Elections]. Al-Sulta al-Wataniyya -Lajnat al-Intikhabat al-Markazia, n.d.

Al-Qasim, Anis. *Min al-Tiyhin ila al-Quds* [From the Wilderness to Jerusalem].Tripoli: Dar al-Nashr al-Libiyya, 1965.

Qleibo, Ali H. "Tribal Methods of Conflict Resolution—The Palestinian Model: Atwah or Sulh Ashaʾiry." In *Practicing Conflict Resolution in Divided Societies.* Policy Studies No. 46. Jerusalem: The Leonard Davis Institute, July 1993, 57–59.

Quandt, William B. *Revolution and Political Leadership: Algeria 1954–1968.* Cambridge, Mass.: MIT Press, 1969.

Quandt, William, Fuad Jabber and Ann Mosely Lesch. *The Politics of Palestinian Nationalism.* Berkeley: University of California Press, 1973.

"Risala Ikhbariyya Sadira ʿAn Shabakat al-Munazamat al-Ahliyya Al-Filastiniyya" [An Information Report from the Network of Palestinian Non-Governmental Organizations]. *Al-Siyasa al-Filastiniyya* 2.7–8 (Summer–Fall 1995): 248–50.

"Risala Min al-Ard al-Muhtalla: Taqrir ʿan Maʿahid al-Taʿlim al-ʿAli fi al-Diffa al-Gharbiyya" [Report from the Occupied Land: Report on Institutions of Higher Education in the West Bank]. *Shuʾun Filastiniyya* 13 (September 1972): 230–34.

Rokkan, Stein. "Center Formation, Nation-Building and Cultural Diversity: Report on a UNESCO Programme." In S. N. Eisenstadt and Stein Rokkan, eds., *Building States and Nations*, vol. 1. Beverly Hills, Calif.: Sage, 1973, 13–38.

Ronen, Dov. *The Quest for Self-Determination*. New Haven, Conn.: Yale University Press, 1979.

Ross, Lauren G., and Nader Izzat Sa᾿id. "Palestinians: Yes to Negotiations, Yes to Violence." *Middle East Quarterly* 2.2 (June 1995): 15–24.

Roy, Sara M. "Gaza: New Dimensions of Civic Disintegration." *Journal of Palestine Studies* 22.4 (Summer 1993): 22–37.

Rubin, Barry. *Revolution until Victory?* Cambridge, Mass.: Harvard University Press, 1994.

Rubinstein, Daniel. "The Jerusalem Municipality under the Ottomans, British, and Jordanians." In Joel L. Kramer, ed., *Jerusalem: Problems and Prospects*. New York: Praeger, 1980.

Ruggie, John Gerard. "Territoriality and Beyond: Problematizing Moderity in International Relations." *International Organization* 47.1, (Winter 1993): 139–74.

Sahlins, Peter. *Boundaries: The Making of France and Spain in the Pyrenees*. Berkeley: University of California Press, 1989.

Sakhnini, ᶜIsam. "Al-Kiyan al-Filastini" [The Palestinian Entity]. *Shu᾿un Filastiniyya* 41–42 (1975): 46–74.

Sahliyeh, Emile. *In Search of Leadership: West Bank Politics since 1967*. Washington D.C.: Brookings Institution, 1988.

Salih, ᶜAbd al-Jawad. *Al-Mushkilat al-Thatiyya lil-Mu᾿assasat al-Taᶜlim al-ᶜAli fi al-Diffa wa Qitaᶜ Ghazza* [The Inherent Problems of Higher Education in the (West) Bank and the Gaza Strip]. Nicosia, Cyprus: Markaz al-Quds li᾿l-Ibhath, 1982.

——— "Al-Tajarrub Min al-Ard al-Muhtalla: Ziraᶜat al-Nujum ᶜAla Ard Filastin" [The Experience from the Occupied Land: Planting the Seeds in Palestinian Soil]. *Shu᾿un Filastiniyya* 63/64 (Februrary/March 1977): 98–108.

Salih ᶜAbd al-Jawad, Salih. "Dirasa fi Qiyadat Harakat Fath" [A Study of the Leadership of the Fath Movement]. *Qadaya* 4 (August 1990): 1–21.

Salim, Walid. "Dirasa Awwaliyya fi Bahth Barnamij al-Lajna al-Mushtaraka" [A Perliminary Study of the Joint Committee Programs. *Al-ᶜAhd* 24 (September 1984): 1–4.

Sandler, Shmuel. "The Socio-Political Origins of the Israel-Diaspora Relationship: The Territorialization of the Zionist Movement, 1917–1935." *Israel and Diaspora Jewry: Ideological Political Perspectives*. Ramat-Gan, Israel: Bar-Ilan University Press, 1991.

Sandler, Shmuel, and Hillel Frisch. *Israel, the Palestinians and the West Bank: A Study in Intercommunal Conflict.* Lexington, Mass.: Lexington Books, 1984.

Saul, John S. *The State and Revolution in Eastern Africa.* New York, 1979.

Sayigh, Yezid. "Turning Defeat into Opportunity: The Palestinian Guerillas After the June 1967 War." *Middle East Journal* 46.2 (Spring 1992): 244–65.

Sha^{c}aban, Ibrahim Muhammad. *Al-Intifada al-Filastiniyya fi ʿAmiha al-Awwal.* Jerusalem: n.p., 1989.

Sha^{c}th, Nabil. "Filastin al-Ghad" [The Palestine of Tomorrow]. *Shu$^\supset$un Filastiniya* 2 (May 1971): 5–23.

Shadid, Muhammad. "Palestinian Civil Society." *The Middle East Journal* 47.2 (Spring 1993): 258–74.

Shafiq, Munir."Limadha Yarfudun al-Filastiniyyun Mashru^c al-Dawla fi al-Diffa al-Gharbiyya wa-Qita^c Ghazza" [Why Do the Palestinians Oppose the Plan of the State in the West Bank and the Gaza Strip?]. *Shu$^\supset$un Filastiniyya* 7 (March 1972): 65–79.

Shafir, S. *Land, Labor and the Origins of the Israeli-Palestinian Conflict, 1882–1914.* Cambridge: Cambridge University Press, 1989.

Shalev, M. *Labor and the Political Economy in Israel.* Oxford: Oxford University Press, 1993.

Shapira, Anita. *Land and Power: The Zionist Resort to Force.* London: Oxford University Press, 1992.

Shapiro, Yonathan. *The Formative Years of the Israeli Labour Party.* Beverly Hills: Sage, 1976.

Sharabi, Hisham, ed. *Theory, Politics, and the Arab World: Critical Responses.* London: Routledge, 1990.

———. *Neopatriarchy: A Theory of Distorted Change in Arab Society.* Oxford: Oxford University Press, 1988.

Sharef, Zeev. *Three Days.* London: W. H. Allen, 1962.

Shemesh, Moshe. *The Palestinian Entity 1959–1974: Arab Politics and the PLO.* London: Frank Cass, 1988.

——— "The West Bank: Rise and Decline of Traditional Leadership, June 1967 to October 1973." *Middle Eastern Studies* 20.3 (July 1984): 290–323.

Shinar, Amnon. "Shchem: Hitpatchut haShetach haBanui beIr Aravit" [Nablus: The Development of the Built-up Area in an Arab City]. In Avshalom Shmueli, David Grosman, Rehavam Zeevi, eds., *Yehuda veShomron: Prakim beGeographia.* Tel Aviv: Cnaan, 1977, 183–91.

Simon, Rachel. *Agudot veMohadonim baGada haMaaravit beTequfat haShilton haHashemi* [Associations and Clubs in the West Bank In the Jordanian Period]. Jerusalem: HaMachon leLimudei Asia veAfrica, 1974.

Singer, Marshal R. "Ethnic Conflict: Alternative Solutions." *Asian Survey* 31.8 (August 1992): 712–22.

Sivan, Emmanuel. *Medieval Theology and Modern Politics.* New Haven, Conn.: Yale University Press, 1985.

Skocpol, Theda. *States and Social Revolutions: A Comparative Analysis of Russia and China.* Cambridge, Mass.: Harvard University Press, 1979.

Smith, A. D. *Nationalist Movements.* London: Macmillan, 1976.

Smith, Tony. "A Comparative Study of French and British Decolonization." In Prosser Gifford and Wm. Roger Louis, eds., *The Transfer of Power in Africa: Decolonization 1940–1960.* New Haven, Conn.: Yale University Press, 1980.

Snyder, Louis. *Global Mini-Nationalisms: Autonomy or Independence.* Westport, Conn.: Greenwood Press, 1982.

Snyder, Louis. "Nationalism and the Territorial Imperative." *Canadian Review of Studies in Nationalism* 3 (1975): 1–21.

Statistical Abstract of Israel 35 (1984). Jerusalem: Central Bureau of Statistics, 1985.

Statistical Abstract of Israel 36 (1985). Jerusalem: Central Bureau of Statistics, 1986.

"Sulayman, Hasan. "Al-Intifada wa al-Masʾala al-Ziraʿiyya ʿfil Filastin-Dirasa Madaniyya Fi Qarya Kafr Nuʿma, Qadaʾ Ramalla." In *Al-Intifada: Mubadara Shaʿbiyya.* Jerusalem: n. p., 1990.

Tamari, Salim. "Building Other People's Homes." *Journal of Palestine Studies* 11.1 (Autumn 1981): 75–95.

———. "Comment." *Birzeit Research Review* 4. (Spring 1986): 79.

———. "Makhatir al-Rataba: Al-ʿIsyan al-Mahdud wal-Mujtamaʿ al-Madani" [The Dangers of Routine: Limited Collective Action and Civil Society]. *Majallat al-Dirasat al-Filastiniyya* 3 (Summer 1990): 12–23.

———. "The Palestinian Movement in Transition: Historical Reversals and the Uprisings." *Journal of Palestine Studies* 20.2 (Winter 1991): 57–70.

Tauber, Eliezer. *The Emergence of the Arab National Movements.* London: Frank Cass, 1993.

Taylor, Michael. "Rationality and Revolutionary Collective Action." In Michael Taylor, ed., *Rationality and Revolution*, Cambridge: Cambridge University Press, 1988, 63–97.

"Al-Thawra wal-Tanzim" [The Revolution and the Apparatus]. *Al-Thawra al-Filastiniyya* 12, (October 6, 1968).

The Hashemite Kingdomn of Jordan Statistical Yearbook 1983/84. N.p., n.d.

The Middle East Record—1968. Jerusalem: Shiloah Institute for Middle Eastern and African Studies and Israel Universities Press, 1973.

Al-Tibawi, Ali."Visions of the Return: The Palestinian Refugees in Arabic Poetry and Art." *Middle East Journal* 17.5 (1963): 507–26.

Tilly, Charles. *From Mobilization to Revolution*. Reading, Mass.: Addison-Wesley, 1978.

———. "Reflections on the History of European State Making." In Charles Tilly, ed., *The Formation of Nation States in Western Europe*. Princeton, N.J.: Princeton University Press, 1975, 70–76.

——— "War Making and State Making as Organized Crime." In P. Evans, *Bringing the State Back In*. Cambridge: Cambridge University Press, 1985, 169–91.

———. "Western State-Making and Theories of Political Transformation." In Charles Tilly, ed., *The Formation of Nation-States in Western Europe*. Princeton, N.J.: Princeton University Press, 1975, 601–638.

Turki, Fawaz. *The Disinherited: Journal of a Palestinian Exile*. New York: Atlantic Monthly Press, 1973.

ʿUd, Munir Ahmad. *Nashra Ihsaʾiyya ʿan al-Taʿlim fi al-Diffa al-Gharbiyya wa Qitaʿ Ghazza* [Statistical Publication Concerning Education in the West Bank and the Gaza Strip]. Nablus: Jamiʿat al-Najah al-Wataniyya, Markaz al-Dirasat al Rifiyya wa Jamʿiyyat al-Dirasat al-ʿArabiyya, n.d.

U.S. Draft of "Israeli-Palestinian Joint Statement," Washington, D.C., May 12, 1993. Reprinted in *Journal of Palestine Studies* 22.4 (Summer 1993): 158–59.

Usher, Graham. "Fath Tearing Itself Apart," *Middle East International*, February 18, 1994, pp. 4–5.

ʿUthman, Munir ʿAbd Allah. *Bayan Nashatat al-ʿAwqaf fi al-Diffa al-Gharbiyya Hilal Sit al-Sanawat 1977–1982* [A Report of the (Department of Endowments) Activities in the West Bank during the Six Year Period 1977–1982]. Jerusalem: Daʾirat al-Awqaf al-Islamiyya al-ʿAmma, 1985.

Walid, al-Qamhawi. *Al-Naqba wal-Banaʾa fi al-Watan al-ʿArabi* [The Disaster and Reconstruction in the Arab Homeland]. Beirut: Dar al-ʿIlm lil-Muʿallimin, 1959.

Waterbury, John. *Commander of the Faithful*. London: Nicolson and Weidenfeld, 1970.

Weitzer, Ronald. "In Search of Regime Security: Zimbabwe Since Independence." *Journal of Modern African Studies* 22.4 (1984): 529–57.

Yaari, Ehud and Zeev Schiff. *Intifada: The Palestinian Uprising—Israel's Third Front.* New York: Simon & Schuster, 1989.

Yiftachel, Oren. "Debate: The Concept of 'Ethnic Democracy' and Its Applicability to the Case of Israel." *Ethnic and Racial Studies* 15.1 (January 1992): 125–36.

Weiss, Ruth. *Zimbabwe and the New Elite.* New York: British Academic Press, 1994.

Wizarat al-Takhtit wal-Ta ʿawwun al Dawli, Waraqat ʿAmal Lil-Ta ʿammul ma ʿa al Munazamat Ghair al-Hukumiyya, Muqaddama min al-Duktur Anis al-Qaq, Wakil Wizarat al Ta ʿawwun al-Dawli [Ministry of Planning and International Cooperation, Working Paper Regarding Relations with the Nongovernmental Organizations, Presented by Dr. Anis al Qaq, Deputy Minister for International Cooperation]. N.p., n.d.

Wunsch, James S. and Dele Olowu, eds. *The Failure of the Centralized State: Institutions and Self-Governance in Africa*, Boulder, Colo.: Westview Press, 1990.

Zamir, Meir. *The Formation of Modern Lebanon.* London: Croom Helm, 1985.

Zolberg, Aristide. "One-Party Systems and Government for the People." *Africa Today* 9.4 (May 1962): 4–7.

INDEX